vocabulary
in a SNAP

100+ Lessons for Elementary Instruction

angela b. peery

Solution Tree | Press

555 North Morton Street
Bloomington, IN 47404
800.733.6786 (toll free) / 812.336.7700
FAX: 812.336.7790

email: info@SolutionTree.com
SolutionTree.com

Visit **go.SolutionTree.com/literacy** to download the free reproducibles in this book.

Printed in the United States of America

21   20   19   18   17   1   2   3   4   5

Library of Congress Cataloging-in-Publication Data

Names: Peery, Angela B., 1964- author.
Title: Vocabulary in a snap : 100+ lessons for elementary instruction / Angela B. Peery.
Description: Bloomington, IN : Solution Tree Press, [2017] | Includes bibliographical references and index.
Identifiers: LCCN 2017010923 | ISBN 9781943874903 (perfect bound)
Subjects: LCSH: Vocabulary--Study and teaching (Elementary)
Classification: LCC LB1574.5 .P44 2017 | DDC 372.44--dc23 LC record available at https://lccn.loc.gov/2017010923

Solution Tree
Jeffrey C. Jones, CEO
Edmund M. Ackerman, President

Solution Tree Press
President and Publisher: Douglas M. Rife
Editorial Director: Sarah Payne-Mills
Managing Production Editor: Caroline Cascio
Senior Production Editor: Tara Perkins
Senior Editor: Amy Rubenstein
Copy Editor: Ashante K. Thomas
Proofreader: Elisabeth Abrams
Cover Designer: Abigail Bowen
Editorial Assistants: Jessi Finn and Kendra Slayton

This book is dedicated to the many selfless teachers I've had the joy of supporting as they've improved their literacy practices.

Acknowledgments

I would like to thank Leanne Geary for her invaluable input. I am also incredibly grateful to all the reviewers who helped me reshape this manuscript.

Solution Tree Press would like to thank the following reviewers:

Leah Barley
Reading Coach
Royall Elementary School
Florence, South Carolina

Joshua DeWar
Second-Grade Teacher
Engelhard Elementary School
Louisville, Kentucky

Kourtney Ferrua
Principal
Wascher Elementary School
Lafayette, Oregon

Loreen Flanary
Kindergarten Teacher
Woodruff Elementary School
Logan, Utah

Linda Glasgow
Third-Grade Teacher
John Nowlin Elementary School
Blue Springs, Missouri

Evelyn Mamman
Director of Title I and Supplemental
Education Programs
New Brunswick Public School District
New Brunswick, New Jersey

Dana McDonough
Second-Grade Teacher
Fostertown ETC Magnet School
Newburgh, New York

Nancy Michael
Second-Grade Teacher
Pembroke Elementary School
Danbury, Connecticut

Abby Sandlin
Third-Grade Teacher
Smyrna Elementary School
Smyrna, Georgia

Visit **go.SolutionTree.com/literacy** to download the free reproducibles in this book.

Table of Contents

3   Robust Roots A–K

7 Testing Terms

8 Varied Voice

About the Author

Angela B. Peery, EdD, is a consultant and author and has been a teacher since 1986. Since 2004, she has made more than one thousand presentations and has authored or coauthored eleven books. Angela has consulted with educators to improve teacher collaboration, formative assessment, effective instruction, and literacy across the curriculum. In addition to her consulting work, she is a former instructional coach, high school administrator, graduate-level education professor, and English teacher at the middle school, high school, and college levels. Her wide range of experiences allows her to work shoulder to shoulder with colleagues in any setting to improve educational outcomes.

Angela has been a Courage to Teach fellow and an instructor for the National Writing Project. She maintains memberships in several national and international education organizations and is a frequent presenter at their conferences. Her book *The Data Teams Experience: A Guide for Effective Meetings* supports the work of professional learning communities, and her most recent publications and consulting work highlight the importance of teaching academic vocabulary.

A Virginia native, Angela earned her bachelor's degree in English at Randolph-Macon Woman's College, her master's degree in liberal arts at Hollins College, and her doctorate at the University of South Carolina. Her professional licensures include secondary English, secondary administration, and gifted and talented education. She has also studied presentation design and delivery with expert Rick Altman. In 2015, she engaged in graduate study in brain-based learning.

To learn more about Angela's work, visit http://drangelapeery.com or follow @drangelapeery on Twitter.

To book Angela B. Peery for professional development, contact pd@SolutionTree.com.

Introduction

Since the 1990s, teachers have begun to realize that "look it up in the dictionary" or "check the glossary" is not an appropriate response when students inquire about a word's meaning. Thankfully, in most classrooms, the weekly lists of words to study for Friday quizzes have been replaced with vocabulary assignments that create better retention. Teachers know that their students need to learn and use more words than ever. Why have teachers come to this conclusion? Three factors have influenced most of the teachers with whom I work.

First, the increasing rate of children living in poverty means that students arrive in prekindergarten or kindergarten programs already displaying a vocabulary deficit. The *thirty-million-word gap*, as it is known, refers to the number of words that students in welfare-dependent families have heard spoken versus the number of words that students in professional families have heard spoken before they enter school (Hart & Risley, 2003). This gap, if not addressed, is compounded over time and becomes a serious impediment to reading comprehension. Studies show that kindergarten vocabulary knowledge accurately predicts second-grade reading comprehension (Roth, Speece, & Cooper, 2002). Anne E. Cunningham and Keith E. Stanovich's (1997) work shows a correlation between first-grade vocabulary knowledge and reading comprehension in high school. Thus, boosting our economically disadvantaged students' vocabulary is incredibly important because they have an early and huge disadvantage that impacts their achievement through their teenage years. (And, ethically, boosting every student's vocabulary should be part of each school's mission.)

Second, academic standards have increased in rigor, and they demand that students have large, general academic vocabularies in addition to advanced, discipline-specific vocabularies. The United States and other nations' adopted standards have been crafted with attention to the workings of our global economy. It's simply no longer possible for the masses in most countries to get a good factory or office job with attractive benefits and comfortable pensions upon leaving secondary school. The world has changed a great deal since the 1960s, and the best jobs now require high levels of literacy and numeracy in addition to nonacademic skills like effective collaboration and technological savvy. Teachers feel pressed for time, as they always have, but they also know that the high level of literacy needed for success in academia and in the workplace requires more attention to vocabulary.

And third, teachers know that students with rich vocabularies do better in many facets of life. Reading comprehension is definitely tied to the strength and size of one's vocabulary, as mentioned previously. Oral expression, which factors greatly into first impressions, is highly dependent on a person's vocabulary. A first impression is often critical to a student's success—for example, a college or job interview depends on making a good first impression. Teachers also know that as students progress through school, the demands in each subject area increase. Those content-area demands require a deep understanding of hundreds of words. Our students, many of whom have been subjected to years of multiple-choice testing of reading and vocabulary, must be reconditioned to learn words not only at a recognition level or with answers from which to choose but also at a deep level for application in speaking and writing.

The Teacher's Perspective

I understand the concerns that teachers have about the size and strength of their students' vocabularies. When I was a full-time classroom teacher, my concerns were mainly about the actual words I should teach explicitly because they were vital to understanding content, and how to best encourage incidental or self-directed vocabulary learning. These areas of concern seem to resonate with the hundreds of teachers I've worked with to improve vocabulary instruction as well.

I also understand that teachers have doubts about the words their instructional materials target for instruction. When I was teaching short stories, essays, drama, and poetry, I questioned the words my literature textbook emphasized. Sometimes I thought, "Who in the world selected these words?" Archaic terms, words used metaphorically, and lists of words to study for the ACT and SAT often seemed so disconnected from what I felt my students needed to know *right then* for academic success.

My doubts were validated when, as a high school English teacher, I discovered that my students lacked a knowledge of words that I assumed they knew well. For example, I was surprised once when my students, who knew the word *summary* and had actually written summaries in my class, couldn't tell me what the word *summarize* meant. This moment, in the first class of the day, allowed me to check with all my students later in the day about their knowledge of inflectional endings. I remember being fairly shocked that ninth graders didn't know the ending *-ize* is used with verbs. (Thus, *summarize* often means "to write a summary"). Upon further probing, I discovered the majority of them didn't know that *-er* or *-or* in a noun often signifies a person, as in *teacher, sailor,* and *actor.*

Because of the gap that I found in their learning, I wove small teaching moments into instruction for the next few weeks as we encountered inflectional endings attached to words of which they had some basic knowledge. I gradually started selecting words that I found necessary for the deep understanding of the text at hand—not necessarily the same words the publisher had selected. Also, I wanted my students to be word-seekers, to find words in the books they chose for independent reading, and to be genuinely interested in growing their own vocabularies. I understood that by requiring my students to read their self-selected books for more than two hours a week in class and for homework, I could support their vocabulary growth by asking them to be cognizant of words they did not know, to record them, and to apply them. I finally settled on a vocabulary log assignment in which students would find several unknown words per week in their reading or in their environments and tackle those words by recording the context, defining each word as it was used in context, and using the word in an original sentence. Periodically, I asked students to do *word talks* during which they shared a word or two with the class and explained why those words were important or interesting. Eventually, I also made a section on my final exam that required students to argue for ten words they thought everyone in their grade level should learn. These assignments weren't perfect, but they were certainly more aligned with how people authentically learn vocabulary through reading and participating in life.

About This Book

With these realities and concerns in mind, I have drawn from some of those improvised lessons and devised a framework for effective vocabulary minilessons. The term *minilessons* refers to short lessons that can be completed in twenty minutes or less. This book offers more than one hundred minilessons for immediate use that target specific words and often suggest related words. The chapters and sections in this book group minilessons in ways that build on similarities. In some cases, the target words appear alphabetically. In other cases, they appear in groups based on word length, sound pattern, thematic relationship, or some other kind of similarity.

Chapter 1 outlines the components that make up these minilessons and explains how to logistically implement each. Chapter 2 offers descriptions of the different research-based, time-tested, instructional strategies that are noted throughout the lessons in this book. Teachers can broadly apply these types of instructional strategies to effective vocabulary instruction. These strategies appear throughout the book within minilessons but are also provided in more depth in this chapter as a reference, and also so you can find your own unique ways to apply them to instruction more broadly if you wish. Chapter 2 also includes short descriptions of relevant digital tools. Chapters 3 through 7 describe specific minilessons for some of the essential vocabulary words I've identified for helping to ensure success for elementary students in academics and beyond. Chapters 3 and 4 focus on roots, and lessons cover roots alphabetically. Due to the disproportionately high number of roots as compared to other types of word parts, chapter 3 addresses roots beginning with the letters a–k, and chapter 4 addresses roots beginning with the letters l–z. Next, chapter 5 offers lessons centered around target words with common prefixes. Chapter 6 similarly offers lessons for words with common suffixes. Lessons for common academic vocabulary and terms encountered in testing appear in chapter 7. Chapter 8 focuses on terms to expand students' word choices beyond the simple or slang terms they often fall back on and overuse.

I recommend digital tools and resources in some minilessons. Websites and applications are suggested only when they seem to fit the content well or add extra support or enrichment. Visit **go.SolutionTree.com/literacy** to access live links to the websites suggested throughout this book. Additionally, an appendix featuring an index of vocabulary words (page 245) lists all words that are included in these minilessons, so you can quickly look up any specific word to see if it's covered in this resource. This feature can support you as you find important vocabulary in content-area classroom materials that you plan to use in instruction.

This book is not a program, a textbook, or a workbook. It does not have to be digested or utilized in any set manner; the way you use what's offered here is up to you. It's a collection of ideas that—when brought to life based on your unique teaching situation—can change the lives of your students for the better. My hope is that you'll find support for what you already do and inspiration for things you could do differently. As teachers know, with larger vocabularies, your students have a greater chance of being successful in their academic work, communities, and future workplaces.

Final Thoughts

Vocabulary in a SNAP is a resource for you no matter where you are on the vocabulary instruction spectrum. If you're just beginning to feel the itch to improve in this area, terrific! If you've been tinkering with vocabulary instruction for a while, you will find detailed ideas here that can supplement what you're already doing. And if you're already an expert teacher of vocabulary, you will find precise suggestions and tools here that save you time and give you new ideas.

Minilesson Management

Obviously, you're interested in what you can do to help your students embrace word learning and enlarge their vocabularies. This book can be a handy resource for you and for other professionals in the building who want to address students' critical need for high levels of vocabulary knowledge. By addressing this critical need, you will be helping students move more clearly toward success in academia and in the world of work.

Vocabulary in a SNAP can fuel teacher inquiry and data collection. After using some of the minilessons, ask your students if they feel they're learning more words. Ask them if they are excited about word learning. Analyze their speaking and writing for improved word choice. Along with trusted colleagues, determine which minilessons, instructional strategies, and digital tools work best, and continue refining vocabulary instruction at your school. This chapter lays out the research basis for the SNAP minilessons, highlights the flexibility and adaptability of this framework, clarifies the structure and components of the minilessons in depth, and explains the logistics of implementing the minilessons in your classroom.

Research Basis

This book does not purport to be the one, end-all, be-all collection of words that will guarantee students finish their K–5 years prepared for all that lies ahead of them. In fact, no such word list exists, and even if it did, it would not take into account all that good teachers bring to instruction in order to meet their students' needs.

The excellent teachers I've observed and supported as a professional development provider heavily influenced this work. The teachers and students I've worked with in settings as dissimilar as West Valley City, Utah, and Zwolle, Louisiana, were first and foremost in my mind. What would I say and do if we were teaching these lessons to their students? How would I work with teachers to adapt the lessons?

I consulted several credible resources to decide which words to include in this book, in addition to consulting many dedicated educators who have been studying vocabulary instruction with me. The following published works have most influenced word selection in this book.

- *A New Academic Word List* by Averil Coxhead (2000)
- *The Reading Teacher's Book of Lists* (5th ed.) by Edward B. Fry and Jacqueline E. Kress (2000)
- *Vocabulary for the Common Core* by Robert J. Marzano and Julia A. Simms (2013)

All word definitions appearing in the minilessons are my own paraphrases and have been developed mainly by consulting the following online resources: Merriam-Webster (www.merriam-webster.com), Dictionary.com (www.dictionary.com), Thesaurus .com (www.thesaurus.com), Cambridge Dictionary (http://dictionary.cambridge.org /us), and The Free Dictionary (www.thefreedictionary.com). I have also often turned to WordHippo (www.wordhippo.com) as a go-to resource for synonyms and example sentences. The instructional strategies throughout align with either the seminal work *Classroom Instruction That Works* (Marzano, Pickering, & Pollock, 2001) or other influential syntheses of effective instructional strategies.

I suggest that you use this book as only one resource to help plan effective vocabulary lessons. Other resources that should impact your decisions about which words to teach include the core instructional texts that you use (textbooks and other texts), the high-stakes tests your students need to prepare for, the wisdom of colleagues who are joining you in this endeavor, your expertise about the most critical content-area words your students need to know, and your experience in effectively meeting your students where they are in their learning.

Flexibility and Adaptability

These minilessons are not a curriculum. They're not a program or a series of lessons that you should use in any particular order. You can use *any* minilesson at *any* time and adapt it as you see fit for *your* curriculum and *your* students. The minilessons are highly flexible. The text shows only *one of many ways* to use the framework to teach specific words. While the minilessons in this book are organized thematically, I recognize that there may be other ways to group them. If you and your colleagues want to take the ideas herein and totally reorganize them, you can do so without compromising effectiveness. Make things make sense for you. Remember, the ultimate goal is for students to see the words, make the words, associate them, tinker with them alongside peers, and individually apply them. All these steps are designed to increase the "stickiness" of the target words so that when students encounter unfamiliar academic vocabulary, they aren't so flummoxed that they can't move forward—the word will have stuck with them. I also encourage you to use the framework to design your own minilessons when appropriate. So consider this book a book of possibilities.

Vocabulary in a SNAP consists of enough minilessons to use a different one several times a week during the entire school year if you wish. I'm not recommending that you implement the minilessons in any specific number or sequence, however. Use your best judgment and, if possible, undertake this work with colleagues and find what kind of implementation works best for your situation. Also, just because you teach a minilesson once doesn't mean that it can't be repeated later for review. Multiple exposures to unfamiliar words are important for long-term memory. Any minilesson can also be a part of your word study instruction when it might best make sense. In short, there are many ways to use these lessons along with your current literature series, balanced literacy model, and so on.

Structure and Components

Each minilesson contains four core steps, which the acronym SNAP represents.

1. **S:** *Seeing* and *saying* each word

2. **N:** *Naming* a category or group each word belongs to or *noticing* connections to related words or word families

3. **A:** *Acting* on the words (engaging in a brief task or conversation about the words)

4. **P:** *Producing* an individual, original application of the words

Each minilesson also contains a Scaffolding section with suggestions for providing additional support, and an Acceleration section with suggestions for offering enrichment opportunities. Additionally, some lessons contain a Beyond the Lesson section to offer ideas for how to reinforce knowledge and use of target words beyond the minilesson itself. Scaffolding, Acceleration, and Beyond the Lesson sections are not technically parts of the lessons themselves—they are offered as extra, optional information to support teachers if they determine these adaptations are necessary in their classrooms.

Minilessons are assigned an estimated difficulty level—either level 1 or level 2. Level 1 is appropriate for lower grade levels (K–3), many English learners, and students in grades 4–5 who struggle with language. Level 2 is appropriate for upper elementary (4–5) and some English learners. However, these are estimates, and each student and classroom will have different ability levels and needs. Many lessons may also be appropriate for some middle school students who are below grade level or who are English learners, but for the majority of students, lessons in this book are applicable for grades K–5. Readers should feel free to use this book with older students as they deem appropriate. See *Vocabulary in a SNAP: 100+ Lessons for Secondary Instruction* (Peery, in press) for lessons designed for secondary-grades students. Teachers may also want to adjust the content of the examples to fit their students' maturity levels and experiences. For example, recent school events might be easily connected to the content of lessons. Teachers will know what's best in their individual classrooms. Allow your students to be your guide, and consider the designations and content in this book only as broad suggestions. Lastly, each minilesson uses icons to identify its components, as the following sections show.

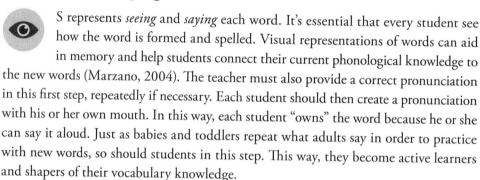

Estimated Difficulty Levels

Level 1: Lower grade levels (K–3), many English learners, and students in grades 4–5 who struggle with language

Level 2: Upper elementary (4–5) and some English learners

Seeing and Saying

S represents *seeing* and *saying* each word. It's essential that every student see how the word is formed and spelled. Visual representations of words can aid in memory and help students connect their current phonological knowledge to the new words (Marzano, 2004). The teacher must also provide a correct pronunciation in this first step, repeatedly if necessary. Each student should then create a pronunciation with his or her own mouth. In this way, each student "owns" the word because he or she can say it aloud. Just as babies and toddlers repeat what adults say in order to practice with new words, so should students in this step. This way, they become active learners and shapers of their vocabulary knowledge.

The recommended strategy for students saying the word is often a choral response in several minilessons throughout this book. However, choral responses can be hard to monitor for individual participation. Do what you feel works best with your students, but do all you can to get every student to form the target words with his or her own mouth. As most of us who teach language know from experience, moving muscles and making sounds with one's own mouth are important in mastering new words.

Naming and Noticing

N stands for *naming* a category or group that each word fits into, *noticing* a connection to other words or concepts, or making other associations with familiar information. Students need to make initial connections in order to get at least a surface-level or temporary meaning of the target words. These meanings are the building blocks on which the next two tasks depend. Also, because comparing and contrasting are basic cognitive operations, having students compare and classify unfamiliar words alongside known words or word families is likely to support them in their first grasp of new vocabulary. Being able to place words into a category or connecting them to other words starts creating cognitive relationships that can be strengthened and expanded. A bonus: this step also addresses connotation in many instances. In the hundreds, perhaps thousands, of students I've worked with over the years, students with smaller vocabularies struggle mightily with connotation.

If you feel you're running short on time for any SNAP minilesson, finish the first two steps and save the following two for later in the day or the next day. The first two steps blend fairly seamlessly into each other, so try to do both of them (at a minimum) for any partial SNAP minilesson.

Acting

The third step, A, is for *acting* on the words by engaging in a brief conversation or some other task using the target words. These activities should be collaborative and engaging. Thus, this segment of instruction generates positive feelings that enhance cognition and increase the students' enjoyment of language in general. The ultimate goal here is to heighten awareness of words while having fun. This segment should be low-stakes, low-stress, and enjoyable enough for even your most struggling and low-literacy students to engage. You want every student to engage in conversation about words at this step of the instructional sequence.

Producing

Lastly, step P is for *producing* an original application of the target words. This is the individual practice piece. Each student uses at least one of the target words in speaking, writing, or both. Teachers can integrate useful digital tools well within this segment. And with this closing piece, the minilesson includes explicit instruction, guided practice, and independent practice, all facilitated with the teacher using proven instructional strategies, and all within only a few minutes of precious class time.

Scaffolding

The ladder icon represents ideas about scaffolding instruction for learners who need more support, especially during the independent practice piece (step P) and sometimes also for the guided practice piece (step A). English learners and students with identified disabilities might benefit from the suggestions here. However, you know your students best. If you don't feel the suggestions the minilessons provide would work well with your struggling, reluctant, or resistant students, devise something that may work better. Keep the ideas that work well; tweak or toss the others.

Acceleration

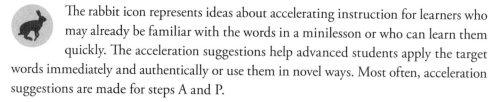

The rabbit icon represents ideas about accelerating instruction for learners who may already be familiar with the words in a minilesson or who can learn them quickly. The acceleration suggestions help advanced students apply the target words immediately and authentically or use them in novel ways. Most often, acceleration suggestions are made for steps A and P.

Sometimes, this section will share words related to the target words. These are words that students should understand fairly easily but are perhaps more difficult or used less frequently than the minilesson's target words.

The suggestions in this section help prevent our high-achieving students and those who are especially interested in words from growing bored because instruction is not meeting their specific needs. The recommendations also spark continued interest in developing advanced students' already well-developed vocabulary. They need to be learning new words, too!

Beyond the Lesson

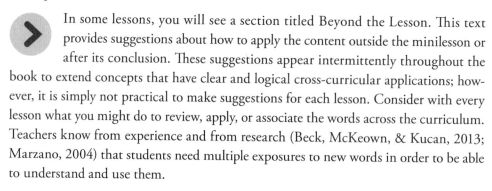

In some lessons, you will see a section titled Beyond the Lesson. This text provides suggestions about how to apply the content outside the minilesson or after its conclusion. These suggestions appear intermittently throughout the book to extend concepts that have clear and logical cross-curricular applications; however, it is simply not practical to make suggestions for each lesson. Consider with every lesson what you might do to review, apply, or associate the words across the curriculum. Teachers know from experience and from research (Beck, McKeown, & Kucan, 2013; Marzano, 2004) that students need multiple exposures to new words in order to be able to understand and use them.

One minilesson will not guarantee that any student can apply any of the target words; however, it will guarantee that students are *exposed* to new words in an engaging, low-stakes situation. In order to move the words into your students' expressive vocabulary (their verbal and written output), consider how you can provide multiple exposures in multiple contexts. You may want to do only one to two minilessons each week, and then commit to using the target words yourself in as many contexts as possible. You'll see that if you use the words repeatedly in talking with students, they will start to use them, too. Think of how babies learn their first words. We all mimic on the way to mastery. Allow your students to do this.

In summary, each SNAP minilesson is a well-planned, flexible, research-based, instructional segment that teachers, paraprofessionals, tutors, and other adults can apply in varied ways for the maximum benefit to students. The structure can fit any words that you want to teach, whether they are general academic words or content-specific words.

Logistics for Implementing SNAP Minilessons

Before delving into the logistics of teaching the minilessons, it's important to reiterate that authenticity and flexibility are built into these lessons. In many places in this book, one minilesson could possibly turn into a short series of minilessons. You could take one minilesson that contains five target words and break it into two minilessons. You can also add related words to any minilesson. Each minilesson's outline or sketch aims to be helpful but again, not prescriptive.

This book is about *coulds*, not *shoulds*. I recognize that you will bring your own passion and artistry to each minilesson you choose. This is a critical part of teaching—responding in the moment to what you see in front of you. If a suggested strategy doesn't sound like it will work with your students, or if it falls flat as you attempt it, adjust it or replace it with your own strategy. Having said that, there are a few basic tenets to follow when implementing these lessons.

Each minilesson in this book should take no more than twenty minutes of instructional time. Instruction needs to move swiftly, and students will need to be familiar with how to transition from a whole-group setting to small groups and to individual work. You should always approach minilesson steps in the order presented (S, N, A, P) and should always include each step. Don't omit any of these steps. If time runs short, cut the minilesson off wherever you are and continue at a later time in the day, the very next day, or as soon as you can. As noted earlier, steps S and N of the minilesson would ideally be done on the same day to give students an initial understanding of the target words. Steps A and P can then be done together as soon as possible (or even at separate times if time dictates). The key is to do all steps so that students have ample opportunity to add new words to their lexicons.

Conducting Step S

This is the visualization and pronunciation step and consists of brief, direct instruction. Step S should take no longer than three minutes. Teachers should write each word and definition in large, clear print on a chalkboard, dry-erase board, poster paper, or similar surface, or display it via interactive whiteboard or projector. Each word must be clearly visible to every student, so sit in the seats in the very back of the classroom before class to ensure the shortest student who is farthest away can still see the words on the board. Do not print the words on handouts and distribute them. Do not have students copy the words into a notebook; this will take too long and slow the minilesson's pace. You may choose to display the words on an ever-evolving word wall or other display, but the point of this part of step S is for students to see the words in their minds, *not* to engage with the words in a way that seems like a normal, everyday assignment. You want an aspect of novelty here; you want to call attention to these words and do all you can to make them seem special.

Ensure that you write the part of speech, as each minilesson notes, alongside each word. The word meaning used in the minilesson is the one for the specific part of speech it notes. For example, if the target word is *transmitted*, the definition given will be for the verb *transmit* in the past tense. The definition or use of the word *transmission* would not be part of the lesson; the lesson would focus on *transmitted*, the verb. Seeing the parts of speech repeatedly helps students become increasingly familiar with how words work grammatically and syntactically and supports much of what happens in the next step of the protocol (noticing associations among words).

Lastly, each student needs to say the words aloud in this step. This can occur a number of ways. You could pronounce all the words first and have students then pronounce the entire list after you. This might be preferable at times if you attach a certain rhythm or cadence to the vocabulary list. Alternatively, you could pronounce a single word, have students repeat it, and then do the same with the other words. Or you could combine these methods. For example, you could say each word clearly and have them listen, then repeat each individual word, and have them repeat. You could do any of these things several times. The goal is for the majority of students to say each word correctly out loud so that their brains and their mouths have experience with producing the word.

If technology is readily available, you may want to have each student speak his or her work into a device and record it. Collecting words said aloud this way can help students even further if they periodically play the words back and listen to themselves. Rudimentary tools such as *whisper phones* (made of curved PVC pipe that students can speak quietly into to hear themselves read aloud) can also be employed to make the saying aloud of the words more dramatic and memorable.

Conducting Step N

Ideally, the first two steps (S and N) are always done together. They (and you!) provide a model to students of correct pronunciation and enunciation and allow students to form the words not only in their minds but with their mouths and while hearing their own voices. Seeing the words, pronouncing them oneself, and making initial connections to prior knowledge and personal experience are what the first two steps are all about.

If it takes more than ten minutes to accomplish those goals, then save the rest of the minilesson for another time. If you are in the middle of step S or N and see that the minilesson may take more than twenty minutes, stop and continue with the other two steps at a later time. Remember, each minilesson should be short and memorable. If a minilesson turns into more of a standard lesson, then the benefits of brevity and novelty may be lost, and the target vocabulary becomes just more information awash in the sea of words that bombard students each day.

Step N relies on brief, direct instruction, and describes the student cognition that teachers should facilitate. In this step, you will help students connect new information to familiar information by focusing on the parts of speech, word components, morphology, etymology, associations, and other connections. The teacher assumes the active role in the classroom during this step, explaining word categories and associations for students and presenting examples. How teachers present this information and what students do with it during the N step are at the teachers' discretion—teachers will know best what is appropriate in their classrooms. You really have a wide variety of choices about the connections and associations you make for your students here, and you can encourage them to make their own associations as well. Susan Neuman and Tanya Wright (2013), vocabulary researchers who have created a complete vocabulary curriculum, note that "clustering words within categories facilitated children's comprehension and provided promising evidence of accelerating word learning" (p. 12). Therefore, organizing words into groups that are semantically or conceptually related in step N should support student learning.

The strategies that you use to help students connect the new to the known in this step can certainly vary, but some methods are almost always appropriate. Using gestures, having students engage in kinesthetic activity, sketching out a quick visual, or showing images—you can employ all these methods successfully here to immediately improve depth of understanding. If you don't feel that the suggested strategy in a given minilesson will work for you, substitute another that will. The most important consideration is that you feel confident presenting the associations and that you do so in an engaging enough way to help students build more context around the words.

Often in step N, you will give examples based on school, home, or community so that students can immediately get at least an initial idea of word meaning. This second step of each minilesson should take only about three minutes but can be incredibly worthwhile. The bulk of students' active engagement in discussing the words and producing meaning will occur during the next two steps of the lesson to deepen students' initially incomplete understanding.

Conducting Step A

A refers to *acting on* the words (engaging in a brief task or conversation about the words). This step is meant to be collaborative and engaging; it is a quick, guided practice piece. This part of the minilesson should last no longer than five minutes. During this step, the teacher should circulate, monitor, and support students as needed. Students are supposed to be talking about, writing about, or playing with new words in this part of the minilesson as a foundation for using the words independently in the final step.

In many of the minilessons, small groups of students will be asked to write something during this step. Be sure that you have the necessary materials ready to go before you begin the minilesson so that this step can be accomplished quickly. Anything written during this step (and in the next one) should be collected but not graded. What students do during the entire SNAP minilesson is formative practice designed not only to enhance vocabulary but to increase student enjoyment of learning about words. Giving a grade or score on any of the tasks would undermine the minilesson's overall goals.

Conducting Step P

This step is the independent practice piece that follows the cooperative learning step (step A). During this step, each student should authentically use at least one target word (but ideally two or more). Each student may use the word or words in a sentence or paragraph or may perform some other task with them. This step should last about five minutes in most cases. It is usually done in writing but can be adapted to be done orally per teacher discretion. You can meaningfully incorporate digital tools during this step to enhance engagement and further support student learning and transfer of knowledge.

Conducting Scaffolding, Acceleration, and Beyond the Lesson

The lessons in the book offer ancillary suggestions for scaffolding and acceleration, and ideas for supporting word learning beyond the lesson also appear from time to time. There are no specific logistics for implementing these pieces. These are intended to be used flexibly as you best see fit for your students.

Final Thoughts

Nothing is hard and fast here; I encourage you to use the lessons in the ways that best fit you and the learners before you. The purpose remains that we are trying to familiarize students with as many academic words as possible. Keep the end in mind, and do the best you can do with the ideas here, but feel free to revise as you see fit. I hope you will find the SNAP minilesson framework and the specific minilessons in this book useful. The remaining chapters include brief introductions and then launch into dozens of minilessons that you can shape to fit your needs. Enjoy!

Supportive Strategies and Technology Tools

Throughout the minilessons that the following chapters describe, I note instructional strategies that teachers may wish to use during steps A and P in specific minilessons. This chapter describes each instructional strategy in detail to benefit you as you dive deeper into the lessons in this book. You may also draw from these strategies for support in identifying ways to customize the lessons to best serve your and your students' needs. Throughout the minilessons, I also mention a number of technological tools, including websites, applications, and games. This chapter includes explanations of these tools, as well. Recommendations for good online videos to illustrate a strategy or tool—when they exist—appear throughout this chapter. Please note that web addresses often change, but all videos were current and functioning as this book went to press.

Choral Response

Choral response is a method of classroom discussion in which students call out responses in unison. Choral response is effective for providing repeated opportunities to deepen declarative knowledge. For example, if you ask a question that requires a short answer, such as one about a definition or a step in a process, you can use choral response instead of calling on volunteers to answer. All students would be asked to say the answer on your cue. Teachers often use a hand signal or count to three before students respond.

This strategy helps students take risks in using their verbal skills because there is safety in numbers. It's hard to be embarrassed about an incorrect answer if your voice is lost in the crowd. A student who is incorrect gets immediate feedback to that effect (from the crowd that responds otherwise) without the teacher having to check with each student individually. And this is one of the downfalls of choral response—it is not the best tool for checking individual understanding. However, used sparingly, it can be highly engaging for students and can enhance their memory of critical information.

The ESU6 Craft Knowledge Video Series has an excellent video titled *Choral Response .mov* (esu6pd, 2011; http://bit.ly/2qwtuvu) explaining and demonstrating choral response.

Comparisons

Students benefit cognitively from comparing, classifying, creating metaphors, and creating analogies. Results of employing these strategies can help boost student achievement from 31 to 46 percentile points (Marzano et al., 2001). Discerning and discussing similar and dissimilar characteristics of concepts or items is a basic building block of analysis. Teachers can direct this type of thinking and discussion or may allow students to do it on their own. Strive to frequently point out similarities and differences. Present students with similarities and differences explicitly when this helps them advance toward the designated learning target. Gradually decrease your support and allow them to become more independent in searching for, naming, and creating comparisons of all forms.

Graphic representations can be helpful. For comparison of two items, a Venn diagram (see page 24) works well. For multiple items, a comparison matrix is beneficial. For classifying or categorizing, a tree chart or Thinking Map called a *Tree Map* (Hyerle, 2009) works well. Metaphors and analogies are harder to put into a graphic format, but David Hyerle (2009) suggests a Thinking Map called a *Bridge Map* for analogies. Visit www .thinkingmaps.com for more information about Thinking Maps.

Concept Circle

Janet Allen (2007) popularized this strategy from Richard T. Vacca and Jo Anne Vacca (1986). When used for word association, this simple graphic organizer helps students analyze connections between words and explain relationships among words and the topic they are learning about. As teachers can choose the topics and the words appropriate for their students, Tyson (2012) notes that the concept circle works well with both elementary and secondary students.

The concept circle itself is simply a circle divided into four sections, like four large slices of pizza. Students record a word in each section as it relates to the topic. In addition to categorizing words, students should explain connections among those words either in writing or orally. Figure 2.1 provides a completed concept circle.

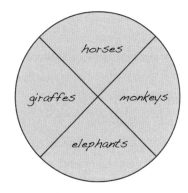

Topic: mammals

Describe or name the concept relationship among the sections.

Source: Tyson & Peery, 2017.

Figure 2.1: Completed concept circle.

Exit Ticket

You can use the exit ticket strategy to help students process new material and to reflect on information. Additionally, students may also reflect on their own thinking and learning processes in writing when completing an exit ticket.

First, design the prompt or question that you want students to respond to. Students will respond at the end of the lesson and give you their written response as a "ticket out the door" or as closure for the lesson (hence the name). Exit tickets serve as an excellent formative assessment that can help you adapt your teaching for the very next lesson. You can share information from the exit tickets the next day in class or even as the information is coming in if you use a digital tool like TodaysMeet (https://todaysmeet.com) or Padlet (https://padlet.com).

Certain prompts always work for exit tickets, such as the following examples.

- Write about one thing you learned today.
- What's the most important thing to remember from today's lesson?
- Discuss how what you learned today would be used outside of school.
- What is something that was hard to understand in this lesson?
- What is a question you still have about today's lesson?
- Summarize today's lesson as if you were telling an absent classmate about it.

Exit tickets take just a few minutes but are a great way to incorporate writing across the curriculum and to ask students to reflect on their learning.

Four Corners

The four corners strategy is one that gets students talking with each other and moving and is a great way to inject energy into instruction. First, you need to generate a statement or question related to your topic. You either need to have four different and specific answers, or you can go with *strongly agree*, *agree*, *disagree*, and *strongly disagree* if the question or statement is intended to check opinions or feelings. If you use a digital student response system like Plickers (https://plickers.com; see page 22), you need to have answer choices A, B, C, and D.

Second, present the statement or question and allow time for students to independently think about an answer before they start talking amongst themselves. Then, students gather in the corner of the room that corresponds to their choice. Once in a corner, ask students to talk with at least one other person there about why they selected the answers that they did. Call the whole class back together and, if time allows, have a student or two from each corner explain why their group chose the answer that it did.

You can use four corners to check background knowledge about a topic, to debate issues, to review previously taught material, and even to review for tests. One variation of this strategy is to ask students in one corner to convince others to come to their corner by providing reasons or evidence about why they should change their answers. Another variation is to have only two choices for an answer—perhaps agree and disagree—and ask students to form two lines or groups, one along one wall and the other opposite of and facing them. Students who are undecided or neutral stand in the middle of the room. You can allow students in the two lines to try to convince students in the middle to move toward one side or the other.

Frayer Model

The Frayer model is a graphic organizer or visual tool used for word analysis and vocabulary building. The model helps students deepen their knowledge of words that have conceptual weight; the model doesn't work as well with terms that have very clear-cut or simplistic definitions.

There are four steps to completing the visual (and to the discussion or thinking that takes place while completing the visual), and each step corresponds to a different box within the model. In the first box, the user defines the term. The next box is for stating the critical attributes or defining characteristics of the term. You may find that students go back and forth between the definition box and the characteristics box as they complete these two steps. This is absolutely normal. In the third and fourth steps, students generate examples and nonexamples of the word, and place these in the corresponding boxes. In this step, students clarify exactly what makes something an example of the term they are studying. Figure 2.2 illustrates this organizer. See the section titled Modified Frayer Model (page 20) for an adapted version of this organizer that includes nonlinguistic images.

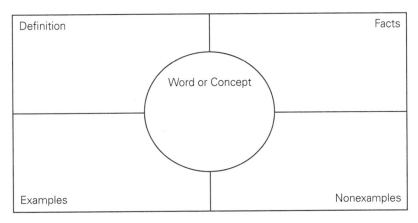

Source: Tyson & Peery, 2017.

Figure 2.2: Blank Frayer model.

*Visit **go.SolutionTree.com/literacy** for a free reproducible version of this figure.*

Jigsaw

Jigsaw is a powerful cooperative learning strategy that Aronson and Patnoe (1997) designed. The jigsaw strategy promotes interdependence among group members. Every student is part of a home group that learns the content and completes the tasks required. Each student is also part of an expert group, which consists of one member from each of the home groups becoming an expert on specific content. That expert will then return to the home group and teach the content to their teammates.

For example, if the groups were learning about William Shakespeare, one member of the home group would become an expert on a specific related topic (for example, his early life, education, dramatic works, or comedic works). Each expert group would meet to discuss and learn its topic, and then members would teach it to their home group members.

Many teachers create a note-taking template or other handouts to guide the work of both the home groups and the expert groups. Jigsaw is a great way to teach large amounts of content quickly and with high engagement. The key is to monitor the groups' activity closely to ensure they are finding the most important material that you want emphasized.

Kahoot!

Kahoot! (https://getkahoot.com) is a free, game-like, classroom-response tool that engages participants and provides feedback instantly on the screen. It is incredibly engaging for students and adults alike. Teachers can use Kahoot! to build multiple-choice questions for students to access from their computers, laptops, tablets, or phones. This will allow them to assess students' learning of target words at the end of a minilesson and also periodically check students' retention of these words. Watching the YouTube video *How to Use Kahoot! in the Classroom* (Tech in 2, 2014; http://bit.ly/2r86G3Z) is a great way to familiarize yourself with this tool.

Membean

Membean (http://membean.com) offers both free and paid versions. It bills itself as a test preparation and instructional strategy tool. Each word you look up on Membean is broken down into its constituent parts, including roots. This breakdown can help support students in doing word analysis on their own. One of Membean's most helpful areas is Roots Trees. These Roots Trees show words in one word family, connected by a common root. Each tree has clickable boxes that define the words. Membean's Word Maps feature is also useful. A student can type any word into the search box and instantly see a concept map of related words, synonyms, and more. The paid version offers self-paced online learning for your students. It provides data to both student and teacher about how many words are being learned.

Modified Frayer Model

The modified Frayer model is an adaptation of the original Frayer model and includes the power of a nonlinguistic image (see figure 2.3). It contains the following components (Tyson & Peery, 2017).

- A definition, synonym, or paraphrase
- The defining characteristics or critical attributes
- The word itself
- Examples
- A visual
- Nonexamples

Before discussing nonexamples, it can be helpful to generate the examples and a visual as students seek to solidify their conceptual understanding. In my personal interactions with students, they report that spending more time on the positives—meaning what the term actually *is* versus what it *is not*—is often very fruitful. It is important for students to learn to distinguish what makes something an example versus trying to generate lots of nonexamples. Push them to articulate what the defining features are.

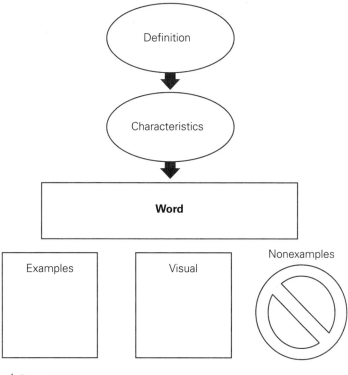

Source: Tyson & Peery, 2017.

Figure 2.3: Modified Frayer model.

*Visit **go.SolutionTree.com/literacy** for a free reproducible version of this figure.*

Padlet

Padlet (https://padlet.com) is an online space for creating a collaborative, digital poster or visual bulletin board. Users can create sticky notes that can include text, images, links, and videos to place on the board. Padlet is a useful, collaborative tool and can serve many purposes. Teachers can create a large Padlet that students revisit over time, perhaps on Greek or Latin roots or on synonyms for a particular overused word like *said*. The YouTube video *How to Use Padlet in the Classroom* (AISLyle, 2015; http://bit.ly/2qCVrNg) is a good introduction to the tool. Vicki Davis, also known as Cool Cat Teacher, offers an excellent, detailed blog post on using Padlet (see Davis, n.d.; www.coolcatteacher.com/how-to-use-padlet-fantastic-tool-teaching).

Pass the Paper

In this strategy, each student has a blank sheet of paper and responds to the teacher's prompt or question quickly (in one minute or less). Then, time is called, and each student passes his or her paper in the direction the teacher has chosen. The last person in the row, section, or class gets up and runs his or her paper to the first person in the sequence so that every person has a paper at all times. The cycle can be repeated several times. You can shorten the writing or responding time to thirty seconds if pressed for time.

Allow students to write as much or as little as they want—as long as they are on topic. Encourage students who don't like to write to quickly brainstorm a list of words or a bulleted list. Everything does not have to be in complete sentences. You can collect the papers and create a Padlet (https://padlet.com) or other display—or even a found poem—with some of what the students wrote. You can share this the next day or keep it displayed to continue reminding students of the content.

Plickers

Plickers (https://plickers.com) is a formative assessment tool much like interactive clicker systems, but without physical click devices. Instead, students hold up signs that have visuals that resemble QR codes. Each visual corresponds to an answer choice (such as A, B, C, or D). You take a photo of the students holding up their answer cards with the app, and, like magic, the app breaks down the data for you, showing you who answered correctly and incorrectly. This tool requires nothing but the free cards that you print from the site and a device that the app can be loaded onto.

Quizlet

Quizlet (https://quizlet.com) is a collaborative online community that has activities for students to use when studying just about any subject. More than twenty million students and teachers use Quizlet per month (Quizlet, 2017). It has collections of practice activities to use as well as the capability for you to make your own materials.

Stand-Up Meeting

A stand-up meeting is a quick way to do a check for understanding in your classroom. It obviously involves standing up, but it can be applied to many situations and can be a tool for helping your students become more self-directed in their work. The strategy is versatile. You can call a stand-up meeting to check on group or individual progress with a long-term assignment or use it to quickly check for understanding of new content you just taught.

First, you must gain everyone's attention and ask them to stop what they're doing temporarily. Then, the entire class stands and gathers in an area you indicate. You can pose a question or topic to discuss in advance or once everyone convenes. See David Orphal's blog post "Stealing Business Ideas for my Classroom" on the Center for Teaching Quality's webpage (Orphal, 2014; http://bit.ly/2jXNBiz) for a good discussion of how one teacher used this strategy in his classroom. (Visit **go.SolutionTree.com/literacy** to access live links to the websites mentioned in this book.)

Teacher Gestures

The term *nonlinguistic representations* became popular with the publication of the book *Classroom Instruction That Works* (Marzano et al., 2001). Briefly, nonlinguistic representations are depictions of knowledge that rely less on language and instead tap into the visual, kinesthetic, tactile, or concrete. Either the teacher or student can produce these manifestations of knowledge. When the teacher produces them, the goal is to help students form an image in their minds, provide them with something they themselves can do to better remember the topic or concept, or to support linguistic forms of knowledge, especially when the terminology may be of concern.

Teacher gestures, then, are a form of nonlinguistic representation. Teachers can often use gestures (or exaggerated facial expressions) to cue students as to the meaning of the linguistic information that accompanies them. For example, Jeff Zwiers (2014), senior researcher at the Stanford Graduate School of Education and director of professional development for the Understanding Language initiative, recommends using hand gestures when teaching students how to correctly use transition words like *however* and *nevertheless* in their writing. Because these words are used only when there are opposites on either side of the word, you can create hand gestures that symbolize that meaning.

Nonlinguistic images have resulted in gains of as much as 43 percentile points (Marzano, 2007). Neurologist and educator Judy Willis (2006) reminds us that offering information visually sets up connections with the occipital lobes of the brain and helps create memory pathways. Teacher gestures are a powerful form of nonlinguistic image that can help students solidify information like nothing else.

ThingLink

ThingLink (www.thinglink.com) is an online tool that allows students to create visuals containing links connecting to other sources such as webpages, videos, and so on. In other words, students can use ThingLink to create layered content, linking together visuals, texts, voice-overs, and more.

Think-Pair-Share

Think-pair-share is a collaborative learning strategy in which two students talk together to solve a problem or respond to a question or prompt. This strategy has two critical steps: cognition and talking after students are paired. The "think" step is often rushed or almost absent. It's critical that you pose the question or prompt, then allow adequate think time, and lastly, ask students to pair and talk. There must be individual cognitive processing before there's collaborative discussion within the pair.

Pairs can be preassigned in order for the strategy to work smoothly. Some teachers have standing pairs that last for a certain time period, like a quarter or semester. You can add another step and have pairs report out at the end of the allotted sharing time.

TodaysMeet

TodaysMeet (https://todaysmeet.com) is a live backchannel that you can use in classes and meetings. Upon accessing the site, you'll see a box that has the words "Pick a Name" above it. To create a space for your class, type in a name, such as Peerys4thBlock, and, if it's available, you will see a check mark appear. You will then go to the box below and fill out how long you want this chat "room" to be open. For one class period, choose one hour. Then, as you conduct the minilesson, display the room you created on the screen. Students can use devices individually to join you in the room by typing in the room's name. Then students give themselves screen names and type comments of up to 140 characters. Those comments will appear on the site and your screen in real time. TodaysMeet is a great way to keep students engaged and use technology authentically.

Venn Diagram

A Venn diagram is a graphic organizer for comparison and is widely used in classrooms (see figure 2.4). First used in mathematics, it helps illustrate relationships in logic and probability. Now used more generally, it is a visual that shows similarities between two items. In the Venn diagram, users record similarities in the part where the circles overlap, and qualities unique to each item in the parts where the circles do not overlap. Visit www .readingquest.org/strat/venn.html to access a good discussion of Venn diagrams.

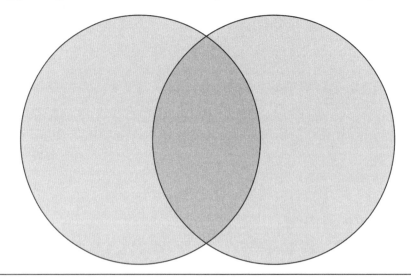

Figure 2.4: Blank Venn diagram.

*Visit **go.SolutionTree.com/literacy** for a free reproducible version of this figure.*

Vocabulary Frame

A vocabulary frame can be hand-drawn on notebook paper, a large index card, or even a large sticky note. To make the frame, students place the term in the middle of the paper. It can be written in all caps or in large lettering to enhance memory. Their own (unresearched) definition is then written in the upper right corner. A sentence that reminds them of the word's meaning is written on the top half of the page. A quick sketch (nothing elaborate) is written in the lower right corner. This strategy allows students to write about the term in their own words and use a visual and context to aid memory.

Vocabulary Log

The vocabulary log strategy—also called vocabulary journal, vocabulary notebook, and word log—is a record of student-selected words, meanings, and applications. Ideally, you should use it during segments of instruction that focus on general academic vocabulary and with independent reading.

With this strategy, the student needs to accomplish five steps: (1) record each word, (2) give its part of speech (as used in the source where it was found), (3) describe the context in which he or she finds the word, (4) give a student-friendly definition, and lastly, (5) attempt to use it authentically. Figure 2.5 provides an example of a vocabulary log in use.

Word	Part of Speech	Context and Source (How was it used when you read, heard, or saw it? Provide enough context for others to understand. Cite your source.)	Definition (in your own words, matching the part of speech)	Application (Write a sentence of your own or use the word in enough context for others to understand the meaning.)
1. *cricket*	Noun	Children's book read to us in class; the character said that he liked to play cricket when he was a child.	A bat-and-ball game played on a field with two teams of eleven players each that play against each other	I would like to learn how to play cricket because it seems fun.
2. *quarantined*	Verb, past tense	On the evening news; the dogs were quarantined.	To separate from others, often to prevent the spreading of disease	The cats were quarantined after they were taken from the dangerous situation.

Source: Adapted from Tyson & Peery, 2017.

Figure 2.5: Sample vocabulary log.

Visit go.SolutionTree.com/literacy for a free reproducible version of this figure.

Word Wheel

A word wheel is a slightly simpler version of a concept circle (see figure 2.6). You can use it with students at any level who struggle with vocabulary and comprehension. When using a word wheel, you can quickly sketch this visual or give it to students on a handout, whichever you prefer.

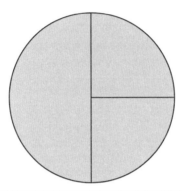

Figure 2.6: Blank word wheel.

*Visit **go.SolutionTree.com/literacy** for a free reproducible version of this figure.*

The target word is written in the left-hand "pie slice" (half of the wheel), and the two slices on the right side that make up the second half of the wheel are where synonyms, pictures, or both for the target word are placed. When I use this strategy with intermediate students and above, I usually provide a synonym for one slice and ask students to work together to come up with another synonym for the remaining slice. With early elementary students, you could include a sketch in the top right slice and a very simple synonym in the bottom right slice. For example, if the word on the left were *companion*, the top right might depict two stick figures holding hands, and in the bottom right, the word *friend* would appear. A fifth-grade class and teacher made the following word wheel (figure 2.7) after reading the book *Wilfrid Gordon McDonald Partridge* by Mem Fox (1984).

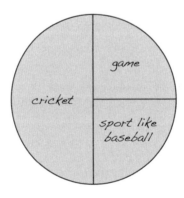

Source: Tyson & Peery, 2017.

Figure 2.7: Word wheel example.

Wordle

Wordle (www.wordle.net) is a site for creating word clouds. You simply type text into the tool, or cut and paste from a text, and the site magically creates a visual that includes all the words, with the most frequent or important words appearing larger than others.

Whip Around

You can use the highly engaging Whip Around strategy as a closing activity or within a lesson anytime you want to quickly check students' comprehension. You first give a prompt or pose a question. It should be something that could be answered fairly quickly and simply. After allowing students think time (or they can jot their answers down), "whip around" the class, calling on students in rapid succession. You can even change the order of how you call on students. For example, you can start calling on students on the right side of the room and suddenly switch to the left. Refer to the YouTube video *CLR: Whip Around* (Cal High News, 2015; www.youtube.com/watch?v=9LJ50g-u4dI) for a good demonstration of this strategy in a high school classroom.

Students can repeat answers given earlier if they like, but encourage them, if at all possible, to try to have a unique response ready or to add to what has already been stated. Students can also say "I pass" if they can't think of an answer, but remember to go back to those who passed to see if they can supply an original answer later or repeat a response that was given. The key for this strategy is to move fast. Don't stop to discuss answers until you have completely gone around the room.

Word Talk With Word Questioning

I learned this strategy from educator and author Janet Allen. To implement this strategy, provide student groups with a list of words from the unit of study. Ask students to discuss them based on their knowledge of the words and the topic and then to respond to the questions you provide.

The following example of a word talk with word questioning is based on the topic of malnutrition and is from Allen's (2014) book *Tools for Teaching Academic Vocabulary*.

- How are vitamin B, milled rice, and beriberi related?

- What possible connection could there be between pirates and vitamin C?

- What is the relationship between growth spurts and empty calorie foods? (Choose two words that would seem to be unrelated.)

- How are scurvy, diets, and picky eaters all related to malnutrition?

- If I discovered a cure for malnutrition, what scientific words would likely describe the process I used?

Final Thoughts

This chapter seeks to be a jumping-off point for you as you explore strategies and tools to improve instruction in all areas, not just vocabulary learning. The strategies and tools herein are mentioned in the lessons that follow, but don't limit yourself to using them only in the ways I suggest. Explore and enjoy!

Robust Roots A–K

Y ou may remember at some point in your own K–12 education completing a unit of study on Greek or Latin roots. My eighth-grade year was the year that my English teacher engaged us in what she called *minicourses*, most of which consisted of a slew of independent work that had to be completed and then bound into some kind of binder for her inspection. I vaguely remember the minicourses on journalism and word study being my favorites. Learning about roots, word families, and affixes in the word study minicourse was a joy for me. However, years later, when I tried to generate similar joy in my classroom, I failed miserably. Why did my students not find roots as mesmerizing as I did? That question I may never be able to answer, but I do know that the student who has knowledge of frequently used roots is the student who has a useful tool in his or her toolkit. The study of roots is definitely worth spending time on and can support our students in preparing for future academic study. This is not just teacher lore; many studies attest to word analysis as a practice that increases both students' vocabulary and their general knowledge of language (Graves, 2006; Graves & Hammond, 1980; White, Sowell, & Yanagihara, 1989).

The study of roots that are present in cognates across several languages can support English learners. Native Spanish, Italian, and French speakers can find many shared word families in English. All teachers should be invested in the study of some of the most common English language roots because knowledge of these roots assists students with mastering content-area vocabulary and supports incidental word learning. Andrew Biemiller and Naomi Slonim (2001) estimate that children acquire about six hundred root word meanings per year from infancy to the end of elementary school. However, we know that not all our students will acquire six hundred root word meanings; some will acquire significantly less (Colker, n.d.; Hart & Risley, 2003; Morgan, Farkas, Hillemeier, Hammer, & Maczuga, 2015). Students who are new to schooling or new to English also face additional challenges. And lastly, students' learning of roots should continue beyond elementary school and exceed six hundred root words per year. Thus, additional instruction about roots, whenever we can squeeze it into our lessons, can support our students in unlocking the meaning of thousands of words.

Root words, sometimes just called *roots*, are words that do not have prefixes or suffixes and cannot be further subdivided. Each root represents the smallest unit of meaning in our language and is the basis for a word family. For example, think about the word *walk*. *Walks*, *walked*, and *walking* are built on the root (also called the base word). Other roots like *ped* are not words unto themselves but are used with other component parts to create words like *pedal* and *pedestrian*.

You may have also heard the word *cognate*. A cognate is a word derived from the same root as another word; in other words, cognates are words that have a common origin. They may occur not only in one language, like English, but in a group of languages. For example, the word *adversary* in English and *adversario* in Spanish are cognates derived from the Latin *adversus*, which means "against" or "opposite of."

It is widely noted that more than 60 percent of the English language is based on or borrowed from Greek and Latin (Dictionary.com, 2015). Even new words that enter our language are often based on Greek or Latin precedents. For example, the word *megabyte* builds on the Greek word *mega* that means "great." It's a combination of *mega* as a prefix and the computing term *byte*. The word *locavore*, which means "a person who eats only locally produced food," builds on the precedent set by words like *carnivore*, derived from the Latin *carnivorus*. Many brand names originate from these two ancient languages. For example, the auto manufacturer Volvo takes its name from the Latin *volvere*, which means "to roll," and its competitor Audi based its name on the Latin *audire*, which means "to hear" (Christa, 2013). Items as diverse as Nike sports apparel, Venus disposable razors, and Xerox copy machines can also trace their brand names to Greek and Latin.

This chapter focuses on some of the most common Greek and Latin roots that students are likely to encounter in school texts. In the lesson titles, the letter r denotes that the minilesson is about one or more roots, and the number indicates the order in which the specific lessons appear (for example, lesson R1, lesson R2, and so on). The roots are grouped alphabetically, covering words that start with the letter a through letter k. Chapter 4 covers the letter l onward. As Timothy V. Rasinski, Nancy Padak, Joanna Newton, and Evangeline Newton (2011) remind us, "The systematic, ongoing, and consistent integration of Latin and Greek roots into vocabulary instruction offers awesome potential for enhancing students' academic growth" (p. 13). My hope is that you can get started on this path toward such awesome potential with the minilessons you find here.

Root: *act*

The root *act* is present in many common words. This minilesson focuses on the root *act* from the Latin meaning "to do." You may want to start the minilesson by reviewing the verb *act* with your students and then building on it for the remainder of the target words. *Act* (a verb) means to do something or to behave in a certain way.

Lesson R1: *action, actor, react, reaction*

In this minilesson, teachers will teach the root *act*, such as in the words *action*, *actor*, *react*, and *reaction*.

Difficulty level: 1

S

The following lists target words students should *see* and *say* for this minilesson.

▸ **Action (n.):** A thing that has been done

▸ **Actor (n.):** A person who has done something; more specifically, a person who performs in movies, theater, television, and so on

▸ **React (v.):** To respond to something; to behave in a certain way in response to something that happens

▸ **Reaction (n.):** A response to something; the way someone behaves

N

All these words are about doing something. The words *act* and *react* often work together. You can role-play to demonstrate an action and reaction to students. Share with them the popular saying, "For every *action*, there is a *reaction*." This applies widely, not just in science, where they may have heard it before.

Remind students of the meaning of the prefix *re-* if this has been covered before, too.

A

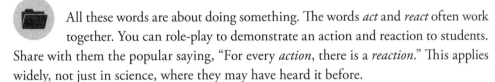

Partner students up and have them take turns being an *actor*. Ask the designated actor to perform an *action*, like making an exaggerated expression or a funny face of some sort. Then ask the pair how the other partner, not the *actor*, *reacted*. Then reverse roles. Do several rounds of this as time allows.

The following are some ideas for the rounds. You can say:

▸ "Make a funny face. See if your partner laughs or smiles."

▸ "Act sad. How does your partner react?"

▸ "Roll your pencil across your desk. Does the pencil fall off the desk? Did your partner stop it from rolling off the desk or pick it up from the floor?"

▸ "Get up and walk away from your partner. What is the reaction?"

P

Ask each student to write sentences using at least two of the following words: *act, acted, acting, action, react, reacted, reacting,* and *reaction.* You most likely used all these forms when you engaged the students in step A or when you defined the words.

Scaffolding

Assist struggling students by asking them to write about what they and their partner just did. This should help them use the words in context.

Acceleration

Enact is a related word that teachers can add to this minilesson for advanced students or for the entire class if appropriate.

▸ **Enact (v.):**

1. To perform or to act something out

2. To make into a law or other rule or statute

Roots: *ann, enn*

These roots, which are alternative spellings of each other, originate in Latin and mean "year." *Ann* is most often used at the beginning of words, like *annual* and *anniversary.* *Enn* is used in the middle of words, like the ones in lesson R2 as well as the words *perennial* and *centennial.*

Lesson R2: *annual, anniversary, millennium, millennial*

In this minilesson, teachers will teach the roots *ann* and *enn*, such as in the words *annual, anniversary, millennium,* and *millennial.*

Difficulty level: 1

S

The following lists target words students should *see* and *say* for this minilesson.

- **Annual (adj.):** Happening once a year
- **Anniversary (n.):** The date on which something occurred in a previous year
- **Millennium (n.):** A period of one thousand years
- **Millennial (adj.):** Relating to a period of or anniversary of one thousand years

N

Consider saying something like the following to your class.

All these words are about time, and specifically, they are about periods of time. Annual means one year has passed. An anniversary is a date marked each year, like a wedding anniversary or an anniversary of moving to a new place or meeting one of your friends. Millennium and millennial have been used frequently since we passed the year of 1999. The year 2000 and beyond is what we call a new millennium—a new period of one thousand years has begun. The year 3000 will mark the next millennium. You may have also heard the word millennial to describe people who reached adulthood in the year 2000 or since. They are people who came of age during this new millennium.

A

Form small groups of students. Ask them to discuss the following questions.

- What is something that happens *annually*, meaning that it happens every year? Come up with as many things as you can think of.
- Does your family celebrate any *anniversaries*? If so, what are they?

P

Have each student write a sentence using two of the target words (or related forms of those words). Have a few share aloud if time allows.

Scaffolding

Provide sentence templates like the following for students to choose from.

- My favorite *annual* event is _____.
- Some people celebrate the *anniversary* of _____.
- *Millennium* means _____.
- *Millennial* means _____.

Acceleration

Related words *bicentennial* and *centennial* may be of interest or may be familiar to some students. Discuss these words as appropriate, or ask advanced students to find out more about them during step A and to share what they find in step P.

▸ **Bicentennial (adj.):** Relating to a two hundredth anniversary or a period of two hundred years

▸ **Centennial (adj.):** Relating to a one hundredth anniversary or a period of one hundred years

Root: *aud*

The following two minilessons focus on the root *aud*, which comes from the Latin word *audire*. *Audire* means "to hear."

Students may be somewhat familiar with the word *audio* because of their experience with electronic devices and the word *auditorium* because it is a place they have visited for school functions. However, the less common word *auditory* is taught along with these two words in this difficulty level 1 minilesson.

Lesson R3: *audio, auditorium, auditory*

In this minilesson, teachers will teach the root *aud*, such as in the words *audio, auditorium*, and *auditory*.

Difficulty level: 1

S

The following lists target words students should *see* and *say* for this minilesson.

▸ **Audio (n.):** Sound, usually used in relation to the transmission or recording of sound

▸ **Auditorium (n.):** A room or space in a building where people go to watch a performance, assembly, and so on

▸ **Auditory (adj.):** Related to your sense of hearing

Ask students if they have seen or heard the word *audio* when using electronic devices or computers. Discuss a recent trip to the school *auditorium* or use the word in a familiar context. You may also connect the word *audience* to *auditorium* if you feel that this will help students. For *auditory*, you can point out how it is very similar to *auditorium* (in this step or the next step). You could say, "In addition to sight, we use our hearing when we go to the *auditorium* to watch a performance. In other words, we use our *auditory* system. That's our sense of hearing."

N

Consider saying something like the following to your class.

So, you can see that all three words share a root or word part, aud. *Many English words use this root, and it always relates to sound and hearing. Remember that* audio *and* auditorium *are nouns. And remember our definition of noun—it's a person, place, thing, idea, or feeling.* Audio *is a thing—it's usually sound that is recorded or played, like the audio that comes out of our computers' speakers. An* auditorium *is a place. It's where we go to have an assembly or see a play.* Auditory *is an adjective. It describes nouns. For example, I could say that I enjoy learning by* auditory *teaching methods. When someone speaks to me out loud, I find that I remember the information better than if I just read about it. In other words, I'm good at* auditory *processing.*

A

Small groups should discuss the following questions.

▸ What are some devices that use *audio*? Look around the classroom for ideas. (Answers may include smartphones, televisions, DVD players, laptop and desktop computers, tablets, home stereos, car stereos, and so on.)

▸ Have you been to an *auditorium* outside of school? If so, what were you doing there? (Answers may include attending a ceremony like a graduation, seeing a play, going on a class field trip, and so on.)

P

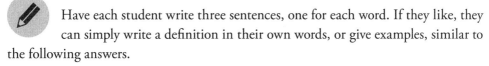

Have each student write three sentences, one for each word. If they like, they can simply write a definition in their own words, or give examples, similar to the following answers.

▸ *Audio* is sound that plays on a device like my iPad.

▸ An *auditorium* is a place where we go to see a presentation or play.

▸ *Auditory* is about your hearing. Teachers have good *auditory* skills.

Scaffolding

Provide students with sentence stems. The blanks can be filled in with single words or with phrases. Examples include:

▸ The word *audio* means _____. An example of *audio* is _____.

▸ An *auditorium* is a place where we go to _____.

▸ If something is *auditory*, it can be heard. Something *auditory* from school today is _____.

Acceleration

Ask students to generate additional words with the root *aud* or to find them online using a search engine or website. Quizlet (https://quizlet.com) retrieves a list of words with visuals if you use the search feature and type the phrase "root word aud." Students can also view the presentation "'Aud' Words" (Gordon, 2014; https://prezi.com/ggdthqwezkdk/aud-words) to access information on this root. Advanced students could pair up and go through the presentation together, perhaps reading it aloud to each other.

Lesson R4: *audible, inaudible, audiology*

In this minilesson, teachers will teach the root *aud*, such as in the words *audible*, *inaudible*, and *audiology*. This level 2 minilesson focuses on three words that may all be unfamiliar but links together two antonyms to enhance memory.

Difficulty level: 2

S

The following lists target words students should *see* and *say* for this minilesson.

- ▸ **Audible (adj.):** Capable of being heard
- ▸ **Inaudible (adj.):** Incapable of being heard; producing no sound
- ▸ **Audiology (n.):** The science of studying hearing

Ask students if they know any related words. Answers might include *audio*, *audience*, *auditory*, *auditorium*, and *audiologist*.

N

Consider saying something like the following to your class.

> The words audible *and* inaudible *are opposites of each other, or antonyms. Notice that the prefix* in- *on the second word makes it the opposite of the first. So, if I were giving you directions for something we were doing in class, I'd want my directions to be clearly* audible. *That means you could all hear what I said. If you couldn't hear the directions, you could say they were* inaudible, *or that I was speaking in an* inaudible *manner.* Audiology *has an interesting word part in it, too. Notice the* -ology. *Words like* biology *and* psychology *use that part, and in each case, it means the study of or the science of something. In* audiology, *it means the study of hearing. When you know the root* aud, *sometimes when it's combined with other familiar word parts, you can unlock the whole word's meaning.*

You may want to underline or box the word part *-ology* so that students' eyes can see it as a word component.

A

Have students work together to list *audible* things versus *inaudible* things. For example, a teacher's lecture and the announcements on the public address (PA) system are *audible*. Movies, TV shows, and music are *audible*. However, a student daydreaming or journaling in class are *inaudible*.

P

Ask students to write short explanations (or synonyms) of all three words that they can share with students who are absent today or to summarize the minilesson. This writing can be done on sticky notes and attached to chart paper, a wall, or a door. Students can also use an online tool like TodaysMeet (https://todaysmeet.com) or Padlet (https://padlet.com).

Examples:

▸ Something that is *audible* can be heard, but something that is *inaudible* cannot be. *Audiology* is the study of hearing.

▸ *Audible* and *inaudible* are opposites. You can hear it if it's *audible* but not if it's *inaudible*. *Audiology* is the science of studying hearing. The *-ology* lets you know that and is in other words like *biology*.

Scaffolding

Allow some students to provide their explanations to you orally instead of in writing as time allows. You can reinforce the meaning of the words by saying, "I'd like to hear you give an *audible* summary instead of a written one."

Acceleration

Ask students to brainstorm and write sentences with related words. Possible answers include *audibly*, *inaudibly*, *audience*, and *audition*.

Root: *auto*

The two minilessons in this section focus on the root *auto*, which originates from the Greek word *autos*, meaning "self" or "same." Many students will likely know the word *automobile* as a synonym for *car* or if they speak Spanish or Italian because of the similarities of the word in those languages to English.

Lesson R5: *autobiography, autograph, automatic*

In this minilesson, teachers will teach the root *auto*, such as in the words *autobiography*, *autograph*, and *automatic*.

Difficulty level: 1

S

The following lists target words students should *see* and *say* for this minilesson.

▶ **Autobiography (n.):** A person's written account of his or her own life

▶ **Autograph (n.):** A person's signature or signing of one's name; often a memento or souvenir from a sports star or other celebrity

▶ **Automatic (adj.):** Working independently or on its own; self-directed

> Be sure to pronounce the *T* in *auto* as a *T* and not with a *D* sound like *audio*. The roots *auto* and *aud* are pronounced differently and have different spellings and meanings. While these distinctions may seem obvious to you as a well-educated speaker of English, it can be confusing for non-native speakers, young students, struggling readers, and students who have auditory processing difficulties.

N

Consider saying something like the following.

> *You may have seen these three words before, and you may even know what they mean, but I'd like to talk with you today about a similarity they all share. Notice the root word* auto *that appears at the beginning of each word. It means "same" or "self," and with these three words, the root* auto *definitely means "self." You would write an* autobiography *yourself; you would be the author. If you became famous for writing your* autobiography, *your readers might come to a book signing and ask for your* autograph. *This is where you'd sign the inside of your book. Signed books by famous authors are often very valuable. Lastly, the word* automatic *means something that works by itself, on its own, sometimes without human direction. Many electric devices these days are* automatic. *For example, I have a coffee maker and an iron at home that are* automatic. *They cut off when they have been on too long, even if I don't switch them off. They do it all by themselves.*

You may ask students if they know related words, like *biography*, the opposite of *autobiography* (which they may have learned in English language arts), or *automobile* as a synonym for car.

A

Place students in triads. Have them complete the following sentences.

▶ I would like to read an *autobiography* by _____.

▶ I would ask _____ for an *autograph*.

▶ Something *automatic* that I use is a _____.

Encourage each triad to allow each person to have three turns, ensuring that each student gets to supply a personal answer for each prompt. Group members can help each other think of answers if necessary.

P

Have each student select his or her favorite two words and write his or her own sentences for those words. Let students know that they can use a sentence they said themselves or that they heard another student say in the triad activity that preceded this step.

Scaffolding

Monitor students who struggle with the writing and point out objects in the room that might help them create their sentences. For example, you could show one or two *autobiographies* from your classroom library or mention those that students have read. You could also point out objects that have *automatic* properties, like the screen saver on an interactive whiteboard or computer, or even the overhead lighting.

Acceleration

Have students access the WordHippo webpage "Words Starting With AUTO" (2017b; http://bit.ly/2rBi0Hi) and scroll through the list of words that start with *auto-*. The advanced students can pick a new word or two to research and learn about—and to possibly share with the rest of the class.

Lesson R6: *autonomy, autonomous*

In this minilesson, teachers will teach the root *auto*, such as in the words *autonomy* and *autonomous*.

Difficulty level: 2

S

The following lists target words students should *see* and *say* for this minilesson.

▸ **Autonomy (n.):** Self-governance, independence, or freedom to do what one wants

▸ **Autonomous (adj.):** Self-controlling, independent, or free

Point out that *autonomy* and *autonomous* are related (one is the noun form, and the other is the adjective form, from the same root). Ensure that students know the accent is on each word's second syllable. These words, especially when encountered during independent reading, may seem hard to pronounce.

N

Consider saying something like the following.

You see that these words have a common word part, in this case aut. *This word component is usually spelled a-u-t-o but may be slightly different depending on the letters that follow. The main thing to remember about words that contain* aut *is that they all relate to the self.* Autonomy *and* autonomous *are about controlling your actions. Often teachers say they'd like* autonomy, *or the freedom to do what they choose in their classrooms.* Autonomous *is the adjective form, so an* autonomous *teacher would be one who could make decisions about what and how to teach. You might even tell your parents that you'd like to be more* autonomous!

You may want to ask students what being more autonomous would be like for them—for example, setting their own bedtimes or curfews, determining how much screen time or device time they are allowed, or deciding when and where to complete their homework.

A

In pairs or small groups, have students brainstorm examples for *autonomous.* You may want to start them off with the following example.

▸ **Things that are *autonomous*:** Deciding that you'll be a vegetarian or vegan; determining what medical treatment you will or will not take; taking a stand on an issue regardless of what your best friends think; choosing how and when to observe your religion

P

Ask each student to choose one of the two target words and write a short paragraph (two to five sentences) about how he or she can apply or has applied each term in his or her own life. You may want to model or share your own example to get them started. For example, I might tell students that an example of *autonomy* for me was when I chose the college I wanted to attend, saved my money, and went there at age seventeen, even though it was an hour from my home and I had no car. I knew that once I arrived there, I would be almost entirely independent or *autonomous.*

Scaffolding

Offer students who struggle with the writing (P step) ideas individualized for them. Give them examples of when you've seen them being *autonomous.* For example, you might say to a student, "Yesterday you were being *autonomous* during silent reading time. You chose your book, got busy reading, and didn't even need any help from me."

Acceleration

Students can work independently or in pairs and view and discuss the slide show "Root Word → AUTO" (studntz, n.d.) on SlideShare (www.slideshare .net/studntz/root-word-auto) during the last part of the minilesson (step P). (Visit **go.SolutionTree.com/literacy** to access live links to the websites mentioned in this book.) Even though this presentation is only ten slides in length, it's not necessary for students to get all the way through it. There's plenty of material to discuss within the first half of the slides.

Beyond the Lesson

You may want to tell your students that if they'd like greater *autonomy* in the classroom, they need to do certain things to convince you they can handle it.

Roots: *ben, bene, beni* and *mal, male, mali*

The following two minilessons focus on the roots that basically mean good and bad: *ben, bene, beni* and *mal, male, mali*. Because these roots have a similar meaning, *mal, male,* and *mali* are included here rather than in the next chapter where roots starting with the letter m occur.

Students may already be familiar with the word *benefit* or *beneficial*. Students may also know the word *maleficent* because of the movie by that title starring Angelina Jolie. See if you can build on their familiarity and move them to a few sophisticated yet less frequently used words.

Lesson R7: *benefit, beneficial, benevolent, malevolent*

In this minilesson, teachers will teach the roots *bene* and *male*, such as in the words *benefit, beneficial, benevolent,* and *malevolent*.

Difficulty level: 1

S

The following lists target words students should *see* and *say* for this minilesson. You can use the following four words with fairly young students because they may already be familiar with the words *benefit, beneficial,* or both.

- ‣ **Benefit (n.):** A gain or profit
- ‣ **Beneficial (adj.):** Resulting in something good or profitable
- ‣ **Benevolent (adj.):** Kind or charitable to others
- ‣ **Malevolent (adj.):** Mean or harmful to others

Consider adding teacher gestures (see chapter 2, page 23) if you feel it will help your students remember the words' meanings. For example, for every word that contains *bene-*, you could add a sweeping gesture with your arms (showing openness), a broad smile, or both since they exemplify a positive reaction to something. In contrast, for *malevolent*, you can cross your arms and demonstrate a frown, which symbolizes a negative reaction.

You may want students to practice *benevolent* and *malevolent* several times, as they are more difficult to pronounce than the other two words.

N

Consider saying something like the following to your class.

> Benefits *you get from something are the good things that you receive. For example, some* benefits *you get from attending our school each day are that you're able to see your friends, you learn new things, and you get help from teachers when you need it. The adjective* beneficial *can describe these* benefits.

Pause to ensure the relationship between these two words is clear. One is a noun, and the other is an adjective, but their meanings are very similar. They cannot, however, be used interchangeably. This is a syntax error students may make. Provide clarification and examples as needed.

Then you might say something like the following.

> Remember, benevolent *and* malevolent *are both adjectives that usually describe people. Again, the word that starts with* bene- *is the positive or good word, and* malevolent, *that starts with* male-, *is the opposite of that. So, a* benevolent *person does kind things, but a* malevolent *person does mean things. I would say that teachers are* benevolent *people, and people who hurt animals are* malevolent, *the opposite of* benevolent. *In a moment, I'll ask you to come up with examples with your group of fictional characters in books, on TV, and in movies that are* benevolent *and* malevolent.

A

Small groups can list *benefits* of familiar activities, like participating in physical education classes, going on field trips, attending assemblies, playing a sport, or eating healthy foods. You may want to assign each group a different activity for which to list benefits so that every group is working on something slightly different.

Then, ask each group to list either *benevolent* characters from movies, TV, and literature or *malevolent* characters, or both, depending on time and how well your groups are working together. Circulate briskly and monitor, as there won't be time to report out after this step. If you need to prompt students, here are some ideas.

> *Benevolent* **characters:** Cinderella's fairy godmother; Charlotte the spider in *Charlotte's Web*; Miss Rumphius in the picture book of the same name; Boo Radley in *To Kill a Mockingbird*

> *Malevolent* **characters:** Cinderella's stepmother and stepsisters; the wolf in "Red Riding Hood"; Cruella de Vil in *101 Dalmatians*; Lord Voldemort in the *Harry Potter* books and movies

P

 Use an adaptation of the four corners strategy here (see chapter 2, page 17). Call out names of characters or historical figures that your class has studied, and ask students to go to one side of the classroom if you call out a benevolent person's name or the other side of the room if the person is malevolent. You may also allow students to stand in the center if they feel neither term applies.

Scaffolding

Provide students with sentence stems. Use the following if you like.

> A *benefit* is something you receive that is good or that helps you. One *benefit* of a good night's sleep is _____. One *benefit* of eating vegetables is _____.

> If something is *beneficial*, that means that it's good for you. For example, it's *beneficial* to ask your teacher for help if you need it. It's also *beneficial* to _____.

> A *benevolent* person often helps others. _____ is a *benevolent* person because _____.

> A *malevolent* person is often mean to others. _____ is a *malevolent* person that we have read or studied about because _____.

Acceleration

Have students use a Venn diagram (see chapter 2, page 24) to compare and contrast two *benevolent* figures from history or literature (or two *malevolent* figures). Alternatively, or additionally, you could have students create a chart with *benevolent* in one column and *malevolent* in the other and have them brainstorm synonyms all the way down each column. Accelerated students could work in pairs or small groups if you prefer.

Beyond the Lesson

 Encourage students to use the word *beneficial* instead of *good* when possible. You could start an anchor chart or small word wall with synonyms for good, starting with *beneficial*.

Lesson R8: *beneficent, benefactor, maleficent, malefactor*

In this minilesson, teachers will teach the roots *bene* and *male*, such as in the words *beneficent, benefactor, maleficent,* and *malefactor.*

Difficulty level: 2

These four words are easily grouped together because of their similar meanings. They are sophisticated words that can add polish to a student's writing.

S

The following lists target words students should *see* and *say* for this minilesson. The adjectives *beneficent* and *maleficent* may require additional time to ensure students can pronounce them correctly. You may want to have students say the words several times and in different orders to help them practice the correct pronunciations.

- **Beneficent (adj.):** Doing good things or producing goodness
- **Benefactor (n.):** Someone who gives money or other support to others
- **Maleficent (adj.):** Doing evil things or producing evil
- **Malefactor (n.):** Someone who does evil to others

N

Make sure students understand that we classify two of the words as nouns and use them to talk about a specific type of person. The other two are adjectives and describe people but can also be used to describe things like policies or, more rarely, events. Tell students to think of *beneficent* as being similar to the word *charitable* and provide examples. So, the American Red Cross is a *beneficent* organization. On the opposite side, thieves and liars would be called *maleficent*. Be sure to give additional examples that students may be familiar with from being in your class.

A

Orchestrate a think-pair-share (see chapter 2, page 23). Ask, "Which people have been *benefactors* in your life? Which people have been *malefactors*?" If you wish, tell them to keep the people's names to themselves or to use pseudonyms if their examples are current teachers or students at your school. Allow students one full minute of think time before pairing. Assign a partner A and partner B. Each partner then has two minutes to talk.

P

Give each student two sticky notes (or use an online application like Padlet or TodaysMeet). On one note, they use the word *beneficent* in a sentence. On the other, they do the same for *maleficent*. Have them post their sentences in a designated space. On the next day, you can share the most effective sentences or simply leave those posted and remove the others. You could also post the notes in a huge T-chart to show more clearly the words' relationship as antonyms.

Scaffolding

Provide a list of *benefactors* and *malefactors* from history, current events, or literature on your interactive whiteboard, poster paper, and so on. Students can refer to this list to help them with the think-pair-share and when writing their sentences. Use the following examples if you wish.

> ▸ **Benefactors:** Paul Revere, Mother Teresa, Bill Gates, Malala Yousafzai
>
> ▸ **Malefactors:** Adolf Hitler, Osama bin Laden

Acceleration

Challenge advanced students to use all four words within their writing during the next week or so. Have them think about ways they can use the words in conversation with teachers or other adults.

Root: *bio*

The Greek root word *bio* means "life." Some common English vocabulary words that come from this root word include *biological*, *biographical*, and even *amphibian* and *symbiotic*. The root can appear anywhere in a word but is most often at the beginning.

Lesson R9: *biome, biology, biography*

In this minilesson, teachers will teach the root *bio*, such as in the words *biome*, *biology*, and *biography*.

Difficulty level: 2

S

The following lists target words students should *see* and *say* for this minilesson.

> ▸ **Biome (n.):** A large community of plants and animals that occupies a specific region
>
> ▸ **Biology (n.):** The study of life or living matter
>
> ▸ **Biography (n.):** A person's written account of someone else's life

N

Consider saying something like the following to your class.

These three words are very common academic words. Biology *is a branch of* science, *and* biome *is actually a term that is often used in* biology *or other life science classes.* Biography, *although used in literature and not science, also has a meaning directly based on the root.* Biology *is the study of living things; a* biome *is a home for living things; and a* biography *is a life story.*

A

Form pairs. Ask each pair to discuss the following.

▸ Do people live in *biomes*? Explain.

▸ Would you like to study *biology*? Why or why not?

▸ Have you read a *biography*? Explain.

P

Have each student write a short summary of his or her discussion in step A, being sure to use every word in context.

Scaffolding

Share the following sentence stems with students if needed.

▸ A *biome* is a place where _____.

▸ *Biology* is a type of _____ about _____.

▸ A *biography* is the story of _____.

Acceleration

Biodiversity and *autobiography* are words that are related to the target words. Accelerated students may want to explore these. Ask them what connections they see to the other words.

▸ **Biodiversity (n.):** The variety of life in a particular biome or other area

▸ **Autobiography (n.):** A person's written account of his or her own life

Roots: *cand, cend*

These roots both originate in the Latin word *candere*, which means "to glow," "to glisten," or "to shine." They are the basis of the words *candle, incandescent,* and *incendiary* and even *chandelier,* where the spelling is slightly different.

Lesson R10: *candle, incandescent, incendiary*

In this minilesson, teachers will teach the roots *cand* and *cend*, such as in the words *candle*, *incandescent*, and *incendiary*.

Difficulty level: 2

S

The following lists target words students should *see* and *say* for this minilesson.

▸ **Candle (n.):** A molded piece of wax, or other substance with a wick that is burned to cause a flame and light

▸ **Incandescent (adj.):** Able to produce light when heated, as in an incandescent light bulb; used figuratively as a synonym for brilliant, passionate, or spirited

▸ **Incendiary (adj.):** Able to cause fire; used figuratively to mean provocative, inflammatory

Students should know the everyday word *candle*, but some English learners in particular may not know this word. If possible, show a small candle. Showing *candle* as the most basic word reiterates the meaning of the root, which has to do with glowing, glistening, or lighting up.

N

Consider saying something like the following to your class.

I think most of you know about candles. *I love* candles *myself, and I burn them at home. But I'm not allowed to use them here in my classroom for safety reasons. I'd like for you to look at all three of these words' parts that are alike—* cand *in* candle *and* incandescent, *and* cend, *a little different, in* incendiary. *They all come from the same Latin root word that means to glow, glisten, or shine.*

Let's think about that a minute. A candle *glows, right, because of its flame? So, I also want you to keep in mind the idea of fire or a flame with these words. It will help you remember their literal meanings as well as their figurative or broader meanings.* Incandescent *is often used to describe someone's personality or knowledge—that it glows outward from them, or that it warms others, or fires them up, as you might say informally.* Incendiary *is often used to describe a person's actions or words—again, you can say that it fires other people up, and not in a good way.* Incendiary *means that someone is stirring things up or inciting people.*

Of course, incandescent *can also mean putting out light—like a lightbulb. This is how the word is used literally. And* incendiary *can literally mean causing a fire, like with matches. Matches are definitely* incendiary, *as are bombs and other devices. However, academic writing often uses these two words figuratively, not literally.*

A

Have students work in pairs and try to use the words *incandescent* to describe literary characters, historical figures, or celebrities. Ask them to justify these uses of the word. Also, have them brainstorm examples of *incendiary* language. Politicians often use such language, as do other figures who are covered in national and international news. Students may also be able to generate literary characters who use incendiary language to incite others. (For example, the Grinch in *How the Grinch Stole Christmas* can be considered an incendiary character.) For more mature students, you could point out that terrorists recruit others by using *incendiary* language.

P

Have each student try a sentence with *incandescent* and another with *incendiary*.

Acceleration

The words *candor* and *candid* also build on this root. These words don't have a literal meaning related to flames, heat, or glowing, but they are often used in academic text and are good words for students to know and to use in their writing.

▸ **Candor (n.):** The quality of being open, honest, and sincere

▸ **Candid (adj.):** Truthful, sincere, outspoken

Beyond the Lesson

Unfortunately, in school situations, *incendiary* language can lead to both verbal and physical conflicts. Use *incendiary* as appropriate for discussing these situations.

Roots: *cede, ceed*

The Latin word *cedere*, which means "to go," "go away," "withdraw," or "yield," forms the base of many words. The minilessons in this section focus on some of the most common words that students will encounter.

Lesson R11: *cede, accede, concede, precede*

In this minilesson, teachers will teach the root *cede*, such as in the words *cede*, *accede*, *concede*, and *precede*.

Difficulty level: 2

S

The following lists target words students should *see* and *say* for this minilesson. Be sure to cover the word *cede* first, because it's not just a root, it's an English word on its own. Then, you can explain and relate the other words to it.

- **Cede (v.):** To surrender or to give up something
- **Accede (v.):** To give in or go along with
- **Concede (v.):** Often a synonym for *cede*; to give up, yield, or surrender
- **Precede (v.):** To go before

Point out the prefix *pre-* (meaning "before") that students may already know, and show how *cede*, *accede*, and *concede* are all very similar in meaning. Remind students that verbs can also have *-ed* and *-ing* forms (*ceded, ceding, acceded, acceding, conceded, conceding, preceded, preceding*). Tell students that any word that has *cede* or *ced* within it could be based on this root.

N

All the words in this minilesson are verbs, and they are all related to the idea of movement, either literally or figuratively. People often use the word *concede* in political contexts (for example, a candidate *concedes* victory to another). *Accede* also often appears in a governmental or political context (for example, a person *acceded* to the government's demands). *Cede, accede,* and *concede* are about giving up, giving in, or relinquishing control, whereas *precede* does not connote handing something over or letting something go.

A

Have small groups of students discuss the four words and see if they can put them in the context of school or family (for example, science class *precedes* mathematics class; a student had to *cede* his cell phone to the principal when the student got caught texting in class).

P

Ask individual students to choose two of the four words that they think they could use in school or at home in the next few days. Have them write an exit ticket about this, or, at a minimum, engage in a think-pair-share. (See page 23 in chapter 2 for more on the think-pair-share strategy.) Alternatively, you could orchestrate a four corners activity with one word being represented at each corner. Provide examples or sentences that each word would fit with, and be aware that *cede* and *concede* may be used interchangeably.

Scaffolding

Monitor the small groups' work in step A. Provide students hints and cues, such as, "What do we do just *preceding* lunch? In other words, what do we do that comes before lunch?"

Acceleration

Add the word *intercede* to the list of words as students complete step P, and encourage advanced students to find out the meaning and use this word in addition to the two that they selected from the original list of four words. Students with knowledge of the prefix *inter-* should be able to figure out that *intercede* means "to go between or to mediate." You can also offer the following synonyms for intercede that advanced students may be interested in: *arbitrate*, *negotiate*, or *conciliate*.

Lesson R12: *exceed, proceed, succeed*

In this minilesson, teachers will teach the root *ceed*, such as in the words *exceed*, *proceed*, and *succeed*.

Difficulty level: 1

The only words in the English language that use the root's other form, *ceed*, are the three in this minilesson. Teach the words in the order that's best for your students; the word *succeed* may be the most familiar, so you could easily start there.

S

The following lists target words students should *see* and *say* for this minilesson.

▶ **Exceed (v.):** To go beyond or further than expected

▶ **Proceed (v.):** To begin or move forward

▶ **Succeed (v.):** To reach the goal that was set; to accomplish something

These words, because they are so similar, are excellent for creating a short chant for choral response. You could also add teacher gestures (page 23). Examples include the following.

▶ *Proceed* means "get started"! (*Put hands on hips; take one step forward.*)

▶ *Succeed* means "reach a goal"! (*Make touchdown signal with arms raised.*)

▶ *Exceed* means "go even further"! (*Put hands on hips; take several steps forward.*)

N

Again, emphasize that these three words share something very special: they are the only three words in English that use the spelling *-ceed*. You can give examples matching each word from recent school or community events. For example, a student athlete may have *exceeded* a state record or *succeeded* in gaining acceptance into the college of his choice.

A

Place students in triads and use the strategy pass the paper (see page 21). One student writes a sentence with *proceed*, then passes the paper to the second, who writes a sentence for *succeed*, and lastly, the same is done for *exceed*.

P

Ask students to write a short paragraph about the three words in their own lives.

Scaffolding

Provide a paragraph template for students to use if they need it. Use or adapt the following one if you like.

▸ One thing I have *succeeded* at this year is _____.
   Lastly, one time I even *exceeded* what I wanted to do was
   when _____.

You can also provide one or both of the following student examples if you think they will help your students.

▸ **For grades K and 1:** One thing that I would like to *proceed* to do soon is to learn how to swim. One thing I have *succeeded* at this year is not being absent at all. Lastly, I even *exceeded* what I wanted to do when I made an A on my math test.

▸ **For grades 2 and up:** One thing that I would like to *proceed* to do soon is to get my learner's permit for driving. One thing I have *succeeded* at this year is not getting any discipline referrals at school because I can control my temper better. Lastly, I even *exceeded* what I wanted to do when I ran the fundraiser for the Humane Society and we got more donations than we had expected.

You can see that students can possibly combine metacognition with these words fairly easily, and it's always beneficial to help students become more reflective.

Acceleration

Provide related words like *successful*, *procession*, and *excessive* and ask students to use these words for their exit tickets instead of the three original words. You may want to display the words and their definitions to save time. Otherwise, you could allow the students to look the words up in an online or hard-copy dictionary.

Beyond the Lesson

There are many opportunities for both you and students to use these words frequently. A student can *exceed* his or her personal goal. The entire class can *proceed* to lunch. Try to use these words as much as possible.

Lesson R13: *recede, secede*

In this minilesson, teachers will teach the root *cede*, such as in the words *recede* and *secede*. These two words differ by only one letter and have very similar meanings. However, people use *recede* more frequently and more liberally than *secede*.

Difficulty level: 2

S

 The following lists target words students should *see* and *say* for this minilesson.

▶ **Recede (v.):** To go or move away; to withdraw

▶ **Secede (v.):** To withdraw formally

You may want to dramatically emphasize the *re* and *se* syllables to highlight the only noticeable difference in the spelling of the words.

N

 Consider saying something like the following to your class.

> So you've noticed that these two words are incredibly similar, differing by only one letter. Their meanings are similar, too, but remember that secede is the more formal and more rarely used of the two words. For example, we sometimes speak of a man having a receding hairline, which means his hair is moving back from his forehead. However, we'd never call that a seceding hairline—the word secede and its forms are more formal and usually relate to some kind of government or political action. Prior to the U.S. Civil War, South Carolina was the first state to secede from the Union, and other states followed. The states that seceded formed the Confederacy and ended up fighting against the Union in the war that followed. So, secede is usually used to mean an official withdrawal from some kind of group or organization. Recede is used more often and in more contexts, like when a hairline recedes, or when flood waters recede.

A

Form groups of students and ask them to discuss the following questions.

▶ Can hills or mountains *recede*? If so, how? Can you describe how?

▶ If two native groups of people were fighting over the same land, and one group gave in to other's demands, would you use the word *recede* or *secede* to describe what it did? Why would you use one word instead of the other?

Generally, *recede* is most appropriate for the first question, as in hills or mountains *receding* from sight, and *secede* is most appropriate for the second.

P

Form two lines of students, facing each other, or an inner and outer circle with students facing each other. For the first round, have one group (line or circle) of students look at the other and discuss one target word; then switch. Have each student talk for one minute about definitions, synonyms, and examples, with the student standing opposite him or her listening only—not interrupting. As students talk, monitor and cue as needed. The goal is to have students say as much as they possibly can to enhance memory.

Scaffolding

Provide additional examples to make the differences between the words clearer. See the WordsinaSentence.com (2016a, 2016b) articles "Recede in a Sentence" (https://wordsinasentence.com/recede-in-a-sentence) and "Secede in a Sentence" (https://wordsinasentence.com/secede-in-a-sentence) for ideas. Adapt the sentences as needed for maximum impact for your students.

Acceleration

Share the related words *recessive* and *recession* with advanced students.

- **Recessive (adj.):** In genetics, related to a gene that does not express itself unless two such genes are inherited; for example, in Labrador retrievers, the gene for the chocolate color is *recessive*

- **Recession (n.):** In general, a movement away from something; in economics, a temporary decline during which trade and business decline; the United States experienced a recession from 2007–2009

Roots: *chron, chrono*

The common root *chron* (or *chrono*) has its origin in the Greek *chronos*, meaning "time." Students may be familiar with the word *chronological* from the first books read aloud to them, because it's often used to discuss the order of events in a narrative.

Lesson R14: *chronology, chronological, chronic*

Difficulty level: 2

S

The following lists target words students should *see* and *say* for this minilesson. Point out the relationship between the first two words.

- **Chronology (n.):** The organizational pattern of how events occur in time

▸ **Chronological (adj.):** The adjective made from chronology; arranged in the order of time

▸ **Chronic (adj.):** Lasting a long time or repeatedly occurring, usually describing an illness

N

Consider saying something like the following to your class.

So, you've probably heard the word chronological *more than you've heard the other two words, but all these words are similar, as they all relate to the concept of time.* Chronological, *again, is an adjective that describes nouns, and it means in the order of time, or in other words, in the order that things actually happened. A* chronology *would be an account or a story that is in that order. I can write a* chronology *of an important historical event, like a battle or a war, or I can read a* chronology *of someone's life. The word* chronic *is a bit different, in that it means something that lasts a long time or something that recurs. Many times, this word relates to an illness. So, I might go to my doctor if I have a* chronic *cough or a* chronic *stomachache. If either ailment keeps coming back, or lasts for a long time, it will be considered* chronic. *You can use the word* chronic *to describe other things, though, that are not related to a person's physical health. For example, we can experience* chronic *flooding, which means that floods happen over and over again, or* chronic *inflation, which means that prices stay high over a long period of time.*

A

Allow small groups to figure out which of the three words best fits each of the following sentences.

▸ One of the king's servants wrote the _____ of the king's lifetime. (*chronology*)

▸ If you have a _____ headache, you should probably see the school nurse. (*chronic*)

▸ The movie keeps shifting back and forth from present to past. It is not in _____ order and was a little confusing. (*chronological*)

▸ The school principal wants to find a way to address _____ absences so that students will get the maximum amount of instruction. (*chronic*)

This exercise will give you an idea of how well students can distinguish where to insert a noun versus an adjective in a sentence.

P

Ask students to participate in a think-pair-share in which they each tell a partner what the hardest word of the three is to remember and why. As partners working together, each pair could try to think of ways to use the words authentically.

Scaffolding

Strategically form pairs for step P to place struggling students or students who aren't as forthcoming verbally with partners that will be able to draw them out and support them.

Acceleration

Advanced students may be interested in the words *chronicle* (or *chronicles*), and *chronicler*. Allow them to explore the following words as time allows.

> **Chronicle (n.):** A published account of important or historical events in the order that they occurred

> **Chronicler (n.):** A person who writes these accounts

Roots: *clud, clus, clos*

These roots trace their meaning to the Latin *claudo*, which means "shut." Variants of this root show up in our words *include*, *exclude*, and even *closet* and, with an alternate spelling, *claustrophobia*.

Lesson R15: *include, exclude, inclusive, exclusive*

In this minilesson, teachers will teach the roots *clud* and *clus*, such as in the words *include*, *exclude*, *inclusive*, and *exclusive*.

Difficulty level: 2

S

The following lists target words students should *see* and *say* for this minilesson.

> **Include (v.):** To have or to contain

> **Exclude (v.):** To keep out, leave out, or shut out

> **Inclusive (adj.):** Including or containing something

> **Exclusive (adj.):** Not letting something in; restricted

The word *include* is probably the most familiar to students. Have them tell you what they think it means—ask them how they would explain it to a friend. Teacher gestures may be a good strategy to use here. Use open arms and then act like you're pulling something close to your chest for *include* and *inclusive*, and then pushing away for *exclude* and *exclusive*.

N

These words are pairs of opposites. *Include* and *exclude* are the opposite in meaning, as are *inclusive* and *exclusive*. If students can remember their prefixes and suffixes, they should note that *in-* means "into," *ex-* means "out of," and *-ive* means "having the quality of," so the words can be analyzed pretty directly. So, using these word parts, *inclusive* obviously means "into" plus "contain" plus "having the quality of." *Inclusive*, then, means being able to contain or bring something in. Walk through an analysis of the word *exclusive* the same way. Explain these words as best as you can for your students, and help them make connections to what they already know about the roots and affixes.

A

Group students in pairs or triads. Ask the students if the following are examples of being *inclusive* or being *exclusive*.

▶ Inviting a new student to sit with you at lunch (*inclusive*)

▶ Having a birthday party and asking everyone in your class to come (*inclusive*)

▶ Including your younger brother or sister in a game (*inclusive*)

▶ Blocking someone's way as he or she tries to join a game at recess (*exclusive*)

▶ Having a private online chat with a few of your friends but not inviting others (*exclusive*)

▶ Buying VIP tickets to an event that allow you to enter a private room with food and drinks that are not offered to everyone (*exclusive*)

P

Ask students to use the words *inclusive* and *exclusive* in a short paragraph. For authenticity and to help better remember these words, students can give examples of times they have been *inclusive* and *exclusive* to other people.

Scaffolding

Allow students who require scaffolding to use *include* and *exclude* in step A instead of the adjective forms, which may be more difficult for them. Provide sentence stems like the following if you feel they would be helpful.

▶ *Include* means to _____.

▶ *Exclude* means to _____.

Acceleration

The root *clus* is present in the following related words. Students who have mastered these words may enjoy trying to use these in sentences in step A in addition to or in place of *inclusive* and *exclusive*.

▸ **Inclusion (n.):** The act of taking in, as in a group

▸ **Exclusion (n.):** The act of shutting out

Beyond the Lesson

Try to use *include* and *exclude* as much as possible for a few days after this minilesson. You could remind students to *include* all group members in their conversation or to *exclude* unimportant details in a summary.

Lesson R16: *preclude, conclude, conclusive, conclusion*

In this minilesson, teachers will teach the roots *clud* and *clus*, such as in the words *preclude, conclude, conclusive,* and *conclusion*.

Difficulty level: 2

S

The following lists target words students should *see* and *say* for this minilesson.

▸ **Preclude (v.):** To keep something from happening or to make something impossible

▸ **Conclude (v.):** To bring something to the end or to arrive at a judgment

▸ **Conclusive (adj.):** Final, decisive, convincing

▸ **Conclusion (n.):** The end of something or a generalization that one has reached

N

This set of words clearly makes use of the root and prefixes that, if well known, can help students determine the word meaning instantly. Students are likely to be familiar with *conclude* and *conclusion*, because both reading and writing lessons often feature them. They may not be as familiar, however, with the broader application of these words, as in drawing a *conclusion* in general. Be prepared to provide examples here that apply to your students and help them connect with what they already know.

Preclude may be the most difficult word—and is the one of the four that may appear the least in text that students encounter. Give your own examples of the use of this word. For example, I might tell my students only an illness with a fever or a serious injury would *preclude* me from coming to school. I could ask them what might *preclude* them from coming to school or playing outside.

A

Have pairs or small groups place the correct word in each of the following sentences. Because two of the words are verbs, remind students that they need to be mindful of endings and tense.

▸ The high cost of the dress _____ me from buying it. (*precludes* or *precluded*)

▸ I _____ that my dogs ran through the house when I saw the muddy footprints. (*concluded*)

▸ The data were _____ and convinced me of the importance of our actions. (*conclusive*)

▸ I had sadly reached the _____ that I needed to say goodbye to one of my best friends. (*conclusion*)

P

Ask students to identify the one word they think will be most difficult to use and to write it down, along with its definition, in a safe place. Challenge them to use it in speaking or writing in the next few days. If time allows, do a Whip Around (see chapter 2, page 27) and let each student state his or her chosen word and give a definition in his or her own words.

Scaffolding

Remind students who require scaffolding that they have probably discussed the *conclusion* of an essay, and that it's the last part, or the end. To *conclude* is to end something or to reach a *conclusion* or final idea about something. Concentrate on the connections to the idea of a composition's *conclusion*.

Acceleration

See the Membean (2017a) article "Root Word of the Day: Clud" (http://membean .com/wrotds/clud-shut) for interesting reading for advanced students. (Visit **go.SolutionTree.com/literacy** to access live links to the websites mentioned in this book.)

Root: *cred*

This root comes from the Latin *credere* that means "to believe." Students are likely to know the word *credit*, which traces its meaning to this root. *Credit*—in terms of money—is a promise to pay. The lender must believe the person granted the *credit* will pay, in other words.

Lesson R17: *credible, incredible, credibility, credence, credentials*

In this minilesson, teachers will teach the root *cred*, such as in the words *credible, incredible, credibility, credence,* and *credentials*.

Difficulty level: 2

S

The following lists target words students should *see* and *say* for this minilesson.

▸ **Credible (adj.):** Believable or trustworthy

▸ **Incredible (adj.):** Unbelievable or seemingly impossible

▸ **Credibility (n.):** The quality of being believed in or trusted

▸ **Credence (n.):** The belief in or acceptance of something as true

▸ **Credentials (n.):** Qualifications, achievements, or personal qualities that make someone suitable for something

N

These words are all about believability of qualifications. Students probably know the word *incredible* but haven't thought much about the opposite of it because they hear and see *incredible* more frequently in conversation and in books. You can tie in both *credible* and *credibility* with the discussion of *incredible*.

For *credence,* give personal examples. I might say to my students that I give little *credence* to Internet rumors like the ones about a celebrity's death but much *credence* to my doctor's recommendations for diet and exercise. I could add to this by saying that my doctor has excellent *credentials* and therefore has earned my trust. Share your own examples as appropriate to help students connect the new words to background knowledge.

A

Allow small groups of students to generate a list of people who are *credible* (and thus show *credibility*). If possible, have them extend these examples by naming the *credentials* for the people they have cited. For example, a teacher can be *credible,* because he or she has a degree to be a teacher. A principal has the license to be a principal. A police officer has the training, badge, and uniform that denote he or she is allowed to be an officer. These are just a few examples.

P

Have each student choose two words other than the word *incredible* to use in original sentences. If time allows, have students swap their sentences with a partner, and ask each student to check his or her partner's work to ensure that it accurately uses the words. If you prefer, conduct a quick Kahoot! quiz here. You could write five multiple-choice items, and ensure that each word is covered.

Scaffolding

Provide sentence frames to students if needed. Examples include the following.

▸ _____ is a *credible* person because _____.

▸ I have a lot of knowledge or experience in _____, and that makes me *credible* when I speak about it.

▸ I have a lot of knowledge or experience in _____, so I have *credibility*.

Acceleration

Introduce students who have mastered these words to the related word *incredulous*, which is an adjective meaning that a person is not willing to believe something. Ask these students if they can use the word authentically.

Beyond the Lesson

Incredible is probably the most frequently used word in this list, and it can even be overused, especially in student writing. However, you can use the word *credible* in class more often. You can ask students if a narrator or a character is *credible*. You can tell a student that his or her excuse for not doing homework is *credible*, and therefore you'll give him or her another day. Try to use *credible* in authentic contexts.

Roots: *cog, cogn*

The Latin word meaning "to learn" or "to know" gives us the root *cogn*, which also appears as *conn* in some words. Students may be familiar with the words *cognition* and *metacognition* from their experiences in school.

Lesson R18: *recognize, recognizable, unrecognizable*

In this minilesson, teachers will teach the roots *cog* and *cogn*, such as in the words *recognize*, *recognizable*, and *unrecognizable*.

Difficulty level: 1

S

The following lists target words students should *see* and *say* for this minilesson.

▸ **Recognize (v.):** To identify or to know something or someone when you see them again

▸ **Recognizable (adj.):** Able to be identified from previous knowledge or experience

▸ **Unrecognizable (adj.):** Not able to be identified from previous knowledge or experience

N

These words are all about knowing something when you see it, or remembering someone or something. Students may know the word *recognize*. Ask them when or how they have used this word or heard it used. Then discuss the adjectives, which are opposites of each other. Remind students that the prefix *un-* makes a word the opposite meaning.

A

Ask small groups to discuss these questions.

▸ How would you *recognize* a friend or family member you hadn't seen in a long time? What would you look for or do?

▸ How could a person be *unrecognizable*? What might he or she have done to make him- or herself *unrecognizable*?

P

Ask each student to write a pair of sentences clearly showing the opposing relationship of the words *recognizable* and *unrecognizable*.

Scaffolding

Be prepared to give examples from literature, movies, TV, or pop culture of people being *recognizable* and *unrecognizable*. For example, some celebrities disguise themselves in order to play a prank, or they become unrecognizable after having plastic surgery.

Acceleration

Challenge advanced students to write only one sentence for step P, still meeting the criteria.

Lesson R19: *cognition, metacognition, cognizant*

In this minilesson, teachers will teach the roots *cog* and *cogn*, such as in the words *cognition*, *metacognition*, and *cognizant*.

Difficulty level: 2

S

The following lists target words students should *see* and *say* for this minilesson.

- **Cognition (n.):** The mental actions of understanding something
- **Cognitive (adj.):** Related to the mental actions of understanding something
- **Metacognition (n.):** Understanding your own mental actions and thought processes
- **Cognizant (adj.):** Being aware of something or knowing about something

N

Students may have heard the word *metacognition*; in fact, you may have used this word with them. However, it is often only briefly defined as "thinking about your thinking," which is a bit of a limited definition. If they are familiar with this word, though, describe the other terms in relation to it, always emphasizing that all four words are related to thinking and knowing, to build on the limited definition. You can also do a word analysis of *metacognition* if you feel your students would be interested in the prefix *meta-*, which in this case means "beyond." So, *metacognition* is to think and then to go beyond your thinking to actually analyze it.

A

Ask small groups of students to discuss the following questions.

- Are you *cognizant* of the fact that your heart is beating or that you're breathing? Explain.
- Are you *cognizant* of the weather? Explain.
- The amount of sleep you get affects your *cognition*. What else affects your *cognition*?

P

Have each student choose his or her favorite word from this group of words. Ask him or her to write a student-friendly definition for the word and to justify why it's the student's favorite. The following is an example of a possible student response:

"to be *cognizant* of something means that you know it's happening. I like this word the best because it has the letter z in it. There aren't many words that have a z, and I like saying the z sound."

Scaffolding

Give students who require scaffolding plenty of synonyms for each word. Use the following if you wish.

- ‣ **Cognition:** *Thought, thinking, knowing, understanding*
- ‣ **Cognitive:** *Mental, conscious, reasonable*
- ‣ **Metacognition:** *Reflection, analysis, deep thinking*

Acceleration

Ask students who have mastered these words how they might use the word *cognizant* with their teachers, friends, and families. As time allows, encourage them to role-play or engage in conversation with this word.

Beyond the Lesson

Because all these words are related to thinking, you can use them frequently in various lessons. Strive to use them whenever possible, and encourage students to use them, too.

Root: *dem*

The root *dem* comes from the Greek *demos* and means "people" or "population." *Dem* shows up in quite a few English words, with the most familiar being those associated with the word *democracy*.

Lesson R20: *democracy, democrat, democratic*

In this minilesson, teachers will teach the root *dem*, such as in the words *democracy*, *democrat*, and *democratic*.

Difficulty level: 2

S

The following lists target words students should *see* and *say* for this minilesson.

- ‣ **Democracy (n.):** A government where people choose their own leaders and share in making decisions

- **Democrat (n.):** A supporter of democracy when used as a common noun; a member of the U.S. Democratic Party when used as a proper noun

- **Democratic (adj.):** Having the principles of democracy; allowing for participation of the people

N

Consider saying something like the following to your class.

Today, we're looking at three words that are closely related, which I'm sure you've heard before—democracy, democrat, democratic. TV news shows and our social studies curriculum often use these three words. As you advance in school, you'll see other words that have similar meanings and that contain the root dem, *which means "people" and "population." I grouped all of these words together for you because they all start with this important root, and I want you to automatically think "people" when you see this root.*

A

Ask small groups to discuss what they know about the concept of *democracy*. What is it? Is the United States a democracy? How do you know? What are some places that are not democracies? How do you know?

P

Have each student use the word *democrat* or *democratic* in an original sentence. If they need help, give examples like the following.

- The two major political parties in the United States are the Democratic and Republican parties.

- We live in a democratic country.

Scaffolding

Review the parts of speech and how to use each word as necessary.

Acceleration

Select a few words listed in the article "Demo & Dem" on the English for Students (n.d.; www.english-for-students.com/demo.html) website, or have students peruse these words. *Democratically* and *antidemocratic* are closely related to the first three target words and may be worth discussing.

Root: *dict*

The Latin root *dict* (or sometimes, *dic*) means "to say" or "to speak." This root forms some of the most familiar words we use in school, like *predict* and *dictionary*. These lessons build on familiarity and push students to learn and use less common words, like *diction* and *edict*.

Lesson R21: *diction, dictionary, predict, prediction*

In this minilesson, teachers will teach the root *dict*, such as in the words *diction, dictionary, predict,* and *prediction*.

Difficulty level: 1

S

The following lists target words students should *see* and *say* for this minilesson.

▸ **Diction (n.):** The style or word choice used in speaking or writing

▸ **Dictionary (n.):** A book or electronic resource that lists the words of a language and gives their meanings; it also usually provides information about pronunciation, origin, and usage.

▸ **Predict (v.):** To think or actually foresee that something will happen

▸ **Prediction (n.):** A statement of what may happen; an educated guess about what is to come

With these particular words, you can probably reference recent classroom experiences to add context to the definitions.

N

These words are all directly and clearly connected to much of the reading and writing we do in schools. All of them may be somewhat familiar, although *diction* may be new for students, depending on their age and previous instruction. Ensure that students understand that *diction* is not something that comes from a dictionary; it comes from a writer's (or speaker's) mind.

Refresh students on the meaning of the prefix *pre-* (or see if they know its meaning) to reinforce the meanings of *predict* and *prediction*.

A

Allow students to work in pairs or triads. Have them discuss the following questions: Do you speak to your teachers or your grandparents with the same *diction* as you do when speaking with your friends? How does your *diction* differ depending on with whom you're speaking? You may want to give them an example of when or how you change your own *diction* (for example, speaking with the principal is different from speaking with one of your neighbors). If you're feeling dramatic, act out part of a conversation with the two audiences you use as examples.

P

Have students work individually or in pairs. Have them discuss the following sentences, filling in the appropriate word for each. They can do this activity verbally or in writing at your discretion.

▸ One thing a good reader does is to _____ what is going to happen next in a story. (*predict*)

▸ A good writer changes his or her _____ to best fit the audience. (*diction*)

▸ A _____ should be based on what you already know. (*prediction*)

▸ Good readers and writers should know how to use a _____. (*dictionary*)

Scaffolding

Be prepared with additional examples of *diction*. Students who attend worship services might connect with an example that uses religious elders in it. Students who have been raised to talk in certain ways to their parents might connect with an example that features parents.

Acceleration

Share the definition of the related words *predictor* and *predictive* with students and see if they can figure out how to use them in context.

▸ **Predictor (n.):** A person who makes educated guesses about what might happen next; for example, a *predictor* could perhaps foretell the winner of the Super Bowl

▸ **Predictive (adj.):** Useful for foretelling or telling about the future; for example, heavy gray clouds are often *predictive* of rain

Beyond the Lesson

Sometimes we have to remind students to use appropriate language at school. You could easily substitute the word *diction* for "language" in such contexts.

Lesson R22: *dictate, dictation, edict*

In this minilesson, teachers will teach the root *dict*, such as in the words *dictate*, *dictation*, and *edict*.

Difficulty level: 2

S

The following lists target words students should *see* and *say* for this minilesson.

▸ **Dictate (v.):** To command or prescribe; to give an order; to say aloud in order to be recorded

▸ **Dictation (n.):** The act of saying words aloud so that they can be recorded in some way, or the action of giving orders

▸ **Edict (n.):** An official order someone in power gives

Be sure to enunciate clearly, especially the long /e/ and the *t* on the end of *edict*.

N

All of these words are about words, often words that someone says as a command or words a person who has authority uses. Students may remember *dictating* stories to a teacher in preschool or kindergarten, so you may want to mention that for additional context. Connect the words to any experiences that you think your students will remember.

A

Put students into pairs and have one student *dictate* to the other; then switch roles. Allow only a minute or two for each student to *dictate*. The listener or recorder can write down what is *dictated* or use a tablet device to record the *dictation* as audio. As for the content of the *dictation*, ask the students to talk about what they did after school the previous day or something equally familiar to all.

P

Students can remain in pairs for this activity. Quickly call on each pair and ask students to give an example of an *edict* that they know of—some rule, law, or order issued in the school, community, or larger society. Provide some examples to get students started. Use the following examples if you wish.

▸ A driver cannot pass a school bus that is stopped and has its lights flashing so that students can cross the street. (*law*)

▸ Students must raise their hands to be called on in class. (*rule*)

▸ The United States can now do business with Cuba. (*order*)

Scaffolding

You can provide a script of two to three sentences for students to *dictate* during step A if you feel it will make things go more smoothly. The idea is for students to simply get a sense of what *dictation* is, so anything that is *dictated* will work.

Acceleration

Share the related word *verdict*, and ask students if they can think of ways to use it in speaking or writing.

> **Verdict (n.):** A decision a jury reaches in a trial that is usually read aloud; can also be used more informally to mean a decision or an opinion

Root: *duc*

This root also traces its history back to Latin words that mean "to lead." If you wish, tell your students they can remember this root when they think of the word *educate* if they think of this word meaning "led to greater knowledge" or "led to deeper understanding."

Lesson R23: *introduce, introduction, produce, production*

In this minilesson, teachers will teach the root *duc*, such as in the words *introduce*, *introduction*, *produce*, and *production*.

Difficulty level: 1

S

The following lists target words students should *see* and *say* for this minilesson.

> **Introduce (v.):** To bring something into use for the first time or to begin something

> **Introduction (n.):** The act of bringing something forth or starting it off

> **Produce (v.):** To make something or cause it to happen

> **Production (n.):** The act of making something or causing it to happen

Point out to students that in some cases the root shows up in words as *duc*, and in other cases, depending on the spelling of the word that is being formed, it may show up as *duct*. You may also want to remind them that *-tion* or *-ion* on the end of a word is a clue that the word is a noun. Be sure they know not to confuse this root with the complete word *duck*, which is not related to this root.

N

This set of words contains two verbs with their corresponding noun forms. Discuss each pair in terms of examples that students will understand from previous classroom experiences. For example, you may want to reference how students begin an expository, persuasive, or argumentative essay with a paragraph that is usually called an *introduction*. Many books also include *introductions*. You may have a book you can hold up and show them as an example. You may have also used the word *produce* in relation to student work—as in an assignment in which students had to *produce* writing, or art work, or something else original.

A

Have students discuss the following in small groups. They should determine whether each is a *production* or an *introduction*.

▸ A cook in a restaurant makes a special recipe. (*production*)

▸ A server in a restaurant convinces you to try a dish you've never tried before. (*introduction*)

▸ Before a movie begins, someone comes on the screen and tells you a little bit about it. (*introduction*)

▸ A neighbor grows flowers in a small yard. (*production*)

P

Ask each student to come up with one example that applies to the words *introduce* and *introduction* and another example that applies to the words *produce* and *production*. If time is short, you could do this part verbally. Go around the room quickly and have each student provide one or the other. Tell students if they can't think of an answer, they can repeat what someone else has said. This will also encourage them to use active listening.

Scaffolding

You can provide the following fill-in-the-blank sentences for students who may struggle coming up with their own examples.

▸ Writing a story is an example of _____. (*production*)

▸ Showing a friend something that he or she has never seen before is an example of _____. (*introduction*)

Acceleration

Ask advanced students what the related word *productive* means. This word often describes a person's capability to do a lot of work, but it can refer to anything that *produces* a lot or is especially generative, such as a field that produces a great amount of a certain crop. Ask students if they can apply this word as well.

Beyond the Lesson

Strive to use the verb *produce* when talking with students about their work. For example, you could ask a writer, "What are you going to *produce* in our writing workshop today?"

Lesson R24: *conduct, misconduct*

In this minilesson, teachers will teach the root *duc*, such as in the words *conduct* and *misconduct*.

Difficulty level: 2

S

The following lists target words students should *see* and *say* for this minilesson.

- **Conduct (v.):** To carry out or to behave

- **Conduct (n.):** How one behaves or acts

- **Misconduct (n.):** Unacceptable or improper behavior

Ensure that students understand the different pronunciations and meanings of *conduct*. For this particular set of words, teacher gestures may be helpful. Simple hand motions, like a wagging finger for *misconduct*, may speak volumes about the meaning of each word.

N

These words are about one's behavior or actions. Students are likely to have heard the word *conduct* used as a noun (and perhaps *misconduct* as well) in school situations previously.

A

Have small groups discuss the following questions.

- How do you *conduct* yourself at school? What actions are acceptable?

- How do you *conduct* yourself at home? What actions are acceptable?

P

Have students think of examples of *misconduct* from school, church, home, or community (whatever seems appropriate). Ask them to write one or two of these and turn it in.

Scaffolding

Students may struggle with the word *conduct* being both a verb and a noun. You can provide additional examples such as the following to help them better understand.

▸ When I'm in the library, I *conduct* myself quietly and calmly.

▸ When I'm in the gym, I *conduct* myself more actively than in the library.

▸ When I'm in the classroom, I try to have excellent *conduct*.

Acceleration

Advanced students may enjoy learning words like *transgression* and *wrongdoing* because they are related to the word *misconduct*. Allow them to explore these words and find other synonyms at Thesaurus.com (www.thesaurus.com).

▸ **Transgression (n.):** An act that goes against a rule, law, or code of conduct

▸ **Wrongdoing (n.):** Behavior that is wrong or even illegal

Lesson R25: *induce, induction, reduce, reduction*

In this minilesson, teachers will teach the root *duc*, such as in the words *induce, induction, reduce,* and *reduction.*

Difficulty level: 2

S

The following lists target words students should *see* and *say* for this minilesson.

▸ **Induce (v.):** To bring about or to influence someone to do something

▸ **Induction (n.):** The act of bringing about something; also, to bring someone into an organization

▸ **Reduce (v.):** To make smaller in size, number, and so on

▸ **Reduction (n.):** The act of making smaller in size, number, and so on

Remind students that the suffixes *-tion* and *-ion* signify nouns. This set of words contains pairs that have the verb form and noun form of the same base word.

N

These words are about human actions that bring about a change. For the word *induce*, some students may have heard the word in relation to a woman having a baby (to *induce* labor). If they know this meaning, they can understand that *induce* means "to make something happen." Another real-life example would be weight loss; many people would like to *reduce* their weight. Again, people have to take action in order for that to happen. Students may have also heard and used the word *reduce* in mathematics lessons. If so, discuss this. *Reduction* always requires that a person does something. You have to take action to *reduce* your weight. You have to do something mathematically when you *reduce* a fraction.

A

Have students work in small groups to brainstorm things that can be *induced* and *reduced*. Provide them some examples to get them started, such as the following:

- A doctor can *induce* labor, as already mentioned.

- A teacher can smile and greet students at the classroom door to *induce* good moods in his or her students.

- A person can diet to *reduce* his or her weight.

- A student can *reduce* his or her homework by using his or her time more wisely at school.

- An organization at school may hold an *induction* ceremony for its new members.

P

Have each student choose two of the target words and write a student-friendly definition for each. You could ask students to think about how they would explain the words to a friend who did not participate in this minilesson.

Scaffolding

Show some images that demonstrate the differences between *induce* and *reduce* if necessary. Images of air pollution, car traffic, and piles of trash would work for *reduce*. An image of a person moving an object or of a person trying to make another person laugh would work for *induce*.

Acceleration

Students may enjoy exploring the words *adduce* and *deduce* that contain the same root and follow the same pattern of making the verb form into a noun form. Again, these words are also about a person's actions.

- **Adduce (v.):** To bring forward in an argument or to cite as evidence

- **Deduce (v.):** To arrive at or conclude based on logic

Beyond the Lesson

You can use *induce* and *reduce* frequently in the classroom. For example, ask students to *reduce* the noise level instead of simply asking for quiet, or prompt a student to get back to work by saying something like, "How can I *induce* you to keep trying?"

Roots: *fid, fis*

This root comes from the Latin *fidere*, which means "to trust" and "to have faith." The common term *bona fide*, meaning "in good faith," comes from this same root.

Lesson R26: *confidence, confident, confidante*

In this minilesson, teachers will teach the root *fid*, such as in the words *confidence*, *confident*, and *confidante*.

Difficulty level: 1

S

The following lists target words students should *see* and *say* for this minilesson.

▸ **Confidence (n.):** A feeling or belief of trust or sureness

▸ **Confident (adj.):** Feeling sure of oneself or of the truth of something

▸ **Confidante (n.):** A very close, trustworthy friend

In my experience, *confidante* is the least used and surely the most unfamiliar word here, but students can easily learn and use it because of its meaning. Be sure to pronounce it correctly several times and to allow students to have fun pronouncing the word, too.

You may have used both *confidence* and *confident* with your students, so remind them of specific examples if you can.

N

Consider saying something like the following to your class.

All these words are about trust or faith in something—in a belief, idea, or person, even if that person is you yourself. The root fid *that you see here is in many English words that have to do with faith and trust.*

A

Put students into pairs. Determine who is partner A and who is partner B. Have partner A respond to the following, and then have partner B do the same. Each person should try to speak fluently and say a paragraph aloud to his or her partner.

Share something you have *confidence* in, something you are *confident* you can do, and someone who is a *confidante* of yours.

You may want to model the speaking first. I would say something like this to my students: "I have *confidence* in my students to always be honest with me. I'm *confident* that I'm a good cook. And one of my closest *confidantes* is my dog Charlie. I can tell him anything. He listens patiently."

P

 Ask students to think about how they can use the three target words in conversation at school or at home in the next few days. You may want to allow a full minute of quiet think time, and, if time allows, ask students to write their plan down on a sticky note or index card. If you don't want to allow writing time, ask each student to share with a new partner (not the partner from step N) after the think time.

Scaffolding

Provide synonyms and antonyms, especially for *confidante*. A confidante is a close friend, a best friend, a pal, a buddy—or, in other words, someone you'd share your closest secrets with.

Acceleration

You may want to share the phrase *bona fide* with students who have mastered these words. The general meanings are "genuine" when describing an object's authenticity or "in good faith" to describe more abstract things.

Roots: *frag, fract*

The two spellings of this root come from Latin words meaning break, breaking, broken, or cracked. *Fractus* is the main Latin word they originate from.

Lesson R27: *fraction, fragment, refract, refraction*

In this minilesson, teachers will teach the roots *frag* and *fract*, such as in the words *fraction, fragment, refract,* and *refraction.*

Difficulty level: 2

S

 The following lists target words students should *see* and *say* for this minilesson.

▸ **Fraction (n.):** A mathematical expression that represents the division of one whole number by another; a part of a whole number or a ratio between two numbers

- **Fragment (n.):** A small part of something that has been broken off or separated somewhere
- **Refract (n.):** To make a ray of light change direction
- **Refraction (n.):** A change of direction that light undergoes when acted on

N

The words *fraction* and *fragment* may be the most familiar to students, at least in their school contexts as being common terms in mathematics and English language arts. *Refract* and *refraction* are fairly easy to connect by saying that they also are about "breaking" or "changing" something. These words are all about dividing something or about making something that's broken or incomplete.

A

Form small groups. Ask students to think about how to use *fraction* and *fragment* to describe things outside of their mathematics and English language arts applications. For example, can a person have only a fraction of the energy that he needs to get a task done? Can you leave a fragment of your heart somewhere? How might these words apply in situations like those?

P

Have each student choose two words of the four and write questions similar to the ones you posed in step A. For example, can a memory be a refraction, meaning that it is interrupted or broken somehow? Encourage students to use metaphorical thinking.

Scaffolding

Provide additional examples as needed. The following are a few.

- Could you use the word *fragment* to describe clothing? How?
- Could you use the word *fraction* when talking about a building, like a school? How?
- Is a rainbow a *refraction*?
- Is your reflection in the mirror a *refraction*?

Acceleration

The related word *fragile* can be integrated into this minilesson.

- **Fragile (adj.):** Easily breakable; delicate

Roots: *ge, geo*

The Greek root word *ge*, commonly appearing in English as *geo*, means "earth," "soil," or "ground." This Greek root is the word origin of a good number of English vocabulary words, including the common words covered in lesson R28: *geography* and *geology*.

Lesson R28: *geography, geology*

In this minilesson, teachers will teach the roots *ge* and *geo*, such as in the words *geography* and *geology*.

Difficulty level: 1

S

The following lists target words students should *see* and *say* for this minilesson.

▸ **Geography (n.):** The study of the earth's surface and its climates, countries, peoples, and natural resources

▸ **Geology (n.):** The science that deals with the earth's physical history, the rocks of which it is composed, and the changes that the earth has undergone or is undergoing

N

All of these words are common in school, especially in the sciences. *Geography* and *geology* are specific disciplines within science. The word *geography* and its adjective form, *geographical*, are the words that students will hear and use most often outside of school.

A

Create small groups. Have students examine all the parts of each word and discuss how the components could help them remember the meaning of each.

P

Have students define each word in writing. Encourage them to use their own words and to create a student-friendly definition. If you like, ask them to include a quick visual with each definition.

Scaffolding

You could use the following sentence stems with students who require scaffolding.

▸ *Geography* is the study of _____.

▸ *Geology* is the study of _____.

Acceleration

The related words *geode* and *geocentric* could be included for accelerated students or for all students, depending on their interest.

- ▸ **Geode (n.):** A stone with crystals inside
- ▸ **Geocentric (adj.):** Representing the earth as the center of the universe

Root: *graph*

The root *graph* comes from the Greek words *graphein, graphikos, graphe, graphia*, and *grapheion*, which all mean "to draw" or "to write." The level 1 minilesson that follows includes words that are probably familiar to native English speakers, even at a young age, but this minilesson may help them apply the root in additional contexts.

The root *graph* means "to write" and originates from the Greek word *graphein*. *Graph* shows up in many words, especially ones that are used in school, like *geography, paragraph, homograph*, and even *graphite* that's found in pencils.

Lesson R29: *autograph, paragraph, photograph*

In this minilesson, teachers will teach the root *graph*, such as in the words *autograph, paragraph*, and *photograph*.

Difficulty level: 1

S

The following lists target words students should *see* and *say* for this minilesson. The following words almost demand that you show actual models of them. With an interactive whiteboard or simply projecting images from a computer, you can show signatures or *autographs*, highlight or box *paragraphs* within a text, and display a few *photographs*.

- ▸ **Autograph (n.):** One's signed name (signature), usually a memento from a famous person
- ▸ **Paragraph (n.):** A group of sentences on one topic, indented
- ▸ **Photograph (n.):** A picture made using a camera

N

Autograph and *paragraph* are both related to writing, and a *photograph* is an image taken of a scene, a person, or a thing. All the words relate to either an image or to words on a page. Ask students if they know other words that contain *graph*. They may say *biography* or *autobiography*. If so, discuss how these words are related to *autograph* and *paragraph*. If necessary, remind them or teach them that *auto* means "self."

A

Ask small groups to discuss the following questions. The following questions rely on the effective teaching strategy of using comparisons.

▸ How is a *photograph* similar to a painting? How is it different?

▸ How is a *paragraph* different from just one sentence? How is it different from a whole passage or a whole story?

P

Have students write a short paragraph using the words *photograph* and *autograph*. If they know other related words, like *biography*, encourage them to use those words too.

Scaffolding

Provide additional examples or visuals if necessary. These words are concrete; students should be able to visualize them well, especially if you use artifacts or images.

Acceleration

Ask students to use an online or print dictionary to find out what the word *calligraphy* means. Ask them how the word is related to *autograph*. Allow them to look at examples of calligraphy and ask what they think of it.

▸ **Calligraphy (n.):** Fancy, decorative handwriting

Lesson R30: *biography, autobiography, bibliography*

In this minilesson, teachers will teach the root *graph*, such as in the words *biography*, *autobiography*, and *bibliography*.

Difficulty level: 2

S

The following lists target words students should *see* and *say* for this minilesson.

▸ **Biography (n.):** A person's written account of someone else's life

▸ **Autobiography (n.):** A person's written account of his or her own life

▸ **Bibliography (n.):** A list of the books and other resources an academic paper or other text uses; appears at the end of that text

N

These words all consist of the root *graph* plus prefixes and suffixes that tell us something else about each word. The prefix *bio-* means "of or relating to life," and the prefix *auto-* means "oneself." While *biography* and *autobiography* have straightforward meanings based on this breakdown, *bibliography* is the word that's different here, because it's not a book like the other two, but instead a list of books. Discuss this word in the context of the others.

A

Ask pairs of students to discuss *biographical* and *autobiographical* texts that they have read. Prompt pairs as necessary with examples. You can also discuss with them movies that fall into these categories. The point here is for them to be certain of exactly what each word means and to not get them confused.

P

Ask students to answer the following questions. If time is short, have them do this orally or with response devices or a digital tool like Plickers (https://plickers.com).

▸ If LeBron James (or another athlete students would know) were to write a book about his life, which of the three words would best fit? (*autobiography*)

▸ If you had to let a teacher know all the resources you used for information for a report, which of the three words would best fit? (*bibliography*)

▸ If you did research about your grandmother or great-grandmother and then wrote a paper about her life, which of the three words would best fit? (*biography*)

Scaffolding

Students can easily become confused between *biography* and *autobiography*. Give them hints to help them differentiate. You can even use a silly rhyme like, "Me oh, my oh, autobio!" This could help a student remember that an *autobiography* is written in first person and is about oneself.

Acceleration

Even though this minilesson focuses on the root *graph*, students may be interested in the word part *biblio*, which often refers to books (and sometimes refers to the Bible). You may want to use the word *bibliophile*. You surely have books in your classroom and can find ways to model this word more than once in the hope that students also learn to use it.

> **Bibliophile (n.):** A person who loves or collects books

Roots: *hydr, hydra, hydro*

The forms of this root mean "water." To add this root before a vowel, use the *hydr* form. Many English words use these roots, and they form numerous compound words like *hydroplane* and *hydrogen, hydrocarbon, hydrocephaly,* and *geohydrologist.* Lesson R31 focuses on some of the most common words utilizing these roots.

Lesson R31: *hydrate, dehydrate, dehydrated, hydrant*

In this minilesson, teachers will teach the roots *hydr* and *hydra,* such as in the words *hydrate, dehydrate, dehydrated,* and *hydrant.*

Difficulty level: 1

S

The following lists target words students should *see* and *say* for this minilesson.

> **Hydrate (v.):** To cause to absorb water

> **Dehydrate (v.):** To cause to lose water

> **Dehydrated (adj.):** Suffering from a loss of water from the body

> **Hydrant (n.):** An upright pipe with a spout, nozzle, or other outlet, usually in the street, used for drawing water, especially for fighting fire

N

Showing a photo or video clip of a water hydrant being used may be a good way to start the discussion of the words because the power of the visual will definitely trigger a connection with the word "water," thus supporting the meanings of the other target words.

A

Have small groups discuss the following questions.

> Are there things in this room that are *hydrated*? Explain. (Possible answers: Plants, people, class pet, air, skin)

> Are there things in this room that are *dehydrated*? Explain. (Possible answers: Paper and pencils are made from *dehydrated* wood; a thirsty person could be dehydrated; the air could be dry and therefore need to be *hydrated*, especially if heat is running)

▸ Does a *hydrant hydrate*? Explain. (Possible answers: Yes, because it sprays water out everywhere; yes, because water is hydration, and water comes out of the hydrant)

P

Have each student choose two of the words and write original sentences with them. You can also pair students up and ask each person to work on two words and have the partner do the other two, but each pair would turn in all four sentences. Alternatively, you could set up a Kahoot! with four items, each representing one word.

Scaffolding

Help students who require scaffolding use the words *hydrated* and *dehydrated*, which are opposites of each other. They may want to write about a time they were hydrated and then another time they were dehydrated, like after sports practice or when being sick.

Acceleration

The word *hydraulics* is related to the words in this minilesson. Share if appropriate.

▸ **Hydraulics (n.):** The science that deals with the laws about liquids in motion

Roots: *jur, jus*

The roots *jur* and *jus* come from Latin and mean "law" or "justice." Students are likely to be familiar with some of these words because they are used so commonly.

Lesson R32: *just, unjust, justice, injustice*

In this minilesson, teachers will teach the roots *jur* and *jus*, such as in the words *just*, *unjust*, *justice*, and *injustice*.

Difficulty level: 2

S

The following lists target words students should *see* and *say* for this minilesson.

▸ **Just (adj.):** Related to what is right or fair

▸ **Unjust (adj.):** Related to what is wrong or unfair

▸ **Justice (n.):** The quality of being right or fair; equity; honesty

▸ **Injustice (n.):** The quality of being wrong or unfair; inequity; dishonesty

N

 These words are pairs of opposites. Something is either *just* (fair) or not (*unjust*). *Justice* can be served, or an *injustice* can be committed. Ensure that students know the word *just* in this minilesson is not the same as the adverb that means "exactly" or "recently."

A

Ask students if things are just or unjust. Use some of the following examples if you like, but be sure to add others that will resonate with your students.

▸ African Americans at one time had to use different water fountains and restrooms than white people. (*unjust*)

▸ Every American should be treated equally. (*just*)

▸ Girls are discouraged from going to school in some countries. (*unjust*)

▸ Workers are legally required to get a break from work after a certain number of hours. (*just*)

P

Have each student write (or say aloud) an example of a *justice* and an *injustice* that he or she knows of. Accept all his or her answers, even if they are fairly insignificant. For example, students might say it's an *injustice* at school that they cannot arrive when they wish or have soda in class.

Scaffolding

If you have students who are immigrants, supply examples from their home countries of *justices* or *injustices* so that they can better grasp the words' meanings. For U.S. students, supply historical examples they may have studied—for example, events from the civil rights movement may be familiar.

Acceleration

Push students who have mastered these words to apply the terms to literature and history and to pull together information they have studied previously. For example, students may be familiar with *injustices* that African Americans experienced in the South during the civil rights movement. Students may have also studied about Cesar Chavez and how he fought against mistreatment of American farm workers.

Lesson R33: *justify, justification*

In this minilesson, teachers will teach the root *jus*, such as in the words *justify* and *justification*.

Difficulty level: 1

S

The following lists target words students should *see* and *say* for this minilesson.

- **Justify (v.):** To give a good reason for something; to prove something is right

- **Justification (n.):** The act of giving a good reason for something or proof that something is right

Students may be familiar with *justifying* their opinions or finding *justification* in text they are reading in class.

N

These words are the verb and noun forms from the same base word. Provide synonyms for *justification*, such as the following: reason, evidence, proof, data, and explanation.

A

Ask small groups of students to brainstorm lists of things they might need to *justify* or give reasons for. Get them started with examples like justifying why they should be allowed to stay up later, have junk food for breakfast, or spend more time with friends.

P

Have each student write a sentence using either target word. If time allows, have each student say his or her sentence aloud. This provides verbal output practice and allows students to say the word an additional time.

Scaffolding

You can provide examples and nonexamples of *justification* for students. For example, they could sort these related words as either yes (related to justification) or no (not related).

- Giving reasons (*yes*)

- Asking questions (*no*)

- Explaining (*yes*)

- Giving proof (*yes*)

- Providing data (*yes*)

- Yelling about being right (*no*)

- Saying bad things about others (*no*)

Acceleration

Justifiable and *justifiably* are the corresponding adjective and adverb. Ask advanced students if they can use these words correctly in context.

Beyond the Lesson

Ask students as often as possible to *justify* their answers.

Final Thoughts

Roots are the basis of many words in the English language. This chapter has introduced some of the most common ones to your students. Remember to highlight these roots (and others) when possible during instruction so that you support your students in unlocking the meanings of hundreds of unfamiliar words.

Robust Roots L–Z

In this chapter, we'll examine roots that begin with the letters l through z. As with other minilessons in this book, you can do any of the words at any time. There is no intended order or specific sequence; trust your professional judgment about what lessons might be most appropriate and when. The numbering system from the previous chapter continues here, with the letter r denoting that the minilesson is about one or more roots, and the number indicating the order in which the specific lessons appear.

Root: *luc*

This root and its other forms *lum* and *lus* originate from the Latin *lux*, *lucis*, and *lumen*. All of these roots mean "light" or, in some cases, "bright." Visit the blog post "Latin Root Word Luc Means Light, Bright" (Kenning, 2012; http://bit.ly/2joGL2u) for an interesting discussion of this root. (Visit **go.SolutionTree.com/literacy** to access live links to the websites mentioned in this book.)

Lesson R34: *lucent, translucent*

In this minilesson, teachers will teach the root *luc*, such as in the words *lucent* and *translucent*.

Difficulty level: 1

S

The following lists target words students should *see* and *say* for this minilesson.

‣ **Lucent (adj.):** Glowing or giving off light

‣ **Translucent (adj.):** Allowing light to pass through

Ensure that students can pronounce these words correctly, with a soft *c* sound and a long *u* sound, not like the word *luck*. When first seeing these words, it can be hard to figure out how to say them.

N

These two words are very similar, different only in the addition of the prefix *trans-* in the second word. Remind students that *trans-* means "across," "beyond," or "through." In the case of these two words, knowing the meaning of the root *luc* and the prefix *trans-* would help a reader figure out the word *translucent* even if the reader knew nothing else.

Give students examples that show the subtle differences between the two words. The moon is *lucent* but not *translucent*. Sheer curtains are *translucent* but not *lucent*. A candle is *lucent* but not *translucent*. Overhead lights are *lucent*, as are televisions. Clear glass is *translucent*.

A

Allow students one minute of think time, and then partner them up for a think-pair-share. (See page 23 for more on think-pair-share.) Ask each student to name things in the classroom that are *lucent* and things that are *translucent*. Direct students' attention to the windows, shades, curtains, projector, or interactive whiteboard if needed.

P

Ask students to write a definition of each term and to place these in their vocabulary logs, personal glossaries, or notebooks as appropriate.

Scaffolding

Monitor the pairs in step A and direct students' attention to objects in the room if they need help. For example, they can look toward an interactive whiteboard (*translucent*) or a lamp (*lucent*).

Acceleration

Ask students who have mastered these words what *semitranslucent* might mean, and allow them to explore this word online. They can also learn a noun form of *lucent*, which is *lucence*. Challenge them to use these words in their speaking and writing.

▸ **Semitranslucent (adj.):** Only partially translucent

▸ **Lucence (n.):** The quality of being lucent or glowing

Lesson R35: *lucid, lucidity, elucidate*

In this minilesson, teachers will teach the root *luc*, such as in the words *lucid*, *lucidity*, and *elucidate*.

Difficulty level: 2

S

The following lists target words students should *see* and *say* for this minilesson.

▸ **Lucid (adj.):** Clear and easy to understand, as in a *lucid* argument

▸ **Lucidity (n.):** The quality of being clear and easy to understand

▸ **Elucidate (v.):** To explain or make something clear

These words may be somewhat hard to pronounce for students, so give them several opportunities to practice. Academic writing often uses the word *elucidate*, so you may want to pay special attention to this word.

N

All these words contain the root *luc*, with two having it as the beginning syllable, and the other one having it as the second. These words, however, unlike the previous set, are about clarity and light in the figurative sense. They are often used to refer to a person's speaking or writing and its clarity.

A

Have small groups of students discuss the following.

▸ When has someone made a *lucid* point or a *lucid* argument with you recently?

▸ What is something you would like to *elucidate* to others?

If necessary, give the groups some examples to get them going. You might want to review important points from a previous minilesson and say something like, "I wanted to *elucidate* the theory of _____ in class" or "I was trying to *elucidate* the argument of _____."

P

Ask each student to choose either the word *lucid*, *lucidity*, or *elucidate* and to write a sentence using it correctly. Students can turn these in or share them using an interactive digital tool.

Scaffolding

Ask students questions related to current events or material studied in class to get them to think about the concept of a clear explanation or argument.

Acceleration

Share with students who have mastered these words the related word *pellucid*, which means "translucently clear," as in *pellucid* water, or "easily understood," as in *pellucid* prose. Challenge them to use this word in step P. It is also sometimes used to describe music or singing.

Beyond the Lesson

Try to use the word *elucidate* in class discussion when you're asking students to explain concepts. For example, you can say things like, "Miley, would you please *elucidate*? Can you say more about that?"

Roots: *man, manu*

This root, which takes two spellings, comes from the Latin meaning "hand" or "by hand." Some words, like *manufacture* and those related to it, derive their meaning from the idea of making something by hand but now usually refer to machinery or automation.

Lesson R36: *manual, manufacture*

In this minilesson, teachers will teach the roots *man* and *manu*, such as in the words *manual* and *manufacture*.

Difficulty level: 1

S

The following lists target words students should *see* and *say* for this minilesson.

> ▸ **Manual (adj.):** Done with or made by one's hands

> ▸ **Manufacture (v.):** To make something by hand labor or by machines; often refers to something made on a large scale, such as to *manufacture* televisions

N

Consider saying something like the following to your class.

> *You may have heard or seen these words before, but let's talk about them a bit.* Manual *as an adjective means "work done with one's hands"—like* manual *labor. Examples of* manual *labor include harvesting crops, repairing automobiles, and building houses.* Manufacture *is a verb and is related to* manual *because it implies that something is made or built, but these days, machines, rather than hands, often make products. However, many of these products used to involve more labor by hand. Machines have been replacing the work that people's hands do over the past hundred years or so. So, things that are* manufactured *include our TVs, kitchen appliances, and cars.*

A

Have pairs or small groups brainstorm more examples of the words' uses or what they might describe. Students may be familiar with the term *manual* transmission in relation to cars or *manual* workers in relation to jobs in the community. They may ask about the word *manual* used as a noun, as in a *manual* for an appliance's operation. Allow them to explore the words without much direction, only stepping in to correct misconceptions.

P

Have each student write a sentence using each word. Each student should have ideas about what to write and how to use the words from the small-group discussion in the previous step.

Scaffolding

Provide sentence stems if needed. Use the following if you like.

- ▸ The word *manual* is used to describe _____.
- ▸ The word *manufacture* means to _____.

Acceleration

Allow the students to visit the WordHippo (2017c) webpage "Words Starting With MANU" (www.wordhippo.com/what-is/words-starting-with/manu .html) to explore related words. As time allows, ask them to share words with the rest of the class.

Lesson R37: *mandate, manipulate, emancipate*

In this minilesson, teachers will teach the root *man*, such as in the words *mandate*, *manipulate*, and *emancipate*.

Difficulty level: 2

S

The following lists target words students should *see* and *say* for this minilesson.

- **Mandate (v.):** To give a person or organization authority to act in a certain way or to instruct them to do so

- **Manipulate (v.):** To handle or control something very skillfully or to influence a person very cleverly

- **Emancipate (v.):** To set free or liberate

Point out the similarities in the words. Not only do they contain the root in the first part of the word, they also all end in *-ate*, which is often a verb ending in the English language. You may also want to orchestrate a chant or choral response that plays on the rhythm of the words when said together: *mandate, manipulate, emancipate*.

N

All of the words are verbs and are grouped together because they are all about actions that happen and that impact others or that have the intent to change others' situations. *Mandate* means to order to act or to give authority to act. *Manipulate* often means to influence another person (and often not in a positive way). You may use the word *emancipate*, which may be familiar to students who have learned about the Emancipation Proclamation, in many contexts to mean to set someone free.

A

Divide the room into thirds (by rows, table groups, and so on). Give each third one of the target words. Ask students to have a stand-up meeting in one area of the room, gathered in a circle, quickly taking turns and trying to use their assigned word in a sentence or by generating an example of when it would be used.

P

Ask students to answer the following, either verbally (by talking with a partner so that all participate) or in writing.

- Which verb is most appropriate to use if an animal in captivity in a zoo is released to the wild? (*emancipate*)

- Which verb is most appropriate to use if we are discussing a new school rule that has been instituted? (*mandate*)

- Which verb is most appropriate to use if a person leaves out important information to try to convince a friend to do something? (*manipulate*)

Scaffolding

Students may skip their turn in the stand-up meeting (see chapter 2, page 22) if they cannot think of examples. If they are attentive, they will learn from others' examples. You can also provide them with examples as they walk toward their assigned meeting group.

Acceleration

Have students who have mastered these words explore synonyms for each word, using trusted online sources or print dictionaries or thesauri. The following verbs are some examples.

- **Mandate:** *Order, direct, command, require, charge, call on*
- **Manipulate:** *Engineer, steer, maneuver, deceive, control, influence, exploit*
- **Emancipate:** *Free, liberate, release, discharge*

Beyond the Lesson

There are many opportunities to use the word *manipulate* in common situations at school. You can ask a student to *manipulate* the lights instead of turning them off or on. You can *manipulate* the controls on an interactive whiteboard or the sound on a laptop or desktop computer. Strive to use the word *manipulate* instead of simpler words when possible.

Roots: *mis, miss, mit, mitt*

This root, with four spellings, traces its history to the Latin words *mittere* and *missus*, meaning "to send." Quite a few common words contain this root, including the ones you see in the lessons here.

Lesson R38: *admit, admission, permit, permission, dismiss, dismissal*

In this minilesson, teachers will teach the roots *mis, miss, mit,* and *mitt,* such as in the words *admit, admission, permit, permission, dismiss,* and *dismissal.*

Difficulty level: 1

S

The following lists target words students should *see* and *say* for this minilesson.

- **Admit (v.):** To let someone enter
- **Admission (n.):** The act of entering or being allowed to enter a place

▸ **Permit (v.):** To allow someone to do something

▸ **Permission (n.):** Allowing someone to do something or authorizing it

▸ **Dismiss (v.):** To send away or to order someone to leave

▸ **Dismissal (n.):** The act of sending away or ordering someone to leave

N

These words often appear in school and community contexts—for example, most students know about *admission* to special events, *permission* slips for field trips, and *dismissal* times at the end of the day. Be sure to build on this familiarity and spend more time discussing the less familiar words *admit* and *permit*.

The words are noun and verb pairs from the same roots, *mittere* and *missus*. Be sure to point out how the noun form differs structurally from the verb form in each case. Remind students that the suffixes *-ion* and *-al* signify nouns.

A

Have small groups of students try to use the verbs *admit*, *permit*, and *dismiss* in original examples. If they struggle, remind them that the verbs can take different forms based on verb tense. For example, you could have *admitted* someone to your birthday party, or a judge may have *dismissed* a case on a TV show.

P

Ask students to focus on the noun forms this time around. Have each student complete a Frayer model for *admission*, *permission*, or *dismissal*. (See page 18 for more on Frayer models.) You could have students work in pairs if you feel it will make this step go more quickly.

Scaffolding

Ask students questions and provide cues like, "Have you ever paid *admission* to enter a place?" and "Think about a time you need *permission* to do something."

Acceleration

Allow advanced students to explore some of the following synonyms.

▸ **Admission (n.):** *Admittance, access, entrance*

▸ **Permission (n.):** *Authorization, approval, authority*

▸ **Dismissal (n.):** *Nonacceptance, rejection, termination*

Lesson R39: *submit, submission, transmit, transmission, emit, emission*

In this minilesson, teachers will teach the roots *mis, miss, mit,* and *mitt,* such as in the words *submit, submission, transmit, transmission, emit,* and *emission.*

Difficulty level: 2

S

The following lists target words students should *see* and *say* for this minilesson.

- **Submit (v.):** To give in or yield or to offer something to others for consideration
- **Submission (n.):** The act of presenting something for review or judgment
- **Transmit (v.):** To pass something along or to relay it to others
- **Transmission (n.):** The act of passing something along or relaying it to others
- **Emit (v.):** To give forth or release something, like a sound
- **Emission (n.):** The act of giving forth or releasing something

N

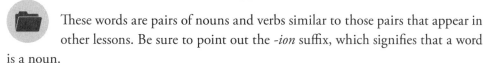

These words are pairs of nouns and verbs similar to those pairs that appear in other lessons. Be sure to point out the *-ion* suffix, which signifies that a word is a noun.

Students may make associations with the word *transmission* if they know about a car's *transmission,* and they may also know the word *emission* as related to cars. Point out that a car's *transmission* is what makes the car move at faster and faster speeds; it is the mechanism by which gears shift. The *emission* system is what gives off byproducts as gasoline is used. Take students beyond these meanings to other applications.

A

Ask small groups of students to focus on the verbs *submit, transmit,* and *emit* and to try to come up with authentic examples for each. You may want to get them started by reminding them that you ask them to *submit* their assignments when they are finished each day.

P

Have each student choose one noun-verb pair and use both words in an authentic paragraph. If you prefer, conduct a Kahoot! with all the target words.

Scaffolding

Provide the following model for step P as needed.

▸ Spaceships have to *transmit* reports to scientists back on the earth. If a *transmission* is late, then the scientists get worried. They may have to send *transmissions* to the spaceship in order to find out what might be wrong.

Acceleration

Another meaning for the word *submit* is when a person gives in or stops fighting something. For example, a person who loves chocolate but is trying to diet might *submit* to his or her craving and eat chocolate one night. Ask students if they can think of other ways to use *submit* in a similar context.

Roots: *not, nota*

This root comes from the Latin *notare* meaning "to mark." With the increasing attention being paid to help students become active readers, many teachers have used the words *annotate* and *annotation* as they teach students how to mark text so it can be referred to later. However, this root has broader application and deserves a bit more exploration.

Lesson R40: *notate, annotate, annotation*

In this minilesson, teachers will teach the roots *not,* and *nota,* such as in the words *notate, annotate,* and *annotation.*

Difficulty level: 1

S

The following lists target words students should *see* and *say* for this minilesson.

▸ **Notate (v.):** To write something down; often used to refer to writing music

▸ **Annotate (v.):** To add notes or symbols to a text

▸ **Annotation (n.):** The notes, symbols, or explanation added to a text

N

These words are all about writing something down, and in the case of *annotate* and *annotation,* to write something down that is in addition to a text that someone else has written. Students who have played musical instruments or who read music may know the word *notate* already; if so, allow them to share their own kid-friendly definitions or examples of it. Make sure that students know that all these words mean to take notes in some way, but the notes can consist of symbols and not just words or abbreviations.

A

 Ask pairs of students to talk with each other about how they have used *annotation* in school. Also ask them if they have used it outside of school—for example, in reading their own books or when studying something for a religious or community group. You may want to share your own examples. I usually show students my annotations in some of my favorite novels.

P

 Have students write a brief exit ticket in which they describe their own methods for or experience with *annotation*. (See page 17 for more on exit tickets.)

Scaffolding

Provide a template for the exit ticket, such as the one in the following example. Students should complete the sentences with details (not just one word).

▸ I have used *annotation* in school when I _____. My favorite way to *annotate* is to _____.

Acceleration

Students who have mastered these words may be interested in the related words *notary* and *notarize*. You may want to ask them if they have heard these words before or have been with an adult when something had to be officially *notarized*.

▸ **Notary (n.):** A person who performs certain legal functions, such as verifying documents; often called a notary public

▸ **Notarize (v.):** To have a document certified or verified by a notary

Lesson R41: *connote, connotation, denote, denotation*

In this minilesson, teachers will teach the roots *not*, and *nota*, such as in the words *connote, connotation, denote*, and *denotation*.

Difficulty level: 1

S

 The following lists target words students should *see* and *say* for this minilesson.

▸ **Connote (v.):** To imply, suggest, or allude to

- **Connotation (n.):** A meaning implied or suggested; not the literal meaning
- **Denote (v.):** To mean something or to be an indication of something, as in a fever *denoting* an infection
- **Denotation (n.):** The literal meaning of a word or phrase; not an implication, suggestion, or allusion

N

These are pairs of verbs with their noun forms and are structured regularly. Point out the *-tion* on the end of the nouns; this is a signifier for words that are nouns.

Connotation and *denotation* are important words, especially as students study literature. Writers carefully choose their words based on *connotation*. Give students familiar examples. For example, the word *slender* has a different connotation than the word *skinny*; it is generally more positive. Likewise, the word *frugal* has a more positive connotation than the word *cheap*. Use examples that will work with your students.

A

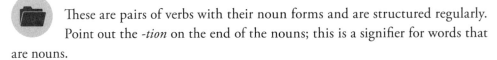

Have groups look at the following sets of words and determine which in each group has a positive connotation and which has a negative connotation.

- *Watch, observe, stare*
- *Curious, interested, nosy, eager to learn*
- *Small, petite, puny*
- *Odor, smell, fragrance*

P

Ask each student to think of some of his or her own pairs or groups of words that have positive and negative connotations and to write them down and turn them in.

Scaffolding

If students struggle in step P, give them these words with negative connotations and ask them to think of synonyms that would have positive connotations.

- An object that is cheap (Possible answers: Inexpensive, basic, gets the job done, useful)
- A person whose behavior is weird (Possible answers: Funny, unique, one of a kind)

Acceleration

 Students who have mastered these words might enjoy playing a bit with *connotation*. Put them in a group and ask them to rewrite (and possibly, act out) this sentence in as many ways as possible: "She walked into the room." They need to replace the verb *walked* with various words with other *connotations*, like *shuffled*, *dashed*, *ambled*, *meandered*, or something similar.

Beyond the Lesson

 You can most likely find ways to ask students about the *connotations* of words in many situations. Be on the lookout for when this might be most appropriate.

Root: *path*

This root has two meanings that seem quite different from each other, both derived from the Greek word *pathos*. The root means either "feeling" or "disease." We get the words *sympathy* and *pathology* from this root.

Lesson R42: *apathy, empathy, sympathy*

In this minilesson, teachers will teach the root *path*, such as in the words *apathy*, *empathy*, and *sympathy*.

Difficulty level: 2

S

 The following lists target words students should *see* and *say* for this minilesson.

- **Apathy (n.):** A lack of interest or enthusiasm
- **Empathy (n.):** The understanding of another person's experience or emotions
- **Sympathy (n.):** The feeling of sadness, sorrow, or pity for someone else's situation

Consider what order to best present these words in, as you will know which are most familiar to your students.

N

 Consider saying something like the following to your class.

The word pathos, *from the Greek, means "feeling," or as we've discussed in our argumentation unit, "emotion." All these words indicate something about emotions.*

Apathy *means a lack of interest in something. You could feel* apathy *in a certain class or toward a certain subject in school. I hope you don't ever feel* apathy *in my class.*

Empathy *and* sympathy *are very similar, and sometimes, people use them interchangeably, even though they have slightly different meanings. If I can "feel your pain," as President Bill Clinton famously said, then I have* empathy. *But if I feel sad for you because something awful has happened to you, then I have* sympathy. *Those two feelings are a bit different.*

A

Have small groups of students generate lists of things they feel *antipathy* for, *apathy* about, *empathy* for, and *sympathy* for. Encourage them to generate at least two examples in each category. Don't allow them to use examples that you've already shared in discussion.

P

Ask students to write sentences using *apathy* correctly. It's fine if they use examples that were discussed in the small group in step A. Ask students to focus on this word because it is used less frequently than the other two target words.

Scaffolding

Check on struggling students and, if necessary, provide them with cues or questions to help them create sentences.

Acceleration

The words *pathetic* and *apathetic* are both derived from the same root. You may want to share these words with advanced students. They can both be useful in speaking and writing.

▸ **Pathetic (adj.):** Causing people to feel sorrow or sadness

▸ **Apathetic (adj.):** Having no feeling or emotion (the adjective form of the noun *apathy*)

Beyond the Lesson

Remind students to show *empathy* for each other in situations where this would be helpful. You can also use the target words when discussing literary characters.

Root: *ped*

The Latin root word *ped* (and its Greek counterpart *pod*) means "foot." This root is the word origin of many English vocabulary words, including the ones you find in these lessons and ones that don't occur as frequently, like *bipedal* (having two feet) and *quadruped* (having four feet).

Lesson R43: *pedal, peddle, pedestrian*

In this minilesson, teachers will teach the root *ped*, such as in the words *pedal*, *peddle*, and *pedestrian*.

Difficulty level: 1

S

The following lists target words students should *see* and *say* for this minilesson.

▸ **Pedal (n.):** The part of a bicycle, car, or other vehicle (and some musical instruments) that a person uses his or her foot to control

▸ **Pedal (v.):** To move by using a pedal

▸ **Peddle (v.):** To go from house to house or place to place trying to sell something (especially small goods)

▸ **Pedestrian (n.):** A person who is walking

N

All these words are related to the idea of walking or moving from place to place. The word *peddle* has come to mean "to sell" but was originally about walking around and selling items. Discuss with students that *pedal* and *peddle* are homophones. They sound alike but have different meanings and spellings. *Pedestrian* is likely the hardest word here, but students probably know the concept, especially if they live in an area where they walk to school. Show a visual of a traffic sign of a *pedestrian* crossing if you feel it will be helpful here.

A

Have small groups of students discuss how *pedal* and *peddle* are alike and different. Encourage them to share examples of *peddling* that they may have seen (for example, street vendors, door-to-door salespeople, and so on).

P

Ask each student to choose his or her favorite word from the four and write a sentence using it. You can display these sentences around the room or by using a technological tool like Padlet (https://padlet.com).

Scaffolding

Make a pedaling motion to help students remember *pedal* versus *peddle*. For *peddle*, you may want to do a hand motion that mimics giving money to another person.

Acceleration

Encourage the students to write more than one sentence for step P. Also, you could introduce them to the following advanced (but related) words.

▸ **Backpedal (v.):** Figuratively, to reverse one's actions or opinion on something

▸ **Peddler (n.):** A person who goes from place to place and sells things; can also be used figuratively to mean someone who promotes his or her ideas

Lesson R44: *impede, impediment, stampede*

In this minilesson, teachers will teach the root *ped*, such as in the words *impede*, *impediment*, and *stampede*.

Difficulty level: 2

S

The following lists target words students should *see* and *say* for this minilesson.

▸ **Impede (v.):** To delay or prevent; to obstruct

▸ **Impediment (n.):** A delay, obstacle, or obstruction; a limitation

▸ **Stampede (n.):** A rush of people, horses, cattle, or other animals

▸ **Stampede (v.):** To rush or charge in a large mass

N

These words are all about movement, either literal or figurative. *Stampede* may be most familiar to students, so you could start with this word and build from it. (There are surely video clips of stampedes that you could use to emphasize the concept of movement that is shared among these words.) You may also want to discuss the figurative meaning of *stampede*; it can mean a rush of emotion, for example, and not necessarily a rush of physical beings or objects.

A

Have small groups answer and discuss the following.

▸ Can heavy traffic be an *impediment*? If so, how?

▸ Could a crowd at a concert *impede*? If so, how? Could they also *stampede*? How?

P

Have each student write an original sentence with each word. Students can draw on the conversation in step A if they like.

Scaffolding

Provide additional examples when needed. Use the following if you like.

▸ **Impede:** Caffeine can *impede* sleep; exercise can *impede* weight gain; not cleaning a wound can *impede* its healing; poor eyesight can *impede* learning in the classroom.

▸ **Impediment:** People can have speech or hearing *impediments*; pouring rain can be an *impediment* to a football game or golf tournament; a tree blocking the road would be an *impediment* to your getting somewhere.

▸ **Stampede:** People can *stampede* at a soccer match; bulls *stampede* in the streets of Spain; memories can flood your mind like a *stampede*.

Acceleration

Students who have mastered these words might enjoy exploring related words like *unimpeded*, *unhindered*, and *unhampered*, which all mean "free" or "unobstructed." You can also encourage these students to think of how they can use the word *stampede* in a figurative manner, perhaps in their own writing.

Beyond the Lesson

You can demonstrate authentic use of *impede* often in typical classroom situations. I might say things like, "William, don't let the lack of a stable Internet connection *impede* your research" and "Tawanda, don't socialize too much and *impede* your progress."

Root: *photo*

This root, which means "light," originates in the Greek words *phos* and *photos*. Even though the word *photo* (or its longer form, *photograph*) means "picture," we need to help students remember that the art of photography is based on manipulating light.

Lesson R45: *photograph, photography, photographer, photogenic*

In this minilesson, teachers will teach the root *photo*, such as in the words *photograph, photography, photographer,* and *photogenic.*

Difficulty level: 1

S

The following lists target words students should *see* and *say* for this minilesson.

▸ **Photograph (n.):** A picture made using a camera

▸ **Photography (n.):** The art of taking pictures with a camera

▸ **Photographer (n.):** A person who takes pictures

▸ **Photogenic (adj.):** Looking attractive in pictures or movies

N

Consider saying something like the following to your class.

Many of you know a lot about taking pictures with your smartphones or other electronic devices. Before we had these devices, we could only take pictures with cameras, and some of you may have used digital cameras before. The words we're looking at today are all related to pictures, or the other word for them, photographs. *The word* photo *is actually short for* photograph, *like* pic *is short for* picture. *And these words all have their roots in the Greek word for light. Light is actually an important component of any good* photograph.

A photograph *is the actual picture, whereas* photography *is the art and science of taking pictures. And, the person who takes pictures is the* photographer. *All these words are obviously directly related. Lastly, the word* photogenic *means that you look good in pictures. Has anyone ever told you that you are* photogenic? *When I was a kid, everyone said that to my sister—that she was so* photogenic. *I never saw a bad photo of her.*

A

Have small groups of students discuss all four words, making sure they can pronounce each correctly. Ask them to share examples of when they have seen *photographers* at work and examples of people who they think are *photogenic.*

P

Ask students to think about when they might authentically use one of the words. Do a Whip Around so they can state this verbally, or, if time allows, state it in writing.

Scaffolding

Visuals may help students understand the differences among the first three words. You could display a *photographic* image, then an image of a *photographer* engaging in his craft, perhaps with an arrow added, pointing to the *photographer* himself.

Acceleration

Have students visit Quizlet's "Photo- Words" page (imb1999, 2017; http://bit .ly/2qwobMu) for a list of words containing this root. Some of the words are quite rare and advanced but may be interesting to your students.

Root: *port*

This common root comes from the Latin *portare*, meaning "to carry" and the word *porta*, meaning "gate."

Lesson R46: *import, export, transport, portable*

In this minilesson, teachers will teach the root *port*, such as in the words *import*, *export*, *transport*, and *portable*.

Difficulty level: 1

S

The following lists target words students should *see* and *say* for this minilesson.

▸ **Import (v.):** To bring goods or services into a country from another

▸ **Export (v.):** To send goods or services from our country into another

▸ **Transport (v.):** To carry something or someone from one place to another

▸ **Portable (adj.):** Able to be carried or moved easily

N

These words are all about movement, and three are verbs, meaning that people or organizations actively do them. Many students will have some familiarity with *import* and *export* and may have studied forms of *transportation*. Thus, the most unfamiliar word might be *portable*. Be sure to explain that *portable* is a word that goes well with the other three words. Things cannot be imported, exported, or transported if they are not portable. (Some objects that are very large may not seem portable, but with the right equipment, they are.)

A

Have small groups discuss the following question.

▸ What are some things that the United States *imports*? (Possible answers: iPhones, iPads, other electronic devices, televisions, certain brands of clothing and shoes)

P

Ask students to look around the room and list things that they think are *imported* from other countries. Have each student jot at least three things down, starting with the sentence stem "I believe the following things are imported: _____, _____, and _____." As time and practicality allow, see if students can look at the items to check for accuracy.

Scaffolding

Remind students that the prefix *im-* is similar to the word *in* and means "bring something in" in the word *import*. Remind them that the prefix *ex-* appears on the word *exit*, and to exit is to go out. This should help them remember that *exports* go out.

Acceleration

If you live in an area near water, your students may be familiar with a *port* (as in the shipping industry). Regardless of familiarity, advanced students may also be interested in the following words. Students can also do some quick Internet research for places in the United States, or their respective country, that are seaports or that have spaceports (like Cape Canaveral, Florida).

▸ **Seaport (n.):** A town with a harbor for ships going in and out of the sea

▸ **Spaceport (n.):** The base from which spacecraft are launched

Lesson R47: *portfolio, report, porter*

In this minilesson, teachers will teach the root *port*, such as in the words *portfolio*, *report*, and *porter*.

Difficulty level: 1

S

The following lists target words students should *see* and *say* for this minilesson.

▸ **Portfolio (n.):** A case or other holder for loose papers or artwork; a place where a writer or artist keeps his or her work so he or she can carry it around when necessary

▸ **Report (n.):** An account or version of something; sometimes given at regular times, such as a monthly report on the school's attendance

▸ **Porter (n.):** A person who carries things, usually supplies or luggage

N

Students may already know (or have heard) the words *portfolio* and *report* in a school context. Make sure that you broaden their ideas about the word *report*, because it doesn't have to be something like a book report or research report. It is often something verbal—like a message carried back. The word *report* literally means "back" and "carry." If students remember the meaning of the prefix *re-*, they can easily break this word down to its larger meaning (outside the context of school).

Basically, all three words have in common the collection of things and the literal or figurative carrying of those things.

A

Show students the following list and ask them to connect each word or phrase to one of the target words.

▸ Stories (*portfolio*)

▸ Paintings (*portfolio*)

▸ Your backpack (*porter*)

▸ Packages to be delivered (*porter*)

▸ Poems (*portfolio*)

▸ Explanation of a trip to another country (*report*)

▸ Results of a medical test (*report*)

▸ Photographs (*portfolio*— although some may also make a case for *report*)

P

Ask each student to choose the word that he or she learned the most about today, write it on a slip of paper, and then explain (briefly) what he or she learned. This exercise could also be done using Padlet (https://padlet.com).

Scaffolding

Give plenty of examples of *report* that don't involve a student writing a paper. I might share with my students that I recently took one of my dogs to the vet's office, where he had blood work and X-rays. I anxiously awaited the vet calling me with the *report* later that day.

Another example is when you take your car for a regular service, yet the mechanic runs a check on all of the car's systems. You wait for the mechanic's *report* to see if anything is wrong.

Acceleration

More advanced students might enjoy exploring a few other words with this root. They can visit Membean's (2017b) article "Root Word of the Day: Port" (http://membean.com/wrotds/port-carry) to access a good (yet small) collection.

Roots: *scrib, scrip, script*

The roots *scrib*, *scrip*, and *script* are from the Latin words *scriber* and *scriptus* that mean "to write." The English words *scribe* and *script* are obviously derived from these roots.

Lesson R48: *manuscript, transcribe, transcript, transcription*

In this minilesson, teachers will teach the roots *scrib*, *scrip*, and *script*, such as in the words *manuscript*, *transcribe*, *transcript*, and *transcription*.

Difficulty level: 2

S

The following lists target words students should *see* and *say* for this minilesson.

▸ **Manuscript (n.):** A document, book, or other text that has not been professionally published

▸ **Transcribe (v.):** To put thoughts, speech, or data into writing; or, in some cases, to translate from one form or language into another

▸ **Transcript (n.):** A written or printed version of material originally presented in another medium, as in the transcript from a press conference

▸ **Transcription (n.):** The act or process of transcribing; also sometimes used as a synonym for *transcript*

N

Consider saying something like the following to your class.

These words are all about a handwritten or printed text. Before a book is published, writers call the book a manuscript. *To transcribe something is to write down what is being said. There are people who sit in hearings in courts and transcribe everything that is being said by the lawyers, the judge, witnesses, and so on. These people are called* transcriptionists. *The document they produce from a court hearing is called the* transcription. *Some television shows and other broadcasts have* transcripts *you can order, so you can read everything that people said on the show. Also, a* transcript *is what the printed record of your grades in high school or college is usually called.*

A

Have small groups of students discuss the similarities and differences between a *manuscript* and a *transcript* and in which situations each might be used. Help them get started with examples if necessary, like the White House Press Secretary releasing a *transcript* after a news conference with the president or a famous author (that your students would know) preparing a *manuscript*.

P

Ask each student to choose a word and make a word wheel with it. The word wheel can contain the word, a visual, and a synonym, or the word and two synonyms. If a student chooses *manuscript*, he or she might sketch an open book in the top right of the wheel and place the synonym *text* in the bottom right of the wheel. (See page 26 for more on word wheels.)

Scaffolding

Struggling students often confuse nouns and verbs that are similar. Be sure to check on these students during step P and ensure they are not using *transcript* or *transcription* where they should use a form of *transcribe*.

Acceleration

Allow students who have mastered these words to visit Membean's article (2017c) "Root Word of the Day: Scrib" (http://membean.com/wrotds/scrib-write) and explore other words with this root.

Beyond the Lesson

In some cases, you can pair students, pose a question, and then ask one student to respond verbally to the question while the other transcribes what is being said. This is a great way to remind students of the word's meaning and to review for a test or quiz.

Root: *sol*

The root *sol*, meaning "sun," is derived from the Latin *solis*. *Sol* can also mean "alone" or "lonely" when derived from the Latin *solus*; however, in this section, we examine only words related to the meaning "sun," such as *solar*.

Lesson R49: *solar, solarium, solstice*

In this minilesson, teachers will teach the root *sol*, such as in the words *solar, solarium,* and *solstice*.

Difficulty level: 2

S

The following lists target words students should *see* and *say* for this minilesson.

▸ **Solar (adj.):** Related to the sun

▸ **Solarium (n.):** A room built to sunbathe, or expose oneself to sunlight

▸ **Solstice (n.):** One of the two times per year when the sun is farthest from the equator, approximately June 21 and December 21

N

These are all words referring to the sun, with *solar* being the most common one. Students may know *solar* from learning about solar energy. *Solar* and *solarium* can be discussed together, especially if you have an image of a *solarium* and can show how it brings the sunlight in.

A

Ask students to discuss the following questions in small groups.

▸ What do you know about solar energy? How is it used?

▸ Why would someone want a solarium at their house or place of work?

P

Have students choose one target word to use in a sentence, and have them turn in their written work.

Scaffolding

Assist students with constructing their sentences as necessary. Also, provide the word *sunroom* as a synonym for *solarium*.

Acceleration

Visit Vocabulary.com's (2015) article "Elements of the Universe: Sol" (http://bit.ly/2rBbRux) for a manageable word list that advanced students may be interested in studying.

Root: *tele*

This root comes from the Greek words *tele*, meaning "far," and *telos*, meaning "end." When it appears in English words, it mostly also means "distant," "far away," or "at a distance"; and is most often found at the beginnings of words. It may be familiar to many students because of the word *television*; *telos* means "end."

Lesson R50: *television, telephone, telescope, telecast*

In this minilesson, teachers will teach the root *tele*, such as in the words *television*, *telephone*, *telescope*, and *telecast*.

Difficulty level: 1

S

The following lists target words students should *see* and *say* for this minilesson.

‣ **Television (n.):** A device that receives television signals and projects them on a screen

‣ **Telephone (n.):** A device that transmits sound or voice (and now photos and video) to another point far away

‣ **Telescope (n.):** A device that you look through and that makes distant objects appear closer

‣ **Telecast (v.):** To transmit or show something by television

Ensure that students actually know the words *television* and *telephone*. Some may be so accustomed to the shortened forms *TV* and *phone* that they are not familiar with the full words. Additionally, while *telecast* can also be a noun, in this lesson, focus only on the verb.

N

Consider saying something like the following to your class.

> The root word tele, *as you might already know, often means "far." Words that have* tele *in them usually mean that something is coming from far away or is going to a place far away. I'm sure you're somewhat familiar with the words* television *and* telephone, *but I want to help you add two related words to your vocabulary,* telescope *and* telecast, *today.*

You might want to show a few Google (https://images.google.com) or Bing (www .bing.com/images) images or a video clip so that students can envision what a *telescope* looks like and how people use it. For *telecast*, provide the synonym *broadcast* (v.) or *air* (v.) for *telecast*. Also, depending on your students' interest, you can share with them the fact that *telecast* and *broadcast* can also be used as nouns.

A

Have students talk about how they can use these words in conversation in school and at home in the next few days. Challenge them to use the full words *television* and *telephone* instead of the abbreviated *TV* and *phone*.

P

 Ask students to use the words *telescope* and *telecast* in written sentences and turn them in. They can write simple definitions of the words if they don't want to create an authentic context.

Scaffolding

 You can provide the following sentence stems for struggling students or for the whole class if you feel they would be helpful.

▸ A person would use a *telescope* to _____.

▸ One of the best shows that is *telecast* is _____ because it _____.

More than one word should go in each blank; encourage students to respond to the stems by finishing each sentence.

Acceleration

You may want to pair up some advanced students and have them peruse the list of words prefixed with *tele* at Wiktionary's (2013) entry "Category: English Words Prefixed With Tele-" (http://bit.ly/2jDgGPf). You can ask them to pick a few words that the rest of the class may enjoy knowing and to share those.

Root: *terr*

The Latin root word *terr* means "earth" or "land." This root is the word origin of quite a few English words, including *terrarium*, which some students may know from creating these little marvels in school, church, Boy Scouts, or Girl Scouts. Students can easily remember the Latin root word *terr* if they learn the word *terrain*, because the *terrain* of any area is what the earth or land is like in that place.

Lesson R51: *terrain, terrestrial, territory, territorial*

In this minilesson, teachers will teach the root *terr*, such as in the words *terrain*, *terrestrial*, *territory*, and *territorial*.

Difficulty level: 2

S

The following lists target words students should *see* and *say* for this minilesson.

▸ **Terrain (n.):** A piece of land, often described by its physical features, like hilly or sandy terrain

▸ **Terrestrial (n.):** Relating to the earth

> **Territory (n.):** A piece of land or a region; often means land that is under control of a government group or other organization

> **Territorial (adj.):** Related to a certain piece or region of land

Ask students if they have ever heard someone call an animal (or even a person) *territorial*. This word sometimes describes behaviors about protecting an area of land or not letting others into it.

Students may also have heard the word *terrestrial* as part of the term *extraterrestrial*, especially if they are fans of science fiction. Talk with them about the fact that the prefix *extra-* means "beyond" and thus, *extraterrestrials* are beings from beyond our earth's boundaries.

N

 These words all share the root *terr*, but teachers should caution students that words like *terrific* and *terrible* appear to have this root, but they don't. The guidance to give students is that when they encounter an unfamiliar word that contains *terr*, they should ask themselves if a word containing a reference to "earth" makes sense in the context. If not, then the word is probably not a word that contains the root but is instead a word with a meaning unrelated to earth or land.

A

Have small groups of students brainstorm things they can describe as *terrestrial*. For example, trees are *terrestrial*—we find them here on earth. However, stars are not *terrestrial*.

P

 Ask each student to choose one of the target words other than *terrestrial* and write at least one sentence using that word.

Scaffolding

You can use simple sketches or visuals from an online image search to emphasize how the target words differ from each other. For instance, a map with lines drawn can show what a *territory* is, and a photo of hills or forest could show *terrain*.

Acceleration

 The opposite of *terrestrial* is *celestial*, meaning "belonging to or from the heavens." Advanced students might like learning this word also.

Roots: *vid, vis*

The roots *vid* and *vis* mean "to see." They originate in the Latin verbs *video* and *visus*. The two spellings in English, as you can see, also originate in the Latin.

Lesson R52: *vision, visible, visibility, visualize*

In this minilesson, teachers will teach the roots *vid* and *vis*, such as in the words *vision*, *visible*, *visibility*, and *visualize*.

Difficulty level: 1

S

The following lists target words students should *see* and *say* for this minilesson.

- **Vision (n.):** The state of being able to see
- **Visible (adj.):** Able to be seen
- **Visibility (n.):** The state of being able to be seen by others; also, a measure of distance that one can see, as when flying in an airplane or being underwater
- **Visualize (v.):** To see in your mind; to imagine

N

These words all contain the root *vis* so that the alternate spelling of *vid* doesn't confuse students. Students may be familiar with several target words. For example, they may know *visualize* from reading instruction. Teachers often talk with students about being able to *visualize* while reading. However, students may not deeply understand the word's definition or be able to apply it in other contexts. Also, even students ages five to seven often know the meaning of the opposite of *visible*, *invisible*. They may have had lots of experience pretending to be *invisible* but again may be unfamiliar with the word in other contexts. You may also want to talk with students about the figurative meaning of *vision* (seeing or foreseeing something in one's mind). A *vision*, then, can be your sense of sight, but it can also be a *vision* only in the mind or imagination.

A

Have small groups of students discuss the words *visibility* and *visualize*, as these are probably the two most difficult. Ask them to come up with a sentence using each word correctly.

P

Ask each student to write an explanation or definition of one word of his or her choosing from the entire discussion. Possible words that may come up include the following: *vision* (literal and figurative meanings), *visible, invisible, visibility, invisibility, visualize,* and *visualization.*

Scaffolding

If necessary, assist students who require scaffolding in steps A and P. You may want to focus them on the words *vision* and *visible* and assist them in writing their individual sentences.

Acceleration

Allow students who have mastered these words to read "Vid, Vis, View—Root Word" on Quizlet (rtalkows, 2017; http://bit.ly/2iCDUpi) and work in pairs and explore the words on Quizlet that contain the roots *vis* and *vid*.

Beyond the Lesson

Visualization can be used in many ways in the classroom. You can ask students to close their eyes and mentally *visualize* what it might be like in certain historical situations, like living in a covered wagon while moving westward or surviving the Great Boston Fire of 1872. When you use this technique, be sure to remind students of the target word.

Final Thoughts

With the completion of the minilessons in this chapter, your students have learned even more critical roots that will help them unlock the meanings of many words they will encounter in school and in life.

Powerful Prefixes

Prefixes, along with sentence-level and paragraph-level context clues, can be helpful as students try to read difficult text. However, in my experience, even high school students don't know all the word parts (roots, prefixes, and suffixes) that they should know in order to best support them as they tackle complex text for class discussion and in their independent reading.

> A *prefix* is a not a word but a word part, attached to a stem to make a new word, often with a very different meaning from the stem alone.

This deficit that our students so readily display as we engage with academic text in our classrooms thus presents us with quite the dilemma. The good news about prefixes is that only twenty of them account for 97 percent of all prefixed words in printed academic text (White et al., 1989). So, if we choose to teach about prefixes and prefixed words, focusing most of our teaching time on the top twenty prefixes just makes good common sense.

The top twenty English prefixes appear in table 5.1 (page 116), with the total percentage of prefixed words each accounts for noted in the third column. You can see that even focusing on only the top three or four prefixes would help your students gain some knowledge of more than 50 percent of all the prefixed words in English. With that fact in mind, this chapter includes a higher number of minilessons for the most popular prefixes and fewer for the less frequently used ones. The first four sets of prefixes listed in table 5.1 (*un-*, *re-*, *in-*, *im-*, *il-*, *ir-*, and *dis-*) comprise the bulk of lessons in this chapter because they are the most frequently used prefixes. A smaller number of lessons covers prefixes *under-*, *over-*, *sub-*, *pre-*, and *fore-*. If you have limited time for teaching vocabulary, or you find that you can't smoothly integrate many vocabulary minilessons into your instruction, consider making these first four sections in this chapter priorities.

Table 5.1: Common Prefixes in English

Prefix	Meanings	Percentage of Prefixed Words in Which It Appears
un-	not, the opposite of	26.4 percent
re-	back, backwards, again, anew, again and again (repetitively)	13.6 percent
in-, im-, il-, ir-	not, the opposite of	10.6 percent
dis-	not, opposite of, remove, apart	7.3 percent
em-, en-	put into, go into, within, cause to be	4.5 percent
non-	not, the absence of	4.3 percent
in-, im-	into, inside, within	3.5 percent
over-	above, too much, upper, outer, extra	3.3 percent
mis-	bad, wrong, failure of, lack of	2.8 percent
sub-	below, under, less than complete, nearly	2.7 percent
pre-	before, in front of, prior to, early	2.7 percent
inter-	between, among	2.6 percent
fore-	before, in front of	2.5 percent
de-	make the opposite of, reduce, remove	2.4 percent
trans-	across, beyond, change, through	1.6 percent
super-	above, over, superior, too much	1.5 percent
semi-	half, partial	1.3 percent
anti-	against, opposite of	1.1 percent
mid-	middle	1.1 percent
under-	beneath, below, less in degree	0.8 percent

Source: White et al., 1989.

See Marie Rippel's (n.d.) blog post "How We Teach Prefixes" (http://blog.allabout learningpress.com/prefixes) or Grammarist's (2014) article "Negative Prefixes" (http://grammarist.com/usage/negative-prefixes) for additional information for teaching prefixes not covered in this chapter. While websites on prefixes abound, these two are some of the best resources that I've found (and I've done plenty of looking).

Prefix: *un-*

The prefix *un-* accounts for more prefixed words in the English language than any other prefix, so it's worth our time and attention. It is very flexible, as it can be used at the beginnings of adjectives, adverbs, and verbs (including *undo* and *unfriend*). However, it is fairly uncommon for verbs to begin with this prefix; it's much more commonly found in adjectives and adverbs.

Lesson P1: *undo, unable, unnecessary*

In this minilesson, teachers will teach the prefix *un-*, such as in the words *undo, unable,* and *unnecessary.*

Difficulty level: 1

S

The following lists target words students should *see* and *say* for this minilesson. Obviously, you can adjust the order of these words if you like; however, consider teaching *undo* first because it is the shortest word and is also likely to be the most familiar.

- ▸ **Undo (v.):** To cancel or reverse the doing of some action
- ▸ **Unable (adj.):** Lacking the skill or means of doing something
- ▸ **Unnecessary (adj.):** Not needed

Provide examples of the words in familiar classroom or home contexts. At school, for example, students may be asked to *undo* (or *unbutton, unzip, untie*) their outer garments when coming in from outside. You might also provide examples from your experience. For example, I might tell my students that I'm *unable* to lift heavy objects over my head and that I find it *unnecessary* to download music to my smartphone. Choose examples that will work for you and your students.

N

Consider saying something like the following to your class.

> So, you can see that all these words have the prefix un- *in common, and that* un- *makes the word the opposite. If I were to do something and then changed my mind about it, I could* undo *it. Let's say I set up some kind of prank for my husband to find when he gets home, but then I feel bad about tricking him, so I* undid *it before he arrived.* Undid *is the past tense of our word* undo—*remember that it can have several forms or endings because it's a verb, and all verbs change their endings to show number and tense. When you put* un- *on the front of a verb or adjective, it takes the original word and turns it into exactly the opposite.* Undo *is the opposite of* do.

A

Do three short rounds of think-pair-share (see page 23 for an explanation of think-pair-share). Have students stand up and move, pairing up with a different partner for each round. Allow only one to two minutes per round. To save time, don't worry about assigning partner A and partner B for each round; simply tell students to jump in and discuss equally, using their best speaking, listening, and collaboration skills. Pairs should discuss one of the following three questions per round.

1. What are some things you would like to *undo*? (Possible answers: A hair braid, style, or cut; something you said or did that wasn't nice)

2. What are some things you are *unable* to do but would like to be able to do? (Possible answers: Drive a car; play a certain sport or game)

3. What are some things that you think are *unnecessary*, but a friend or a parent might disagree with you? (Possible answers: It's *unnecessary* to eat breakfast every day [parent might disagree]; it's *unnecessary* to sit with your friend at lunch [friend might disagree])

P

Have each student choose a favorite *un-* word from the minilesson today (this could be another word that came up during the minilesson, not necessarily a target word). Ask students to write that favorite word in a special place (perhaps the back of a notebook, in a journal, and so on) and to remember to use it. If you have dry-erase desktops, you could have each student write his or her favorite word in the top right or left corner and leave it there for a few days so he or she can see it (and use it!).

Scaffolding

You may have to provide more examples and discussion in step S than originally planned. Be alert to students who still seem confused after one or two examples.

You may also want to see the quiz in the Acceleration section and use it as a whole-class activity, stopping to answer questions as needed. It can provide additional support for learning additional words with this prefix. While this lesson borrows from the Acceleration lesson, stopping to answer questions can make it a scaffolding activity.

Acceleration

EC English Language Centres (McCarthy, 2010) offers an article "Words Starting With 'Un'" (http://bit.ly/2iJitBL) containing a quiz that your advanced students might like to try. (Visit **go.SolutionTree.com/literacy** to access live links to the websites mentioned in this book.)

Lesson P2: *unavailable, unapproachable, unattainable*

In this minilesson, teachers will teach the prefix *un-*, such as in the words *unavailable*, *unapproachable*, and *unattainable*.

Difficulty level: 2

S

The following lists target words students should *see* and *say* for this minilesson.

‣ **Unavailable (adj.):** Not free to be used or obtained, or not free to do something

‣ **Unapproachable (adj.):** Not friendly or welcoming

‣ **Unattainable (adj.):** Not able to be reached or achieved

Quickly remind students that the prefix *un-* makes what comes after it the opposite of what it was originally, as in the words *friendly* and *unfriendly*. You may also want to note that each word uses the suffix *-able*, and remind students of its meaning (or see if they recall its meaning). The suffix *-able* means having the power, skill, means, or opportunity to do something.

N

Consider saying something like the following to your class.

> *All three of these words are adjectives and are somewhat similar in meaning, as in they all imply that you want something you can't get. Something or someone that is* unavailable *to you means that you just can't get to it. Often our principal is* unavailable *to me because she is busy talking with a parent. And if you're in the lunch line and they sell out of chicken nuggets, those are* unavailable *to you. They're simply no longer around. There is no way you can get chicken nuggets if they are* unavailable *at that moment.*
>
> Unapproachable *is similar but is often used to describe a person who seems like he or she doesn't want to have any contact with you. It means that a person puts off a certain vibe that he or she does not want to be talked to. An animal could be* unapproachable, *too—like a grizzly bear in the forest, looking at you and growling—you wouldn't want to get close!*
>
> *Lastly,* unattainable *is often used in terms of a goal or some other kind of achievement. For example, when I was a student, I thought that being the best athlete in my grade level was* unattainable, *so I decided to turn my energies to my studies, and I set many goals that were* attainable *for me. For example, I won a poetry contest one time.*

A

Have small groups of students match the following words and scenarios to the word they think is most closely related. Make sure they can say why they feel the word they choose for each scenario is the best. (Alternatively, consider using visuals instead of these scenarios, or supplement these scenarios with visuals.)

- ▸ You see a "do not disturb" or "privacy" sign on the door. (*unavailable*)

- ▸ Concert tickets that you want are sold out. (*unavailable*)

- ▸ A stray dog is growling and baring its teeth as you walk toward it. (*unapproachable*)

- ▸ Sending a human into outer space was once thought to be _____. (*unattainable*)

- ▸ One of your neighbors is outside, stomping around and cursing under his or her breath. (*unapproachable*)

P

Ask students, "When are you *unavailable*? When are you *unapproachable*?" Have them answer these questions in a few sentences. Possible answers could include the following.

- ▸ I am *unavailable* when I'm sleeping. There is no way I want to be bothered.

- ▸ I am *unapproachable* when I'm sick. I don't like people bothering me when I don't feel well, and they will see me frowning.

Use Padlet (https://padlet.com) or TodaysMeet (https://todaysmeet.com) if you want students to use a digital tool that allows them to see their peers' work in real time.

Scaffolding

Because the words are so similar, some students may be confused about meaning, or they may not be able to discern the critical differences. Consider providing visuals if you think they will help students better understand the words. For example, you might show a photo of a ladder that appears to continue for infinity to represent the word *unattainable*.

Acceleration

Ask students to brainstorm synonyms for one or more of the target words. Some possible answers include the following.

- ▸ **Unavailable:** *Nonexistent, inaccessible, unreachable, undeliverable, busy, tied up*

- **Unapproachable:** *Aloof, distant, detached, withdrawn, uncommunicative, unresponsive, unsociable*

- **Unattainable:** *Unreachable, unachievable, unobtainable, impossible, unwinnable*

Beyond the Lesson

Remind students of times you're *unavailable* to them—for example, when you're conferring with a student writer or are leading a guided reading group.

Lesson P3: *undecided, uncertain, unwilling*

In this minilesson, teachers will teach the prefix *un-*, such as in the words *undecided, uncertain,* and *unwilling.*

Difficulty level: 2

S

The following lists target words students should *see* and *say* for this minilesson. Again, remind students that the prefix *un-* negates what comes after it. Your reminders will help them remember what *un-* can do when placed on many words. Also, point out that the following words all have different forms after the *un-*.

- **Undecided (adj.):** Not determined; or, if describing a person, not having one's mind made up

- **Uncertain (adj.):** Not known or definite; still in doubt or "up in the air"

- **Unwilling (adj.):** Refusing to do something; not eager to do something; reluctant

Undecided looks like the past tense of a verb, but people often use it as an adjective. *Uncertain* literally means "not certain," so give students synonyms as needed for certain (the word could mean "not for sure" in student terms). And *unwilling* also looks like a verb with its *-ing* ending. It, like *undecided,* is an adjective, though. Modeling word analysis for your students will help them become more and more likely to do this on their own.

N

Obviously, these are all words with the prefix *un-*, but they also have other things in common. This set of words is about not doing or not knowing. They are also all adjectives, so they are describing words. Remind your students over and over that adjectives give details, clarity, and specificity to nouns. This will help them remember adjectives' function and also should help them use stronger adjectives in their writing.

A

Have small groups brainstorm things that could be *undecided*, *uncertain*, and *unwilling*. You may want to have them make three columns and list their ideas in each one, such as in the example in figure 5.1.

Undecided	Uncertain	Unwilling
• Someone who isn't sure yet if he or she wants to ask another person out for a date • Not knowing what you'd like to order for dessert at a restaurant	• Tomorrow's weather • My plans for after school today	• A cat or dog that doesn't want a bath • A toddler who doesn't want to take a nap

Figure 5.1: Small-group brainstorming example.

P

Ask each student to commit to using two of the words in conversation in the next few days. If time allows, ask each student to write his or her plan down quickly and hand it in. If you don't have time for writing, have students partner with someone who wasn't in their small group in step A and share their plans aloud.

Examples could include the following.

> ▸ I'm going to use the words *undecided* and *uncertain* when people ask me questions if I'm not sure of the right answer or if I haven't made up my mind about something.

> ▸ I plan to use the words *undecided* and *unwilling*. For example, I'm *undecided* about what to wear to school tomorrow, and I'm *unwilling* to wear different shoes from today, because these are my favorites.

Scaffolding

If struggling students are quiet during step A, it's fine for them to sit back and listen, as long as the group is generating examples. If a group is stuck, you can provide an example or two. In step P, you can provide sentence templates like the following.

> ▸ I'm going to use the word _____ when
> I _____.

> ▸ I can use the word _____ in school. (Explain how.)

> ▸ I can use the word _____ at home. (Explain how.)

Acceleration

Ask pairs or individuals to brainstorm synonyms and antonyms for the target words. Examples follow.

▸ **Synonyms for *uncertain*:** *Indefinite, debatable, in doubt, unsure, unsettled*

▸ **Antonyms for *uncertain*:** *Sure, positive, predictable, reliable*

▸ **Synonyms for *undecided*:** *Wavering, unsure, mixed up*

▸ **Antonyms for *undecided*:** *Decisive, sure, positive, agreeable*

▸ **Synonyms for *unwilling*:** *Refusing, hesitant, reluctant, shy away from*

▸ **Antonyms for *unwilling*:** *Willing, ready, agreeable, eager*

Lesson P4: *unacceptable, unanswerable, unimaginable, unspeakable, unthinkable*

In this minilesson, teachers will teach the prefix *un-*, such as in the words *unacceptable, unanswerable, unimaginable, unspeakable,* and *unthinkable*.

Difficulty level: 2

S

The following lists target words students should *see* and *say* for this minilesson.

▸ **Unacceptable (adj.):** Not meeting the requirements; not satisfactory or allowable

▸ **Unanswerable (adj.):** Cannot be answered, explained, or proven wrong

▸ **Unimaginable (adj.):** Cannot be believed or described; mind-boggling

▸ **Unspeakable (adj.):** Not able to be expressed in speaking or writing; not able to be defined; often means horrific (too bad to be expressed in words)

▸ **Unthinkable (adj.):** So unlikely that it seems impossible

Students may know *unacceptable* from a school context in which they have heard teachers speak of *unacceptable* behavior. However, the other words are probably less familiar. Provide examples of your own with each definition. For example, some questions are *unanswerable*, like "What is the meaning of life?" People often use *unimaginable*, *unspeakable*, and *unthinkable* with negative connotations, as in *unimaginable* pain, *unspeakable* horrors, and *unthinkable* crimes. If possible, use examples from local news or worldwide current events that students might be readily connected with.

N

This is a large group of words, but the words have many similarities. Each word is prefixed with *un-*, which should be familiar to students if you've done other minilessons from this section. Also, all the words are suffixed with *-able*, which immediately lets us know they are most likely adjectives, so we know they modify nouns. The words are also all about positives and negatives. Something *acceptable* is generally good, while something *unacceptable* is not. Something *unanswerable* may seem negative because of its ambiguity; there will never be a satisfactory answer. *Unimaginable* can be off the scale in terms of positive or negative. For example, winning the lottery may be *unimaginable*, but in a positive way, while losing all your possessions in a flood or fire is *unimaginable* in a negative way. *Unspeakable* and *unthinkable* are often used for the negative, but you could have an *unspeakable* love for someone or an *unthinkable* wish to leave your home forever and head for a deserted island. These two words have a bit more ambiguity and flexibility than the others, and your more advanced students may understand that concept.

A

Use an adapted jigsaw method by creating five groups and asking each group to become an expert on only one word in about five minutes. (See page 19 for more on the jigsaw method.) It would be best for each group to have one device with Internet access and for a group leader to search online for synonyms of, examples of, and images related to the group's assigned word. For example, googling the phrase "synonyms for *unimaginable*" yields the words *unthinkable, inconceivable, indescribable, incredible, unbelievable, unheard of, unthought of, untold, mind-boggling, undreamed of*, and *beyond one's wildest dreams* in the first result. Searching Bing (www.bing.com /images) for "images for unimaginable things," yields, among the movie and pop culture references, some images of nature and of people's faces that groups can use to demonstrate meaning.

Have each group select one person (ideally not the leader) to share with the class in one minute or less what the group learned to help it better understand the assigned word. If time is running short, save this reporting out and step P for the next day.

P

Have each student select two words (one can be the word discussed in step A) and use them in context in at least one sentence each. Examples include:

▸ In the United States, it's *unacceptable* to eat with your hands in many instances when dining out with friends.

▸ Whether or not there is a heaven may just be *unanswerable*.

▸ The horrors of war in the Middle East are just *unimaginable* for me.

▸ Murder is an *unthinkable* crime.

▸ Women in some parts of the world are subjected to *unspeakable* abuse.

▸ It's *unthinkable* that I would ever be a millionaire.

Scaffolding

 Draw students' attention to the base word in each adjective: *accept, answer, imagine, speak, think*. These are words they know well. Show them how the suffix *-able* makes each word mean "capable of" and the prefix *un-* negates that quality. So, the word *thinkable* means that it is possible to think of whatever is being described, but *unthinkable* means it's impossible to think of it.

Acceleration

 You could use advanced students as group leaders in step A. Caution them to lead the searches and the discussion but not to do all the work themselves. All students should feel comfortable offering words, phrases, and images that they like.

Lesson P5: *unhelpful, uncooperative, unreasonable, unreliable*

In this minilesson, teachers will teach the prefix *un-*, such as in the words *unhelpful, uncooperative, unreasonable*, and *unreliable*.

Difficulty level: 2

S

 The following lists target words students should *see* and *say* for this minilesson.

▸ **Unhelpful (adj.):** Not giving aid or assistance

▸ **Uncooperative (adj.):** Not doing what someone else is asking

▸ **Unreasonable (adj.):** Not guided by good sense or fairness

▸ **Unreliable (adj.):** Not likely to work or not able to be relied on or trusted

Students may know the words *unhelpful* and *uncooperative* from school contexts, but if not, they are easily related to the words *help* and *cooperate*. Remind students how you have used the words *help, helpful, cooperate, cooperation*, and *cooperative* in the past. Also, they may know the word *reasoning* or *reasonable* from mathematics instruction.

N

 This set of words is another set of adjectives, and they can be used in many instances in speaking and writing in the world of school and career. The

suffixes *-able* and *-ful* may be familiar, so be sure to reiterate or discuss their meanings, and also share with students how the suffix *-ive* is similar, meaning "related to" or "pertaining to."

A

Allow small groups to discuss the following scenarios. Ensure that the groups are discussing the specific differences among the target words.

- ▸ If a person sees a lost pet on the highway, and he doesn't stop, is he being *unhelpful* or *uncooperative*? (*unhelpful*)
- ▸ If a person refuses to do something that a teacher asks him or her to do, is he or she being *unreliable* or *uncooperative*? (*uncooperative*)
- ▸ If a computer works sometimes when it's turned on, but not every time, is it *unreliable* or *unreasonable*? (*unreliable*; a computer, unlike a human, cannot reason)
- ▸ If a friend wants to study with you and wants total silence, is he or she being *unhelpful* or *unreasonable*? (*unreasonable*)

P

Ask each student to choose the target word that is most unfamiliar or that he or she has used the least and write it down. Then either have students engage in think-pair-share (see page 23 in chapter 2) to discuss how they can apply this word in the future, or, as time allows, have them write on that same topic and turn their brief writing in to you.

Scaffolding

Showing students visuals that depict the words may help students understand the differences between these words. Being *unhelpful* implies that one has the capacity to help but is choosing not to; being *uncooperative* implies that one has been directly asked to do something but still refuses. *Unreasonable* implies anger. *Unreliable* means undependable. Perhaps you have an example from the school that would work with *unreliable*. For example, many schools in which I work have *unreliable* Internet connections.

Acceleration

Students who have mastered these words may enjoy finding visuals that go along with each word and its antonym: *unhelpful* and *helpful*; *uncooperative* and *cooperative*; *unreasonable* and *reasonable*; *unreliable* and *reliable*. For example, a toddler throwing a fit would be a good visual for *uncooperative*, and the opposite visual might depict toddlers playing happily in a sandbox together.

Beyond the Lesson

Use the word *uncooperative* when you need to redirect students' behavior instead of using simpler words.

Prefix: *re-*

The second most common prefix in English is *re-*, which has several meanings. In this section, we'll focus on three of the meanings: "back," "again," and "anew." These three meanings have the potential to unlock hundreds of words.

Lesson P6: *retell, recall, recount, retrace, return*

In this minilesson, teachers will teach the prefix *re-*, such as in the words *retell, recall, recount, retrace,* and *return*.

Difficulty level: 1

S

The following lists target words students should *see* and *say* for this minilesson.

▶ **Retell (v.):** To tell a story again or differently

▶ **Recall (v.):** To bring something back into one's mind or to share it with others; to remember

▶ **Recount (v.):** To tell someone about something; to give an account of an event or experience to another

▶ **Retrace (v.):** To go back over something one has already done; for example, to *retrace* footsteps in looking for something; can also mean to do something just as someone has done it before you

▶ **Return (v.):** To go back or to send back

Return may be the most familiar word to students, so you may want to begin your instruction with it. *Retell* may also be familiar but in a literal sense only; in the early grades, students have to *retell* stories many times. Be sure to talk with students about the broader meaning of *retell*, however, as in to *retell* history or to *retell* a story with another perspective.

N

All these words are verbs. Remind students verbs often mean that a person is performing an action. Go through each word and reassure students that if they know the meaning of *re-* (in this case, "back"), they can isolate the base words and determine a meaning. They just need to think broadly, because they may have only very literal understandings of these words. For example, to *recount* means to recall and share the details of an event or experience—not to (literally) recount items. *Recount, retell,* and *retrace* can be used in very similar ways. Be prepared to give students several examples of their use. For example, you may *retrace* your steps to your lost library book; you might also *retrace* the steps you just completed in a mathematics problem to look for errors.

A

 Have students work in small groups and ask them to generate an image for each word. If possible, each image should focus on how the word is different from other words in the list.

P

Ask each student to determine which word is the most unfamiliar to him or her and to use it in a sentence showing its meaning. This can be done in writing or via a technology tool like Padlet (https://padlet.com) or TodaysMeet (https://todaysmeet.com).

Scaffolding

Be prepared with plenty of examples illustrating how to use each word to give to students in case they need them. Use some of the following if you like.

▸ I felt I had to *retell* my story of the weekend so that my friends would see my perspective.

▸ I use my journal to *recall* fond memories.

▸ My grandmother always loved to *recount* stories of her youth, when she lived on a farm.

▸ My friend *retraced* the steps of the Inca and hiked the historic Inca Trail in Peru.

▸ I had to *return* to my car to get my forgotten book.

Acceleration

Share the advanced but related words *recollect* and *recollection* with students who have mastered the words for this lesson. Ask them to attempt to use the following words in speaking or writing in the near future.

▸ **Recollect (v.):** To remember or recall

▸ **Recollection (n.):** The action of remembering or recalling

Lesson P7: *review, revise, revision, rewrite*

In this minilesson, teachers will teach the prefix *re-*, such as in the words *review, revise, revision,* and *rewrite*.

Difficulty level: 1

S

The following lists target words students should *see* and *say* for this minilesson.

▸ **Review (v.):** To look at, examine, or assess (something) formally while thinking about how to change it

▸ **Revise (v.):** To change something after thinking about it or talking with others

▸ **Rewrite (v.):** Literally, to write (something) again; more broadly, to improve something or offer a new version of it, as in to *rewrite* history

N

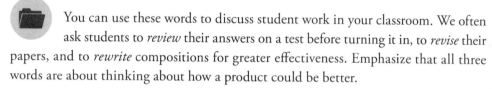

You can use these words to discuss student work in your classroom. We often ask students to *review* their answers on a test before turning it in, to *revise* their papers, and to *rewrite* compositions for greater effectiveness. Emphasize that all three words are about thinking about how a product could be better.

A

Have small groups choose the best word for each of the following scenarios.

▸ Sitting with a partner to look at a paper he or she thinks he or she is done with and offering suggestions (*review*)

▸ Taking a favorite story, poem, nursery rhyme, or fable and creating an updated version of it (*rewrite*)

▸ Rereading one of your own essays and making changes to it (*revise*)

P

Ask each student to write a short paragraph using all three words. Because the words are so commonly used in schools, students should be able to do this.

Scaffolding

Provide sentence stems for students if needed. Use or adapt the following.

▸ When I *review* my own work, I _____.

▸ One thing I try to remember when I *revise* my writing is _____.

▸ A story that I would like to *rewrite* is _____.

Acceleration

Provide students who have mastered the words in this lesson with the following words, and challenge these students to use these additional words.

▸ **Amend (v.):** To make minor changes or to update something

▸ **Alter (v.):** To make changes to something, often used to refer to clothing

You may also want to allow these students to explore synonyms for *revise*. See WordHippo's (2017a) article "What Is Another Word for Revise?" (http://bit.ly/2k5d89K) to access a list of synonyms. (Visit **go.SolutionTree.com/literacy** to access live links to the websites mentioned in this book.)

Lesson P8: *reappraise, reinspect, re-examine*

In this minilesson, teachers will teach the prefix *re-*, such as in the words *reappraise, reinspect*, and *re-examine*.

Difficulty level: 2

S

 The following lists target words students should *see* and *say* for this minilesson.

▸ **Reappraise (v.):** To assess something or determine the value of something again, after an initial assessment; often used for property such as houses or other buildings

▸ **Reinspect (v.):** To examine something again

▸ **Re-examine (v.):** To study something further or again, and possibly, to make a change

Note the hyphenation that usually occurs and is preferred with *re-examine*. You may want to explain to students that words starting with the letter e often use a hyphen when a prefix that ends in e, like *re-* and *pre-*, is added.

N

 These words are fairly close synonyms of each other, and people often use the first two in the context of real estate or property value. Share that particular context if you feel it will help your students understand the terms better. Students can use the words in many situations, however, and should be encouraged to use them as broadly as possible. Because these words are more sophisticated than *review* and *revise*, they can really add to a writer's voice when used in compositions.

A

Have small groups think about the base words of the set: *appraise, inspect*, and *examine*. The prefix *re-* makes the base word mean "again." Ask them to sort the following synonyms by matching them with the base words or saying that they don't match any of them.

- ▸ Scrutinize (*inspect* or *examine*)
- ▸ Ignore (*none*)
- ▸ Accuse (*none*)
- ▸ Assess (*appraise*)
- ▸ Question (*none*)
- ▸ Evaluate (*appraise*)
- ▸ Study (*examine*)

Then, ask students to apply the *re-* prefix to the words, if possible. Ask them if they would use any of the words made with *re-* and when they might use them. The goal here is to get students to think about how broadly they can apply this very useful prefix.

P

Ask students to choose one target word and its base word (without the prefix) and to use each in context. For example, the doctor *inspected* my wound. However, after I mentioned that I had come in contact with a barbed wire fence, she *reinspected* it, and I had to get a tetanus shot.

Scaffolding

Remind students that *redo* is perhaps the simplest synonym to help them remember the meaning of *re-* and that it can apply to many words, like these.

Acceleration

Have students who have mastered these words explore the following related words, and encourage them to use the words in step P or in their speaking and writing.

- ▸ **Reweigh (v.):** To consider something again and possibly change it or reverse it
- ▸ **Recalculate (v.):** To compute or figure again, sometimes using different data

Beyond the Lesson

You can use these words frequently when you encourage students to check their work before turning it in.

Lesson P9: *repeat, restate, rehash, reutter*

In this minilesson, teachers will teach the prefix *re-*, such as in the words *repeat, restate, rehash,* and *reutter.*

Difficulty level: 2

S

The following lists target words students should *see* and *say* for this minilesson.

- **Repeat (v.):** To say or do something again, either once or over and over again
- **Restate (v.):** To say something again but in a different way
- **Rehash (v.):** To put old ideas or materials into a new form that is basically the same as the original
- **Reutter (v.):** To say something again

N

Point out that all these words are verbs, and in this case, they are action verbs. They can actually be seen and heard. The words *repeat* and *restate* are likely to be the most familiar to students, so ask them what those words mean, and how those words are commonly used. Teachers often ask students to *repeat* an answer aloud in class, for example, and they often direct students to *restate* a main idea after reading. Then share with them that *rehash* and *reutter* are very similar to these two more common words. *Rehash,* however, often has a negative connotation. To say that a writer or speaker is *rehashing* old ideas is often a criticism. You might tell students that you don't enjoy reading essays that do nothing but *rehash* ideas that were presented in class. *Reutter* is perhaps the least commonly used word and could be used effectively in writing, especially with dialogue.

A

Allow groups to sort the following synonymous phrases by grouping them with the word they most closely match. Allow them to debate the best match-up, since some words and phrases can go with more than one target word.

- To do something several times the same exact way (*repeat*)
- To say something again (*repeat, restate,* or *reutter*)
- To remake old ideas or material (*rehash*)
- To paraphrase something you read (*restate*)

P

Have students answer one of the following questions in a sentence or two.

▸ How are the words *restate* and *rehash* alike? How are they different? What other words do you think are related to these two words? (Possible answers: *Rephrase, rework, reword, summarize, paraphrase, recap*)

▸ How are the words *repeat* and *reutter* alike? How are they different? What other words do you think are related to these two words? (Possible answers: *Replay, rerun, reproduce, echo*)

Scaffolding

Focus students on the fact that all these words can apply to speaking aloud. They have many applications in the discussions that go on in classrooms. They can also apply to many conversations at home. For example, tell students that if your mother asks you repeatedly to clean your room, you could respond with, "Mom, you don't have to *reutter* your request. I understood it the first time." (And let students know that their advanced vocabulary may buy them a little more time before they actually have to clean their rooms.)

Acceleration

Students who have mastered these words could probably easily learn the following two words, which basically mean "to repeat" but sound much more sophisticated in speaking and writing.

▸ **Replicate (v.):** To copy exactly or reproduce

▸ **Duplicate (v.):** To copy exactly; comes from the Latin word meaning "to double"

Lesson P10: *recycle, restore, refurbish*

In this minilesson, teachers will teach the prefix *re-*, such as in the words *recycle, restore,* and *refurbish*.

Difficulty level: 1

S

The following lists target words students should *see* and *say* for this minilesson.

▸ **Recycle (v.):** To change waste (or something you would throw away) into something you can use or to return something to its earlier stage in a process or cycle

- **Restore (v.):** To return something to the way it was before
- **Refurbish (v.):** To make something fresh and new, like redecorating your bedroom

N

Recycle is probably familiar to your students. Use this familiarity to help them understand the related words *restore* and *refurbish*. Like the word *recycle*, they contain *re-* as a prefix, and the other part of the word in each case (*cycle*, *store*, and *furbish*) may not give students a solid idea of what the whole word means. Students may know that *re-* means "back," "again," or "anew," but to them the word *store* probably means a place where someone goes to buy things.

A

Ask small groups to discuss the following: What are some things that are *restored*? What are some things that are *refurbished*?

P

Have students create a word wheel (see page 26) for one of the words. They can use a visual or a synonym on the top right of the wheel.

Scaffolding

If students need more support during step P, you can provide the following sentence stems.

- Something we *recycle* at school is _____.
  (Possible answers: Paper, cardboard, plastic)

- Something I've seen that has been *restored* is _____.
  (Possible answers: Electricity after a storm, privileges after serving detention or making amends, a historic building)

- Something I've seen that has been *refurbished* is _____.
  (Possible answers: A local movie theater or restaurant, a room in a house or at school)

Acceleration

Share the word *revamp* as a synonym for *refurbish*. You could also share the word *renovate* as a related word.

- **Revamp (v.):** To give a new appearance to something or to improve it
- **Renovate (v.):** To make something more modern or to repair it, as in a building

Lesson P11: *renew, renewal, revitalize, revitalization, rejuvenate, rejuvenation*

In this minilesson, teachers will teach the prefix *re-*, such as in the words *renew, renewal, revitalize, revitalization, rejuvenate,* and *rejuvenation.*

Difficulty level: 2

S

The following lists target words students should *see* and *say* for this minilesson.

- **Renew (v.):** To start doing something again after stopping or to re-establish something, like a relationship

- **Renewal (n.):** The act of doing something again or of re-establishing something

- **Revitalize (v.):** To give something new life or a boost of energy; to refresh

- **Revitalization (n.):** The act of giving something new life or a boost of energy

- **Rejuvenate (v.):** To make someone or something look or feel younger, fresher, or livelier

- **Rejuvenation (n.):** The act of making someone or something look or feel younger, fresher, or livelier

N

All these words are about making something new, fresh, or seemingly young again. Also, point out that the words are in pairs of verb form first, then the noun form of the same word.

You may want to give examples illustrating how to use the words in verb form especially, since the implication of action can sometimes be more easily understood. I might tell my students that I need to *renew* my driver's license, *revitalize* my exercise routine, or *rejuvenate* my skin with a facial at the salon.

A

Ask small groups of students to think of examples for *renew, revitalize,* and *rejuvenate.* It's perfectly fine if their examples mimic the ones you gave in step N, but try to get them to go beyond those, too.

P

Have students answer the following questions in writing or using a technological tool like Plickers (https://plickers.com). The correct answers have an asterisk.

▸ Which of the following might need to be *renewed*?

    a.   An expired food item

    b.   An old friendship*

    c.   An illness

    d.   A movie

▸ Which of the following could be *revitalized*?

    a.   Someone's diet*

    b.   A test you took

    c.   A book

    d.   New clothes

▸ Which of the following could be *rejuvenated*?

    a.   New clothes

    b.   Medicine

    c.   A brand-new car

    d.   A wilted house plant*

Scaffolding

These words are so similar that students could find them confusing. Allow them latitude in how they attempt to use the words.

Acceleration

Revive is another related word, and it also contains the root *viv*, which is sometimes spelled *vit* as in *revitalize*. Advanced students might be interested in both the word *revive* and the information on the root.

▸ **Revive (v.):** To restore to life or consciousness; to activate or to set into motion

Prefixes: *in-, im-, il-,* and *ir-*

These four forms, which take different spellings depending on the base word they are joined with, mean "not" or "the opposite of." *Im-* is used in front of the letters b, m, and p. *Il-* is used in front of l. *Ir-* is used in front of r. The rest of the time, *in-* is used. *In-* and *im-* can also mean "into," but in this set of lessons, we'll stick to the words in which the prefixes mean "not" so as not to confuse students.

Lesson P12: *improper, illegal, illicit*

In this minilesson, teachers will teach the prefixes *im-* and *il-*, such as in the words *improper*, *illegal*, and *illicit*.

Difficulty level: 2

S

The following lists target words students should *see* and *say* for this minilesson. The following words are ordered based on a perceived level of severity.

▸ **Improper (adj.):** Not following the rules; unacceptable

▸ **Illegal (adj.):** Against the law; criminal

▸ **Illicit (adj.):** Forbidden by rules, law, or custom; taboo

Something *improper* may not be *illegal*. Something *illegal* can be minor or major; this particular word covers a wide range of actions. However, *illicit* usually has a severely negative connotation. Even if something is not *illegal*, being illicit is always bad enough that it may not be appropriate to talk about it in polite company. These shades of meaning are important if students are to use sophisticated vocabulary appropriately, especially in their writing.

N

Again, we have another set of adjectives that can add precision and sophistication to speaking and writing. Remind students that adjectives modify nouns, and in this case, they all describe a human behavior. For example, taking a cell phone call in a movie theater is *improper*, but it's not *illegal* or *illicit*. Driving over the speed limit is both *improper* and *illegal*, but probably not *illicit*. A public official who takes bribes is behaving in an *illicit* manner (and in this case, also *illegally*). Provide a couple of examples for each target word.

Improper is the word students can probably use the most often, and *illegal* probably comes in as a close second. So, encourage them to think about when the word *illicit* might be applied. It's the rarest word of the three and can appear when discussing history, current events, and literature.

A

Put students in pairs or triads. Ask them to discuss the following scenarios. Which word best fits each? Even though *illegal* and *illicit* have some overlap, encourage them to think about which word is best, not just accurate. Something *illicit* is not just *illegal*, it also has the quality of being especially surprising or taboo.

> ▸ A student runs down the hallway, screaming the whole way. (*improper*)
>
> ▸ A person who is not handicapped uses a handicapped-only parking space. (*illegal*)
>
> ▸ A student copies her classmate's answers to a homework assignment and submits the work to her teacher as her own. (*illicit*)
>
> ▸ One country is secretly sending weapons to another. (*illicit*)
>
> ▸ A student comes to school dressed in clothing more appropriate for the beach. (*improper*)

P

Have each student create his or her own sample scenario for each word, either in writing or, if time is short, verbally. Students may also share some of these aloud in groups if time allows.

Scaffolding

Students can use examples from the discussion in step A as they write in step P if they can't generate additional examples.

Acceleration

Impolitic is a related word. Share the definition of this word with students and see if they can generate examples of when it could be applied.

> ▸ **Impolitic (adj.):** Not showing wisdom or caution; foolish

Lesson P13: *impulsive, immoderate, immodest, irrepressible*

In this minilesson, teachers will teach the prefixes *im-* and *ir-*, such as in the words *impulsive, immoderate, immodest,* and *irrepressible.*

Difficulty level: 2

S

The following lists target words students should *see* and *say* for this minilesson.

> ▸ **Impulsive (adj.):** Acting based on emotion, not reason
>
> ▸ **Immoderate (adj.):** Not sensible; exceeding reasonable limits

> ▸ **Immodest (adj.):** Improper, bold, or indecent

> ▸ **Irrepressible (adj.):** Uncontrollable; not able to be restrained or
> contained, as in irrepressible laughter

N

Some students may have heard you (or other teachers) use the word *impulsive*, so this word might be the most familiar. Tell students that all these words are describing something that is hard to control or seemingly uncontrollable. You may want to show a short video clip of *irrepressible* laughter so that they can actually see what this looks like. The word *immodest* is used with both behavior and clothing, and you may also want to consider showing an image of *immodest* clothing (but not too immodest!). Most schools have dress codes, so using the word *immodest* in this context may help your students remember the gist of the word. For *impulsive*, you can probably think of examples from class, such as a student doing something mildly disruptive like shooting crumpled paper into the wastebasket, tapping another student with a pencil, or even calling out when not directed to do so.

A

Have small groups discuss their own examples of *impulsive* behavior (of themselves, or of family members of friends) and *irrepressible* laughter. Start the whole class off with a couple of your own anecdotes to help get students thinking.

P

Review the meanings of *immoderate* and *immodest*, and give examples if necessary. Then ask each student to have a go at using each word. Students' attempts can be written or spoken aloud to a partner. I might tell my students that I like to play rock music in my car at a definitely *immoderate* volume and that I don't like to see pop culture icons in *immodest* clothing.

Scaffolding

Find as many images as you can that you can associate with these words. Ensure that struggling students have access to these, even though they will also be good aids for all your students.

Acceleration

See how many additional words starting with *imm-* or *im-* students who have mastered the words in this lesson can think of. You may want to start them off with *immovable* and *imperfect* and see what else they can come up with. Allow them to use technology if it's accessible and won't take too much time.

Prefix: *dis-*

This prefix is from the Latin, meaning "apart," "asunder," "away," and "utterly." This prefix reverses the intention of the base word that it's attached to, similar to *im-*, *il-*, *in-*, and *ir-*.

Lesson P14: *disagreement, disobedient, disrespectful*

In this minilesson, teachers will teach the prefix *dis-*, such as in the words *disagreement*, *disobedient*, and *disrespectful*.

Difficulty level: 1

S

The following lists target words students should *see* and *say* for this minilesson. These three words (or their base words) may already be familiar to even five- and six-year-olds because staff and students often use them in the classroom and school as related to behavior.

▸ **Disagreement (n.):** An argument or difference of opinion

▸ **Disobedient (adj.):** Not following laws, rules, or directions

▸ **Disrespectful (adj.):** Showing a lack of courtesy, or being rude

As you pronounce each word, you may want to add elements of rhythm or rhyme, since the first two words end in a similar sound. Point out that all the words start with the prefix *dis-*, which means "the opposite of" or "not." When *dis-* is added to a word, it turns it into the opposite of what it was without the prefix.

N

Consider saying something like the following.

> *You may have heard me use these words with you. You may have heard your family members use these words. They all relate to people not getting along. If I have a* disagreement *with someone, maybe like my brother, sister, or cousin, that means we have different opinions. For example, my favorite ice cream is chocolate. I would* disagree, *or be in* disagreement *with, a person who likes vanilla better.*

> *Now,* disobedient *and* disrespectful *are stronger words than* disagreement. *We can disagree and still be polite to each other.* Disobedient *means "not to obey" and is used to describe a person who is not following rules. If I asked you to raise your hand before speaking in class, and you decided not to do that, then I could say you were being* disobedient. *The word* disrespectful *means "not showing respect." I always prefer that my students be* respectful *in class, not* disrespectful. *When you call someone a name, or jump in front of them in line for lunch, that's* disrespectful.

A

Create small groups and ask students to work together to choose the one word that goes best with each of the following scenarios. Be sure all three words are still displayed for all to see.

- ▸ A student yells at another student for no reason. (*disrespectful*)
- ▸ A person is driving over the speed limit. (*disobedient*)
- ▸ Two of your friends want to go out for pizza, but you want Mexican food. (*disagreement*)
- ▸ A student is running in the hallway. (*disobedient*)
- ▸ You want to stay up late, but your parents say no. (*disagreement*)

P

Ask students to think of one, two, or three of their own scenarios like the ones used in step A. If you have time, you can have them swap with other students to see if they can stump each other or answer correctly.

Scaffolding

Monitor the groups closely during step A. Change the scenarios to better fit your students' experiences if necessary, or use examples from recently read materials.

Acceleration

Advanced students can create additional scenarios during step A if time allows. They can also be encouraged to create more than three scenarios during step P.

Lesson P15: *disappointed, disinterested, dissatisfied*

In this minilesson, teachers will teach the prefix *dis-*, such as in the words *disappointed*, *disinterested*, and *dissatisfied*.

Difficulty level: 1

S

The following lists target words students should *see* and *say* for this minilesson. The word *disappointed* may be the most familiar word to your students from this list.

- ▸ **Disappointed (adj.):** Feeling that something didn't meet your expectations or wasn't as good as you hoped

> ▸ **Disinterested (adj.):** Not caring to learn about something

> ▸ **Dissatisfied (adj.):** Not happy or not pleased with something

Pronounce and define each word; then have students pronounce each. Be sure to teach or review the meaning of the prefix *dis-* as needed.

N

Say something like the following (but personalized for your students).

> *All these words are about feelings. They're adjectives, so they describe what a person is feeling. You might be* disappointed *that you didn't get a birthday present that you wanted or that we didn't have a day off from school when it snowed. Being* disappointed *means that you are let down, but you can get over it pretty quickly.* Disinterested *is a bit different. It means that you don't really care to learn more about something. When I was in school, I was* disinterested *in history. I didn't like doing the reading and taking the tests. But when I got older, I loved it! I was no longer* disinterested. *Lastly, the word* dissatisfied *means you were pretty unhappy with something. For example, if I went to a fine restaurant for a special meal and I didn't like it, I would be* dissatisfied. *I might even ask for my money back!*

As time allows, ask students to provide examples from their lives that would demonstrate the meanings of the words. Consider using teacher gestures (most likely facial expressions) to teach the subtle differences among the three words. Because *dissatisfied* conveys perhaps the strongest emotion, you may want to use arm motions, too—for example, waving your arms in a crisscross fashion.

A

Create small groups and ask students to work together to choose the one word that goes best with each of the following scenarios. Be sure you display all three words for all to see.

> ▸ A breaking news story cuts off your favorite TV show. (*disappointed*)

> ▸ Your friend is going to visit, but then his family says he has to stay home. (*disappointed*)

> ▸ You don't really like a subject so you don't study it very much. (*disinterested*)

> ▸ Your mother says your room has not been cleaned to her standards. (*dissatisfied*)

> ▸ Your favorite sports team loses a game. (*disappointed*)

P

Ask students to think of one, two, or three of their own scenarios like the ones used in step A. If you have time, you can have them swap with other students to see if they can stump each other or answer correctly.

Scaffolding

Provide examples of *disappointed*, *disinterested*, and *dissatisfied* characters from literature, television, or movies to help students further visualize the emotions. If you could display a visual of each character, the facial expression may support student learning.

Acceleration

Provide the synonym *discontent* for *dissatisfied*. Ask students to use both *dissatisfied* and *discontent* in sentences and share with a partner or the entire class as time allows.

Beyond the Lesson

You can act out being *disappointed* when students don't meet your expectations. Be overly dramatic, and say the word repeatedly.

Lesson P16: *disappear, displace, disregard*

In this minilesson, teachers will teach the prefix *dis-*, such as in the words *disappear*, *displace*, and *disregard*.

Difficulty level: 1

S

The following lists target words students should *see* and *say* for this minilesson. The most familiar word here is probably *disappear*. All the words are easy to pronounce, though, so ensure that students say them loudly and proudly, and perhaps multiple times. Be sure to teach or review the meaning of the prefix *dis-* as needed.

▸ **Disappear (v.):** To pass out of sight or to go away

▸ **Displace (v.):** To move something out of its normal place or position

▸ **Disregard (v.):** To ignore or not pay attention to

N

Consider saying something like the following to your class.

The three words we're looking at today are all verbs, meaning they are what a person or object does. These are action words. I think most of you know

disappear. *That means when something goes away, or at least it goes out of sight—we can't see it anymore. So, when the sun goes down each evening, it* disappears. *To* displace *means to move something out of its normal place. You know that if you've seen flooding, the water* displaces *soil, signs, and even homes. It moves them out of their normal positions. And to* disregard *is to ignore something or to act like it's not happening or it's not there. Sometimes my students* disregard *me! They act as if I'm not even speaking to them! That doesn't happen very often, though, thank goodness.*

As time allows, ask students to provide examples from their lives that demonstrate the meanings of the words.

A

Put students in pairs or triads. Ask them to come up with gestures or pantomimes to help them remember each word's meaning. You may want to assign each group only one word and save time for each group to perform. Student-produced nonlinguistic representations like this are often incredibly memorable for those who perform and for those who watch.

P

Ask students to commit to using one of the words in their speaking and writing in the next few days. Have them write what their plan is. These plans can be done on sticky notes and posted in the room for reference. Each student can then take his or her note down when the plan has been completed.

Possible student response: "I'm going to use the word *disregard* in the next few days. I think I will let my teachers know that I never mean to *disregard* them. I will also tell my family that I won't *disregard* the dog and I will feed him when I'm supposed to every evening."

Scaffolding

Provide a sentence frame for step P if necessary, such as the following.

▸ I plan to use the word _____ this week. I will use it at school when I _____, or I will use it at home when I _____.

Acceleration

Provide the synonyms *dislocate* and *dislodge* for *displace* or have students search for "displace" in an online thesaurus. They can scroll through the various synonyms to see which might interest them. Alternatively, they can go to Snappy Words (www.snappywords.com) to explore one target word and its relationship to other words.

By typing each word into the search box, students can view a concept map made from that word.

Prefixes: *under-, over-,* and *sub-*

These prefixes are not nearly as common as the others we've already covered in this chapter. However, because *over-* and *sub-* are opposites, they can easily be studied together since they can be attached to the same base words to create words that also mean the opposite of each other. And, building on that foundation, the prefix *under-* has the same meaning as *sub-*, so it can be easily added to the mix, and students are still thinking only about two core meanings—"over" or "above" and "under" or "below."

Lesson P17: *overachiever, underachiever, subpar*

In this minilesson, teachers will teach the prefixes *under-, over-,* and *sub-*, such as in the words *overachiever, underachiever,* and *subpar.*

Difficulty level: 1

S

The following lists target words students should *see* and *say* for this minilesson.

▸ **Overachiever (n.):** A person who performs better than expected; often used with academic achievement

▸ **Underachiever (n.):** A person who performs worse than expected; often used with academic achievement

▸ **Subpar (adj.):** Below average or less than what's normal or expected

N

These words can all be related to someone's performance. People often use them to describe academic or athletic achievement. Legendary basketball player Michael Jordan was actually cut from his high school team, and therefore we can call him an *overachiever.* Tim Tebow was a great college football star but didn't succeed in the National Football League; therefore, we could call him an *underachiever* or say that his NFL performance was *subpar.* Ask students if they can name other examples from the world of sports or another field, like music.

A

Allow students to work with partners. Ask students to discuss with their partner times when they felt they either overachieved or underachieved. I might share with my students the fact that I was a very clumsy child, but I loved gymnastics, and I overcame my clumsiness to compete and be part of a school gymnastics team. This is my example of being an *overachiever*. However, in college, I was an *underachiever* in calculus. Even though I had the aptitude for it, I didn't work very hard and ended up failing the course.

P

Have each student choose one of the three words and write a sentence using it in context correctly. These sentences can be turned in as exit tickets (see page 17) or displayed with Padlet (https://padlet.com) or a similar digital tool.

Scaffolding

Employ teacher gestures (see page 23), and use hand motions as much as possible when you say the words or ask the students to use them. Raising your arms high with *over-* and then pushing them down low with *under-* and *sub-* will reinforce the meanings.

Acceleration

Share with students who have mastered these words a few other words they can use immediately, like *overwhelming* and *underwhelming*. You can even be a bit sarcastic or dramatic with these words in order to encourage students to use them. For example, I might say something like, "I was so *underwhelmed* by that movie. I can't believe people pay ten dollars for the privilege of seeing it."

Beyond the Lesson

Tell students repeatedly that you won't accept *subpar* work. Provide other examples from outside of school when *subpar* performance isn't accepted, as when auto manufacturers recall cars because of a problem with a part or when an athlete underperforms at a critical moment.

Lesson P18: *submerge, underestimate, overestimate*

In this minilesson, teachers will teach the prefixes *under-*, *over-*, and *sub-*, such as in the words *submerge*, *underestimate*, and *overestimate*.

Difficulty level: 1

S

The following lists target words students should *see* and *say* for this minilesson.

▸ **Submerge (v.):** To put something down in water or another liquid

▸ **Underestimate (v.):** To guess or predict that something is lower or less than it really is

‣ **Overestimate (v.):** To guess or predict that something is higher or more than it really is

Be sure to tell students that these can all also be adjectives if you add the letter d to the end. They become, in essence, past tense verbs or what we'd call a participial adjective. So, an object (like a submarine) could be *submerged* in the ocean. A grocery bill could have been *underestimated*. The amount of tile or carpet needed for a home-improvement project could be *overestimated*, and then you'd be stuck with way too much tile or carpet.

N

Again, these words are built with prefixes that are opposites of each other. *Under-* and *sub-* always mean "under" or "below." *Over-* always means "over" or "above," or, if you want to be less literal, "beyond." Teachers may use the words *underestimate* and *overestimate* in mathematics instruction; if so, capitalize on this familiarity. These two terms are also often associated with money. The connection to money may be the one that resonates best with your students.

A

Have small groups of students list as many examples as they can of things that might be *underestimated* and *overestimated*. If they stay focused on things that require money, that's okay. You can give a couple of nonmonetary examples before students move to step P.

P

Ask each student to write a short summary or explanation of all three words. You can frame it by asking, "What would you tell a classmate who is absent today about these words?"

Scaffolding

Help students who require scaffolding the most with the word *submerge*. Give them lots of examples, such as the following.

‣ You can *submerge* your head when you swim.

‣ You *submerge* dishes if you wash them by hand.

Acceleration

Preview WordHippo's (2017d) article "Words Starting With SUB" (http://bit .ly/2jxtogx) to view a good collection of words that start with *sub-*. Share with students. Students needing acceleration may enjoy exploring these words.

Lesson P19: *overstate, overrate*

In this minilesson, teachers will teach the prefix *over-*, such as in the words *overstate* and *overrate*.

Difficulty level: 1

S

The following lists target words students should *see* and *say* for this minilesson.

▸ **Overstate (v.):** To say something too strongly or to exaggerate

▸ **Overrate (v.):** To think something is better than it is or to have too high an opinion of something

We can also use both words as adjectives when they are in the past participle forms (*overstated, overrated*). The word *overrated* is common and may be the best one to emphasize here.

You may want to use teacher gestures as you present the words, or present the words in a rhyme. Use the following rhymes as a chant or for a choral response (see page 15) if you like.

▸ To *overstate* is to say too much or exaggerate.

▸ Something *overstated* is kind of like *overrated*.

▸ To *overrate* is to say something's great. (But it's really not!)

N

These words not only rhyme, they mean very similar things. To *overstate* something is to exaggerate it, as when someone says, "I'm freezing!" the person is not literally at 32 degrees Fahrenheit, or he would be dead. In this case, the person is actually using hyperbole, so if your students know that term, you can say that hyperbole is an example of one type of *overstatement*.

To *overrate* something is to think it's better than it is or to have an opinion that is later proven to have been too high or unfounded. Some describe actors, musicians, athletes, and other performers as *overrated* if they are initially successful but flame out fast.

A

Ask students to work in pairs and see if they can come up with things they think are *overrated*. For example, certain brand-name merchandise is sometimes hyped up and overpriced. Students may be able to generate many examples of this type.

P

Ask each student to write an example of each word. This can be in a complete sentence or not—whatever you feel is best and have time for. If students have access to and know how to use ThingLink, they can create an interactive image of one of the words and put the definition on the image where they wish.

Scaffolding

Because the words are so similar, students may get confused about which one is most appropriate for a certain context. Remind them that for *overstate*, a person actually has to say something—to state is to say. To *overrate*, you can state the information or just keep your opinion in your head.

Acceleration

Teach students who have mastered these words another synonym for *overrate*: *overvalue*.

▸ **Overvalue (v.):** To think too much of or to have a higher opinion of something than it deserves

Prefixes: *pre-* and *fore-*

Together, the prefixes *pre-* and *fore-* account for about 5 percent of all prefixed words in English. They are basically synonymous, both meaning "before" in many instances. However, the prefixes can take on different shades of meaning when used with different base words. *Pre-* can also mean "prior to," "in advance of," "early," "beforehand," "before," and "in front of." *Fore-* can also mean "front" (as in *forearm* or *forehead*) or "superior" (as in *foreman*).

Lesson P20: *preview, foretell, foresee, foreshadow*

In this minilesson, teachers will teach the prefixes *pre-* and *fore-*, such as in the words *preview*, *foretell*, *foresee*, and *foreshadow*.

Difficulty level: 1

S

The following lists target words students should *see* and *say* for this minilesson.

▸ **Preview (v.):** To see, hear, or show something before it is officially public, or to look at something beforehand, like a story in your textbook

▸ **Foretell (v.):** To predict the future or an event in the future

▸ **Foresee (v.):** To see something in your mind before it really happens

▸ **Foreshadow (v.):** To signal or warn of something to come

N

These words are all about knowing or showing that something is going to happen before it actually happens. Students may know *foreshadowing* as a literary term. If so, then they can readily understand that the author is the one who chooses to foreshadow. He or she decides what clues to give the reader about what will happen. They may also know that when you go to a movie theater, there are *previews* before the main feature. In other words, the audience is *previewing* what a full movie will be like. Connect with this meaning as well if it helps your students.

Foretell and *foresee* are a bit different. To *foresee* something is to visualize it before it actually happens. If you tell others about this kind of prediction, then you are *foretelling*.

A

Allow students to discuss *foretell* and *foresee*, as these are most likely the unfamiliar words on this list. Ask them if they have ever known anyone who could *foretell* the future or *foresee* disasters. Share an anecdote of your own if appropriate. Many students may have a story from their family about someone accurately *foretelling* of a death, accident, or disaster.

P

Ask each student to choose three of the target words to use in sentences. Have students hand in their work. Allow them to work and talk with each other during this step if possible. Encourage students to check with each other about using the words accurately.

Scaffolding

Provide sentence stems like the following if you wish. Allow students to create as many sentences as they can in about five minutes. If you use these stems or similar stems, make sure students copy the complete sentence that appears first in each pair to help them further internalize sentence structure.

▸ To *preview* something is to see it before others. An example of *previewing* is _____.

▸ To *foretell* something is to say it before it actually happens. An example of *foretelling* is _____.

▸ To *foresee* something is to know in your mind that it's going to happen. An example of *foreseeing* is _____.

▸ To *foreshadow* is to give clues about what's coming up. An example of *foreshadowing* is _____.

Acceleration

Writers often use both *pre-* and *fore-* in books, speeches, historical documents, and so on. Advanced students might be interested in learning or reviewing the following words. You may want to call their attention to the correct pronunciation of *preface*, since the letter e is not pronounced as a long e like other words with the same prefix are.

▸ **Preamble (n.):** An introduction to a document, as in the U.S. Constitution

▸ **Preface (n.):** An introduction to a book, usually by the author

▸ **Foreword (n.):** A short introduction in a book, by someone other than the author

Beyond the Lesson

You can use the word *preview* frequently in class discussion. You can say that something today is a *preview* for tomorrow's lesson, for example, or that the title of an article is a preview to its content.

Lesson P21: *prevent, prevention, preclude, preclusion*

In this minilesson, teachers will teach the prefix *pre-*, such as in the words *prevent, prevention, preclude,* and *preclusion*.

Difficulty level: 1

S

The following lists target words students should *see* and *say* for this minilesson.

▸ **Prevent (v.):** To keep something from happening (before it happens)

▸ **Prevention (n.):** The act of keeping something from happening

▸ **Preclude (v.):** To make something impossible; a synonym for *prevent*

▸ **Preclusion (n.):** The act of making something impossible; a synonym for *prevention*

N

Here we have pairs in the verb form and noun form. The noun forms should be identifiable to your students if they know the suffix *-ion* signifies a noun. Tell students that since they probably already know the word *prevent*, they can quickly learn *preclude*, and preclude is a more sophisticated word. You may want to give them several examples like the following.

> ▸ The heavy rain *precluded* our going to the picnic.

> ▸ People told him that his lack of height was a *preclusion* to playing professional basketball.

Ask students to substitute *prevented* and *prevention* in sentences like these and see if they still make sense. (They may not be the best-sounding sentences, but if they make sense, then the words are used correctly.)

A

Ask small groups to discuss times that they were *prevented* or *precluded* from doing something they really wanted to do—like attending a party.

P

Have each student write an original sentence with any form of *preclude* as a noun or verb—*preclude, precluded, precluding, preclusion*. Because students most likely never used this word, allow them to practice.

Scaffolding

Provide a sentence stem if you wish, such as:

> ▸ Nothing would *preclude* me from _____.

> ▸ The weather *precluded* us from _____.

Acceleration

Challenge students who have mastered these words to use all forms of *preclude* that are listed during step P.

Final Thoughts

Prefixes are important components of word meaning, and unfortunately, they often stump our students. By completing the minilessons in this chapter, your students have become more familiar with the most common prefixes in our language and will thus be better prepared to approach unfamiliar words that begin with prefixes.

Super Suffixes

A suffix, like a prefix, is a word component added to a base word to make a new word. While prefixes are added to the beginnings of words, suffixes are added to the ends of words. The word *beauty* becomes *beautiful* with the addition of one of the most frequently used suffixes, *-ful*. The suffixes *-er* and *-or* are added to bases or roots to create all sorts of words that denote a person's occupation or role, like *teacher, singer, dancer, writer, doctor, aviator, curator,* and *surveyor*. Other suffixes, though lesser used, immediately give us information about a word's meaning. For example, *-dom* added to *free* lets us know about a state of being, *freedom*, and added to *bore*, it denotes a less pleasant state of being, *boredom*. Suffixes can make new words by adding either inflectional or derivational endings.

Inflectional endings account for 65 percent of all suffixed words (White et al., 1989). Inflectional endings give us grammatical information about any word they are added to. They add a letter or group of letters to base words to make different grammatical forms of the words, helping us determine how a word functions in a sentence. Verbs are inflected for number, tense, and to make participles and gerunds. For example, when the suffix *-ed* is added to a verb form, we know that the verb is in past tense. When *-ing* is added to a verb form, we know that the verb is either serving in the present progressive tense or functioning as a participle or gerund. The sentence "I'm shopping online instead of doing my homework" uses the word *shopping* in the present progressive tense to describe what I'm doing right now. The sentence "Shopping as I went along, I really enjoyed the tour of Rome" uses the word *shopping* as a participle to describe my actions. And lastly, "Shopping is one of my favorite pastimes" employs *shopping* as a special kind of noun called a *gerund*, which in this sentence serves as the subject of the sentence. When *-s* and *-es* are added to nouns, the nouns become plural. Adjectives are inflected to make their comparative and superlative forms, as in *nice, nicer*, and *nicest*.

Inflectional endings for nouns and verbs are taught and learned in the earliest years of school, but students who struggle with language often have holes in their understanding that become apparent in later years. Students sometimes misapply *-s* or *-es* for plurals of nouns when words are actually irregular plurals (for example, saying "freshmans" instead of *freshmen*). Other rules, such as when to change a base word's spelling by doubling a consonant before adding an ending (for example, *stop, stopped*, and *stopping*), also create confusion among students who are still learning the rules of English and those who experience difficulty in reading and writing for whatever reasons.

Derivational endings, as you can perhaps infer from the word *derivational*, are needed to turn a noun like *beauty* into the adjective *beautiful* or the adverb *beautifully*. They reflect more than number or tense, and they change one part of speech to another. Students may know a base word like *create* yet misunderstand the related words *creator, creative*, and *creatively* because they don't have a good grasp of derivational endings.

Surely, you've had students who struggle with words that contain suffixes but know the base word to which the suffixes are affixed. Sometimes students are confused because adding the suffix changes the base word's spelling (as is the case with words like *beautiful, happiness, possibility*, and *permission*). Sometimes students don't understand basic facts of grammar and syntax, such as knowing that most words that end in *-ly* are adjectives and that *-tion* and *-sion* appear on the ends of nouns.

Regardless of the reasons that students may struggle with suffixes, teaching more about suffixes can help prepare students for the difficult academic text they encounter as they move through school. A poor grasp of derivational suffixes has been noted as a weakness that struggling secondary and college readers share (Nagy, Berninger, & Abbott, 2006), so arming students with as much information as possible can certainly do them no harm. See table 6.1 for information about common English suffixes. Note that this table does not include inflectional endings, which are more common and are different from suffixes that have meanings within themselves.

Table 6.1: Common Suffixes in English (Not Including Inflectional Endings)

Suffix	Meanings	Percentage of Suffixed Words in Which It Appears
-ly	characteristic of, like, or resembling	7 percent
-ar, -er, -or	one that does or has	4 percent
-ion, -ation, -ition, -ation	act of, process of, or result of	4 percent
-ible, -able	can be done, capable of	2 percent

-al, -ial	characterized by	1 percent
-y	characterized by	1 percent
-ness	state of, condition of	1 percent
-ity, -ty	state of	1 percent
-ment	action, process, means of, or instrument of	1 percent
-ic	of, relating to, or characterized by	1 percent
-ous, -eous, -ious	possessing the qualities of or characterized by	1 percent
-en	made of	1 percent
-er	for comparative form of adjectives	1 percent
-ive, -ative, -itive	for the adjective forms of nouns	1 percent
-ful	full of	1 percent
-less	without or lacking	1 percent
-est	for the superlative form of adjectives	1 percent

Source: White et al., 1989.

This chapter focuses on suffixes and their various uses, and the minilessons here address some of the common challenges students face with suffixes. Because there are far fewer suffixes than prefixes in English, you'll notice that this chapter is not as extensive as the one on prefixes. Also, the suffixes that do exist are often more precise in meaning than any given prefix is. Therefore, you'll find that these minilessons are incredibly focused and can most likely be done in very brief periods of time.

Irregular Plurals

The words in the following minilesson name groups of people or things but form their plurals without the use of -s or -es. Thus, they are called *irregular plurals*. This particular minilesson uses words that refer to people.

Lesson S1: *man, woman, child, chairman, chairwoman, freshman*

In this minilesson, teachers will teach the irregular plurals for people, such as *man, woman, child, chairman, chairwoman,* and *freshman.*

Difficulty level: 1

S

 The following lists target words students should *see* and *say* for this minilesson.

▶ **Man (n.):** An adult human male; the plural is *men*

- **Woman (n.):** An adult human female; the plural is *women*
- **Child (n.):** A young human being (before puberty); the plural is *children*
- **Chairman or chairwoman (n.):** A person who is the head of a group or who leads a meeting; the plurals are *chairmen* and *chairwomen*; often *chairperson* is used instead in order to use gender-neutral language
- **Freshman (n.):** A first-year student in high school and college; also used to describe someone who is new or a novice, as in the *freshman senator*; the plural is *freshmen*

The word *human* is an exception to this pattern. The plural is *humans*. Share this exception with students if you feel it won't confuse them.

N

Consider saying something like the following to your class.

Some of the words we're looking at today seem simple. However, I want you to concentrate on how these words change from their singular to plural forms and how those plurals are spelled.

All the words are about people—the first few are actually the common nouns that name types of people—men, women, children. The words chairman *and* freshman *are fairly common, also, so I've included them here. Most well-educated people know the words* chairman *and* freshman *and know how to use them appropriately.*

A

Put students in pairs, and have each pair generate other examples. Pairs may come up with *fireman, policeman,* and *mailman.* Orchestrate a short discussion not only of these words' plural form but also about their nonsexist counterparts: *firefighter, police officer, mail carrier.* There are also sports words like *baseman* and *lineman* and military words like *airman.*

P

Ask students to choose any two words that end in *-man, -men, -woman,* or *-women* from the discussion and use them in sentences. The goal here is to give them experience using two of the words they may not have previously used very often.

Scaffolding

Students who require scaffolding may struggle with the plural forms and incorrectly use the singular when the plural is needed, and vice versa. A T-chart or other helpful visual with the singular form on one side and the plural on the other could support students.

Acceleration

Students who have mastered these words may be interested in the following two advanced words. Challenge them to find uses of these words.

▸ **Layman (n.):** A person without specialized knowledge or training; in a religious context, a person who is not a member of the clergy

▸ **Tradesman (n.):** A worker skilled in a particular craft, like a carpenter

Latin Plurals

A few words in the English language have peculiar endings in their plural forms. These endings come straight from their old Latin declensions. Table 6.2 shows many of these words, but only a few of the most commonly used words in schools have been targeted for lesson S2. Refer to the Oxford Dictionaries' article "Plurals of English Nouns Taken From Latin or Greek" (Oxford University Press, 2017; http://bit.ly/2iyquWz) to access a good discussion of these endings.

Table 6.2: Chart of Latin Plurals

Singular Form	Plural Form
Addendum	Addenda
Alga	Algae
Alumnus, alumna	Alumni, alumnae
Amoeba	Amoebae
Antenna	Antennae
Bacterium	Bacteria
Cactus	Cacti
Curriculum	Curricula
Datum	Data
Fungus	Fungi
Genus	Genera
Larva	Larvae
Memorandum	Memoranda
Rhombus	Rhombi
Stimulus	Stimuli
Syllabus	Syllabi
Thesaurus	Thesauri
Vertebra	Vertebrae

Lesson S2: *curriculum, syllabus, thesaurus*

In this minilesson, teachers will teach Latin plurals, including the words *curriculum*, *syllabus*, and *thesaurus*.

Difficulty level: 2

S

The following lists target words students should *see* and *say* for this minilesson.

▸ **Curriculum (n.):** The academic content taught in a specific course or series of lessons; the plural is *curricula*

▸ **Syllabus (n.):** An outline of the content that will be covered in a class; the plural is *syllabi*

▸ **Thesaurus (n.):** A book or online resource that gives synonyms (and often antonyms) for words; the plural is *thesauri*

N

Remind students that they have probably heard teachers use all these words. They are all common, basic academic words that educated adults know and use. They are words that are common in school; perhaps you even have a thesaurus in your classroom that you can show to students.

A

Convene small groups and ask them to talk about how they would teach these words (including the plurals) to their classmates. What examples would they use? What would they say to define the terms?

P

Ask each student to choose two of the target words and to write sentences using the words in their singular or plural forms.

Scaffolding

Remind students who require scaffolding that you have a *curriculum* in your class. Give them examples of parts of your curriculum. If you use a monthly calendar or something similar to a syllabus, show them or remind them of this. If you have a thesaurus in the room to point out or can show one online, do so.

Acceleration

Students who have mastered these words may enjoy exploring two other words from table 6.2 (page 157). These two words are used quite often in academia and in the business world.

- **Addendum (n.):** Extra material added to the end of a book or other document; a supplement

- **Memorandum (n.):** A record or written statement, usually in the workplace

Singular Forms Ending in *-is*

There are a few common academic words in the English language that, in the singular, end in *-is*. Changing *-is* to *-es* makes the plural form of these words. The plural and singular are also pronounced differently from one another. The well-educated person knows both how to spell these words and how to pronounce them. These two lessons contain the words your students are most likely to use in K–12 and beyond.

Lesson S3: *basis, crisis, emphasis, hypothesis*

In this minilesson, teachers will teach singular forms ending in *-is*, such as in the words *basis, crisis, emphasis,* and *hypothesis*.

Difficulty level: 2

S

The following lists target words students should *see* and *say* for this minilesson.

- **Basis (n.):** The underlying support or principles on which something is based

- **Crisis (n.):** A time of trouble or danger or a time when a critical decision must be made

- **Emphasis (n.):** Something that is given great importance or value

- **Hypothesis (n.):** A theory based on available evidence

N

These words are some of the few nouns in our language that end in *-is*, which makes them somewhat unique. Students will probably be familiar with both *basis* and *hypothesis* because they hear them used in various school subjects. Ensure students know that a hypothesis for scientists does not mean the same as when we use the word *hypothesis* in a nonscience context, but do let them know that the word is often used outside of science in everyday life.

Be prepared to give them relevant examples of all the words. In school, we often talk about the *basis* of an argument, some kind of historical *crisis* (like the Great Depression, the Syrian refugee *crisis*, and so on), and the *emphasis* an author places on something.

A

Have students work in pairs and generate an example of each word from school or their daily lives outside of school.

P

Ask students to choose two of the four target words to use in sentences, and have them turn these in.

Scaffolding

Provide students who require scaffolding with additional examples, such as the following.

- **Basis:** The *basis* for school rules is safety; the *basis* of a written argument is the claim.

- **Crisis:** Natural disasters like hurricanes, floods, major storms, and earthquakes are *crises*.

- **Emphasis:** An author can place *emphasis* on things by using certain words; an artist can *emphasize* certain colors and textures.

- **Hypothesis:** An educated guess; scientists make *hypotheses* frequently and test them to see if they are true.

Acceleration

Check out Aaron V. Humphrey's (2006; www.telusplanet.net/~alfvaen/latin .html) online article about the plurals of Latin and Greek words that exist in English, and share some of this information with advanced students.

Lesson S4: *analysis, synopsis, thesis*

In this minilesson, teachers will teach singular forms ending in *-is*, such as in the words *analysis*, *synopsis*, and *thesis*.

Difficulty level: 2

S

The following lists target words students should *see* and *say* for this minilesson.

- **Analysis (n.):** A close examination of the structure or parts of something or the process of breaking something down into its elements

- **Synopsis (n.):** A summary of something

- **Thesis (n.):** A statement or position, usually one that will be proven in an essay or speech

N

 This set of words is another of the few in English that end in *-is*, and you can see that they are words used more frequently in academia than outside it. Teachers often ask students to write an *analysis* of something, especially a work of literature. Students also write *synopses* of various things, such as documentaries, other films, and works of literature. The word *thesis* is often used to refer to the main point of an essay. It's important to let your students know that they will encounter these words frequently as they move through school, and in college, they will be expected to know them.

A

Have small groups discuss which word to use if:

▸ A teacher asks you to write a paper in which you describe all the steps that led to the Revolutionary War (*analysis*)

▸ Someone asks you to state your position on rare animals being placed in zoos (*thesis*)

▸ A teacher asks you to summarize the book you just read with a partner (*synopsis*)

P

 Ask each student to make his or her own examples of the use of each word. This may go more quickly if students work in pairs, but with each student writing his or her own copy.

Scaffolding

Give students short statements or synonyms to remember for these words.

▸ **Analysis:** A breakdown

▸ **Synopsis:** A summary; just the facts

▸ **Thesis:** A viewpoint; a position; your main point

Acceleration

 The verb form of *analysis* is *to analyze*, and the verb form of *synopsis* is *to synopsize*. Advanced students may enjoy learning and using these words, too.

Double Consonants

The rule for doubling consonants is that you double a consonant in the base form of a verb when adding *-ing* for the present participle or when adding *-ed* for the past participle when either a one-syllable verb ends with consonant-vowel-consonant or a two-syllable verb ends with the *second* syllable stressed. The minilesson in this section differs from the others in this book because it's about a spelling rule and not specific words.

Lesson S5: Spelling Words With Double Consonants

In this minilesson, teachers will teach words with double consonants, such as *running, stopping*, and others.

Difficulty level: 1

S

The following are rules that teachers will include in instruction about when to double consonants to change a verb form to the present or past participle.

▸ When a one-syllable verb ends with consonant-vowel-consonant, as in the words *sit* and *fan*

▸ When a two-syllable verb ends with the *second* syllable stressed, as in the words *begin* and *refer*

N

Present several more examples, both of when to double and when not to double. See the article "Spelling: When to Double a Consonant Before Adding -ed or -ing to a Verb" (Speakspeak, 2017; http://bit.ly/2jvn1vZ) or "Doubling the Final Consonant Before Adding -ed or -ing" (Learner's Dictionary Ask the Editor, 2015; http://bit.ly/2jFDAmC) for good information about doubling that you can use during this step. (Visit **go.SolutionTree.com/literacy** to access live links to the websites mentioned in this book.)

A

Get students up and moving. Each student can wear or hold a sign that features either a verb, *double the consonant*, or *-ing*. Using the following verbs, have students match up in either twos or threes depending on whether a verb needs a double consonant to make the *-ing* form (the present participle) of the verb. Use all verbs. For example, a student with the word *run* would need to partner with a *double the consonant* person and an *-ing* person.

▸ Run (*three*)   ▸ Walk (*two*)   ▸ Hug (*three*)

▸ Kick (*two*)   ▸ Hug (*three*)   ▸ Spin (*three*)

▸ Jump (*two*)   ▸ Pitch (*two*)   ▸ Find (*two*)

▸ Shout (*two*)   ▸ Sing (*two*)   ▸ Begin (*three*)

▸ Nap (*three*)   ▸ Win (*three*)

You can also do a theme like sports words (*throw, pitch, kick, pass, punt, clip, foul, run, shoot, bunt, block*) or music words (*rap, spin, scratch, hum, sing, rip, drum, tap, beat, scream, riff, pound*). Choose words that make sense for you and your students and for the number of students you have in class.

P

Have each student write a short paragraph in which he or she uses two present progressive tense (*-ing*) or past tense (*-ed*) verbs with at least one containing the doubled consonants. Tell the students to write about something they've done recently. For example, I might tell my students that I would write about *swimming* in the ocean and *eating* at a huge buffet when I went on vacation last summer.

Scaffolding

You can find a foldable for scaffolding this activity in Belinda Kinney's (2013) blog post "Word Endings Foldable {Freebie}" (http://bit.ly/2iU1itN). This blog is about teaching second grade, but the activity is certainly adaptable for students in grades three and higher who haven't mastered this concept.

Acceleration

Challenge students who have mastered these words to find other words that need to have the consonant doubled before adding the ending.

Problematic Plurals

Students often have trouble correctly spelling and using some of the problematic plurals in our language. The lesson in this section addresses words with irregular plurals for different animals.

Lesson S6: *fish, deer, goose, sheep, fox, wolf*

In this minilesson, teachers will teach irregular plurals for words for different kinds of animals, such as the words *fish, deer, goose, sheep, fox*, and *wolf*.

Difficulty level: 1

S

The following lists target words students should *see* and *say* for this minilesson.

▶ **Fish (n.):** An animal with gills and fins that lives its whole life in water; the plurals are *fish* and *fishes*

▶ **Deer (n.):** A grazing animal with antlers; the plural is *deer*

- **Goose (n.):** A bird larger than a duck; has a long neck and webbed feet; the plural is *geese*
- **Sheep (n.):** An animal with a thick, woolly coat and horns; the plural is *sheep*
- **Fox (n.):** An animal of the dog family with a pointed nose and bushy tail; the plural is *foxes*
- **Wolf (n.):** An animal of the dog family, living and hunting in packs; the plural is *wolves*

Use images of the animals as you discuss them so that students who haven't seen certain animals can picture them. Some words may be familiar to students only if the animals have appeared in books you have read with them.

N

Consider saying, "These words are all common animals that appear in stories, fables, and even nursery rhymes. All the words except *fox* make their plural forms in a way other than adding *-s* or *-es*."

A

Put students in pairs and ask them to brainstorm other animal names. Encourage them to write down the singular and plural forms or to search online for them if necessary. If you need to get them started with a couple of examples, you could use *mouse* and *mice*, and *moose* and *moose*.

P

Allow each student to pick his or her favorite singular and plural out of the list of target words and write a sentence with each. For extra fun, they can quickly sketch the animal.

Scaffolding

There is no hard and fast rule with this list of words, so students will have to do their best to remember them. Ask each student which ones he or she finds the hardest. How you help students commit these to memory is at your discretion. Refer to the strategies in chapter 2 for ideas.

Acceleration

Students who have already mastered the terms may be interested in exploring them for groups of these animals and other animals, like the words *flock*, *herd*, *school*, and *pack*. EnglishClub's (n.d.) webpage "Animal Vocabulary" (http://bit.ly /2jUTOYm) offers many of these. You may want to consult the more complete list at

Fact Monster's (2017) webpage "Animal Group Terminology" (www.factmonster.com /ipka/A0004725.html) if you teach upper elementary students.

Adjectives With *-ly*

Don't believe all the tips and shortcuts your teachers may have taught you. The suffix *-ly* often appears in adverbs, but it's more common in adjectives than you may have previously thought. Words like *early, friendly, likely, unlikely, lively,* and *deadly* are just a few adjectives—not adverbs—that end in *-ly*. See the article "Most Things That End in -ly Are Adverbish. These Aren't" (n.d.; http://bit.ly/2kWObgm) if you'd like to refresh your own memory of *-ly* adjectives.

Lesson S7: *friendly, unfriendly, lively, lonely, lovely*

In this minilesson, teachers will teach adjectives about mood or temperament with *-ly*, such as in the words *friendly, unfriendly, lively, lonely,* and *lovely*.

Difficulty level: 1

S

The following lists target words students should *see* and *say* for this minilesson.

▸ **Friendly (adj.):** Kind, pleasant, being a friend

▸ **Unfriendly (adj.):** Unkind, unpleasant, not being a friend

▸ **Lively (adj.):** Active, outgoing, full of energy

▸ **Lonely (adj.):** All alone, unloved, unhappy

▸ **Lovely (adj.):** Beautiful, attractive, charming

These are all useful words for your students in both writing and speaking.

N

These words are all adjectives, and like all adjectives, they are used to describe nouns. These words can all describe people's moods or temperaments. Additionally, *lovely* and *lively* can describe many things like a *lovely* view or a *lively* conversation.

A

Put students in small groups. Have them brainstorm characters from literature or figures from history (or both) who could be described by all the adjectives in this minilesson. Alternatively, students could cite characters from movies and TV shows if you think this would provide more ideas to choose from. The goal is for them to apply the words to people, and because *unfriendly* is on the list, you may not want them to use classmates as examples.

P

Have each student pick a pair of words and write about an example of each. Students may use examples from step N or create new examples.

Scaffolding

You may want to help students with structuring their sentences. You could show them sentence frames like the ones in the following list to help them write sophisticated sentences that use semicolons if you feel they would be up for the task. Of course, they can always make separate sentences if you feel this is best.

▸ _____ is a *friendly* person; _____ is an *unfriendly* person.

▸ _____ is *lively*; _____ is *lonely*.

Acceleration

See the blog post "Non-Adverbs That End in -LY" (Wasko, 2014; http://bit.ly /2tTe7dO) for a list of words ending in *-ly* that are not adverbs. You may want to direct advanced students to study the lists included in this blog post.

Lesson S8: *burly, surly, dastardly, ghastly, grisly*

In this minilesson, teachers will teach advanced adjectives with *-ly*, such as in the words *burly, surly, dastardly, ghastly,* and *grisly*.

Difficulty level: 2

S

The following lists target words students should *see* and *say* for this minilesson.

▸ **Burly (adj.):** Large, strong, stout, sturdy; describes appearance

▸ **Surly (adj.):** Rude, bad-tempered, unfriendly, grouchy; describes mood or temperament

▸ **Dastardly (adj.):** Very mean, wicked, cruel; describes mood or temperament

▸ **Ghastly (adj.):** Horrible, dreadful, shocking; describes events; synonym for *grisly*

▸ **Grisly (adj.):** Horrible, gruesome; describes events; synonym for *ghastly*

N

These words are all terrific adjectives to use in one's writing, as they are a bit out of the ordinary. The first three words most often describe people, and the last two are often used to describe events, like a *ghastly* error or a *grisly* murder.

For the first three words, try to give your students examples from literature, history, and world news to help them internalize the meanings. Lennie from *Of Mice and Men* is a *burly* character, as is Michael Oher in the movie *The Blind Side*. The witch in "Hansel and Gretel" is definitely a *surly* character. Lord Voldemort in the *Harry Potter* series is a *dastardly* character. Images from the civil war in Syria may be too *ghastly* or *grisly* to look at. The details of a murder may be too *grisly* to share on the evening news. Offer your students examples like these.

A

Convene small groups of students. Assign each group a couple of the target words. Have them brainstorm lists of characters from literature, movies, and TV that can be described with the words.

P

Have each student pick his or her favorite adjective from the target words. Ask students to write a sentence using the word correctly and, as time allows, ask them to do a quick sketch that goes along with their sentence and also shows the meaning of the word they selected.

Scaffolding

Support struggling students with synonyms such as the following for the target words.

- **Burly (adj.):** Large
- **Surly (adj.):** Angry
- **Dastardly (adj.):** Wicked
- **Ghastly (adj.):** Shocking
- **Grisly (adj.):** Terrible

Acceleration

Allow advanced students to explore other words using the WordHippo (www .wordhippo.com) site. For example, they could type in *burly* into the "What's another word for" field and click "find it" to discover words such as *brawny*, *hefty*, and *beefy*.

Adverbs With *-ly*

In many words in the English language, the suffix *–ly* signifies use as an adverb, telling how, how much, how often, or something about time, place, or degree.

Lesson S9: *basically, acceptably, adequately, accurately*

In this minilesson, teachers will teach adverbs with *-ly*, such as in the words *basically, acceptably, adequately,* and *accurately*.

Difficulty level: 1

S

The following lists target words students should *see* and *say* for this minilesson.

▸ **Basically (adv.):** Done in a way that meets the minimum or includes only the essentials

▸ **Acceptably (adv.):** Done in a satisfactory way

▸ **Adequately (adv.):** Done in an acceptable way; sufficiently

▸ **Accurately (adv.):** Done carefully; done without error

N

You can use these words to describe a student's work or performance. *Accurately* has the most positive connotation, because the other three words indicate only a low level or the minimum performance.

The word *accurately* can be used in all disciplines. A historian can share an account of an event *accurately*. A mathematician must work *accurately*. A writer must *accurately* report things. And lastly, a scientist must *accurately* measure and observe things.

A

Ask students to discuss the following two questions.

1. What are some things that need to be done *adequately*?

2. What are some things that need to be done *accurately*?

P

Ask each student to think about something he or she can do only *basically* or *adequately* but would like to do better. Have students write a sentence or two explaining this.

Scaffolding

Help students see how these words are made from the adjective forms *basic*, *acceptable*, *adequate*, and *accurate*.

Acceleration

These words may also be of interest.

- **Sufficiently (adv.):** Done well enough
- **Capably (adv.):** Done in a competent way

Lesson S10: *approximately, completely, totally, entirely*

In this minilesson, teachers will teach adverbs with *-ly*, such as in the words *approximately*, *completely*, *totally*, and *entirely*.

Difficulty level: 1

S

The following lists target words students should *see* and *say* for this minilesson.

- **Approximately (adv.):** Nearly approaching a certain state or goal
- **Completely (adv.):** Wholly, entirely, or fully; lacking nothing
- **Totally (adv.):** Absolutely and completely
- **Entirely (adv.):** Wholly, completely, or fully

N

Completely, *totally*, and *entirely* are synonyms for each other. However, *approximately* differs a bit from the other words. Tell your students that *approximately* means "almost" whereas the other words mean "100 percent." These are all words that are adjectives describing an amount but are used with adjectives that describe something's quality.

A

Ask small groups to discuss the following questions.

- Which word or words could you use to describe a full moon? (*completely, totally, entirely*)
- Which word or words would you use if you were almost finished writing a paper? (*approximately*)
- Which word or words could someone use if he or she invited you to a party but not at an exact time? (*approximately*)

P

Have each student write a sentence with the word *approximately* and a sentence with any other vocabulary word for this minilesson. The sentences can relate to each other or not. For example, I tell my mom that I will go to bed at *approximately* 9:00 p.m. She tells me I can stay up a little bit later if I *completely* clean my room first.

Scaffolding

Tell students that *completely*, *totally*, and *entirely* are all ways to say "fully" or "100 percent." *Approximately* means "a best guess," or "almost," or "not quite fully."

Acceleration

Other words that mean *completely* include *wholly* and *thoroughly*. Challenge advanced students to find other synonyms too.

- ▸ **Wholly (adv.):** *Totally; 100 percent*
- ▸ **Thoroughly (adv.):** *In depth* or *in detail*

Lesson S11: *clearly, forcefully, convincingly, concisely, conclusively*

In this minilesson, teachers will teach adverbs with *-ly*, such as in the words *clearly, forcefully, convincingly, concisely,* and *conclusively*.

Difficulty level: 2

S

The following lists target words students should *see* and *say* for this minilesson.

- ▸ **Clearly (adv.):** Plainly and understandably
- ▸ **Forcefully (adv.):** Powerfully
- ▸ **Convincingly (adv.):** In a way that others agree with; persuasively
- ▸ **Concisely (adv.):** Briefly or in a short (abbreviated) manner
- ▸ **Conclusively (adv.):** Decisively; in a manner that gets rid of doubt

N

These adverbs are all used when making or evaluating arguments. It should be fairly easy to walk students through the adjective form of each (*clear, forceful, convincing, concise,* and *conclusive*) and show how the suffix turns each into an adverb.

A

Ask small groups of students to discuss the following.

▸ Would you rather hear a speaker make an argument *clearly* or *forcefully*? Which is more important to you?

▸ Why is it important for a speaker to speak *concisely* when making an argument?

P

Ask each student to choose two words and try to use them in authentic sentences.

Scaffolding

Students who have mastered these words can write sentences based on the group discussion in step A.

Acceleration

Direct students to WordHippo. They can explore interesting synonyms here. For example, if they type in the word *convincingly*, they will see words like *assuredly* and *conclusively*.

Lesson S12: *manually, automatically*

In this minilesson, teachers will teach adverbs with *-ly*, such as in the words *manually* and *automatically*.

Difficulty level: 1

S

The following lists target words students should *see* and *say* for this minilesson.

▸ **Manually (adv.):** Worked or done by using the hands

▸ **Automatically (adv.):** Done without thinking or without using human force

N

Many schools now have automatic lighting, and this is a great example to use to support teaching this pair of words, which is essentially a pair of opposites. Explain to students:

> Manually *means that you do something by hand. So, if I have to flip a switch for lights to come on, then I've done it* manually. *If they come on* automatically *when there's movement in the room, they are obviously not* manual, *but instead,* automatic.

You can also use toilets as an example. Students have most likely experienced *automatic* lighting or *automatic* flushing toilets in school, at the mall, at the movie theater, and so on.

A

Put students in pairs. Assign each pair one word. Have each pair write one sentence using the assigned adverb correctly. As time allows, do a Whip Around, and ask each pair to read aloud its sentence. For extra fun, have each pair read it aloud together, chorally, and ask the other students to give a thumbs-up if they feel the word was used correctly.

P

Ask each student to write a sentence with the word that his or her pair did *not* use. These can be turned in on paper or displayed using Padlet (https://padlet.com) or another digital tool.

Scaffolding

Students may have trouble using adverbs correctly in sentences. Help them place the adverb right after the verb if this will help.

Acceleration

You may use the term *manual labor* along with this minilesson. Manual labor is physical work that people do, especially in contrast to that which machines do, and to that working animals like donkeys and camels do.

Lesson S13: *silently, confidently, dejectedly, contentiously*

In this minilesson, teachers will teach "writerly" adverbs with *–ly* that describe how a person is doing something, such as in the words *silently, confidently, dejectedly,* and *contentiously.*

Difficulty level: 2

S

The following lists target words students should *see* and *say* for this minilesson.

▸ **Silently (adv.):** Without making a sound

▸ **Confidently (adv.):** Having a strong belief; surely

▸ **Dejectedly (adv.):** In a sad way or with low spirits

▸ **Contentiously (adv.):** In an argumentative way

N

These words are all about how a person gets ready to do something or thinks about something. They all refer to a person's mood or actions.

A

Ask small groups of students to choose the word that best fits each scenario.

- ▸ If you were sneaking up on your brother or sister to play a prank (*silently*)
- ▸ If you were sure you would win a race (*confidently*)
- ▸ If you strongly disagreed with someone (*contentiously*)
- ▸ If you got sick and couldn't go on a trip (*dejectedly*)
- ▸ If you were sad because your friend was mean to you (*dejectedly*)

P

What is something you've done *confidently* lately? Have each student answer this question, using the target word, in one or more complete sentences.

Scaffolding

Encourage struggling students to use *silently* or *confidently* for their sentence in step P, as these words are probably the ones they can learn first or best.

Acceleration

Ask students who have mastered these words to come up with opposites for these adverbs. Examples include:

- ▸ **Silently:** Loudly, noisily
- ▸ **Confidently:** Uncertainly, doubtfully, hesitantly
- ▸ **Dejectedly:** Happily, joyfully
- ▸ **Contentiously:** Agreeably

Lesson S14: *normally, abnormally, concretely, abstractly*

In this minilesson, teachers will teach adverbs with *–ly* that are pairs of opposites, such as in the words *normally*, *abnormally*, *concretely*, and *abstractly*.

Difficulty level: 1

S

The following lists target words students should *see* and *say* for this minilesson.

- **Normally (adv.):** Done in the usual or expected way

- **Abnormally (adv.):** Done in an unusual or unexpected way

- **Concretely (adv.):** Done in a manner that is specific and relates to a real thing

- **Abstractly (adv.):** Done in a manner that is unspecific and relates to something intangible, like a concept or a theory

N

Just as *normal* and *abnormal* are opposites, so are their adverb forms. *Normally* is the common way you would do something; *abnormally* would be a way that is uncommon. *Concrete* and *abstract* are also opposites, as are their adverb forms. *Concretely* is about doing something physically; *abstractly* is about doing something in your head or in another way that people can't see or touch.

A

Ask pairs to discuss the following question and respond to the prompt.

- What would it mean if it were to rain or snow *abnormally*? Describe possible events that could occur. (Possible answers: A drought, floods, feet of snow, or even avalanches)

P

Have each student choose one of the other three target words to use in a sentence.

Scaffolding

Have students who require scaffolding complete a concept circle (see page 16), working together if you wish. They can take any one of the target words and brainstorm three related words. They can use an online dictionary or thesaurus if necessary. For example, students can write the word *concretely* in one piece of the concept circle, and words like *visible, visibly, touchable, viewable, exactly,* and *definitely* in the other parts.

Acceleration

Have advanced students list things that can be used or done concretely versus abstractly, or explore these words and their synonyms on the WordHippo (www.wordhippo.com) website.

Suffixes Used for People's Roles

The following words end in *-er*, *-ar*, and *-or*. The suffixes usually mean "one who" or "person." So, a *writer* is "one who writes." A *sailor* is "one who sails" or "a person who sails."

Lesson S15: *teacher, helper, partner, author, scholar*

In this minilesson, teachers will teach suffixes, including *-er*, *-ar*, and *-or*, for roles of people we find in the classroom or school, such as in the words *teacher, helper, partner, author*, and *scholar*.

Difficulty level: 1

S

The following lists target words students should *see* and *say* for this minilesson.

▸ **Teacher (n.):** A person who instructs and leads others

▸ **Helper (n.):** A person who gives aid or assistance to others

▸ **Partner (n.):** Someone that you share the work with or who helps you do something

▸ **Author (n.):** The writer of a book or other text

▸ **Scholar (n.):** An educated person

N

These words are all things that a student can actually be at any time in your classroom. They are synonyms for the word *student*.

A

Have pairs of students role-play some dialogue using as many of the words as they can. They should use the words to describe each other if possible. You can demonstrate first with one student. Choose one who will be good at playing along. You could say, "Juan, you are quite the *scholar* today! Your writing was amazing!" And you would hope that Juan would say something like, "Yes, I'm trying to be an *author* as a career" or "Thank you. You've been a good *teacher* to me."

P

Have students choose one of the following verbs they would like to do. Ask them to identify the related noun that describes a person who does this, write one sentence using the noun, and look up the correct spelling of the noun or check their spelling with a friend.

‣ *Skate*   ‣ *Ski*   ‣ *Invent*

‣ *Surf*   ‣ *Dance*   ‣ *Investigate*

‣ *Sing*   ‣ *Design*   ‣ *Travel*

‣ *Act*   ‣ *Sail*

‣ *Swim*   ‣ *Drive*

For example:

‣ "For one day, I would like to be a (or an) _____
because _____."

‣ For one day, I would like to be an investigator so I could solve a murder mystery.

‣ For one day, I would like to be a surfer so I could ride the waves.

Scaffolding

Focus on familiar jobs or roles for students who require scaffolding, like teacher, reader, writer, actor, singer, and so on.

Acceleration

Ask, "What are other synonyms for *teacher*? *Author*?" See how many terms students can brainstorm.

Lesson S16: *waiter, cashier, baker, butcher, grocer*

In this minilesson, teachers will teach the suffix *-er* for roles of people in the community, such as in the words *waiter, cashier, baker, butcher,* and *grocer.*

S

The following lists target words students should *see* and *say* for this minilesson.

‣ **Waiter (n.):** A person who serves you at a restaurant

‣ **Cashier (n.):** A person who handles payments

‣ **Baker (n.):** Someone who makes baked goods like breads and cakes

‣ **Butcher (n.):** Someone who cuts up and sells meat in a store

‣ **Grocer (n.):** A person who sells food and common household items in a store

You may want to show images of people in these roles, especially if you think your students may be unfamiliar with some of them.

N

These people are people that we see often in our community. They perform important jobs.

A

Ask small groups to discuss the following questions.

- ▶ Would you most likely see a *cashier* at a store, a church, or a school?
- ▶ Would you most likely see a *waiter* at a store, a movie theater, or a restaurant?
- ▶ Would you most likely see a *baker* at a school, a bakery, or a dance party?
- ▶ Would you most likely see a *butcher* at a movie theater, a soccer game, or a store?
- ▶ Would you most likely see a *grocer* at a school, a bank, or a store?

Alternatively, you can form five groups, have each group discuss only one question (for a minute or two), and then have each group report out.

P

Have students answer the following questions: Of all these jobs, are there any that you might want to have? Which is your favorite? Which is your least favorite? Why?

Scaffolding

Help students connect base words to the target words. For example, a *cashier* handles cash. A *waiter* waits on you at a restaurant. A *baker* bakes things. A *butcher* butchers meat. A *grocer* sells groceries at the grocery store.

Acceleration

Ask students who have mastered these words to brainstorm other words that end in *-er* and represent jobs in the community. Examples include *banker*, *driver*, *lawyer*, *manager*, and *petsitter*.

Lesson S17: *spectator, commentator, instigator, agitator*

In this minilesson, teachers will teach the suffix *-or* for roles of observers and those involved, such as in the words *spectator*, *commentator*, *instigator*, and *agitator*.

Difficulty level: 2

S

The following lists target words students should *see* and *say* for this minilesson.

- **Spectator (n.):** A person who looks on or watches something; an observer

- **Commentator (n.):** A person who discusses (comments on) things

- **Instigator (n.):** A person who brings about or starts something

- **Agitator (n.):** A person who stirs up other people; often means trying to cause social or political unrest

N

These words all end in *-or*, which is rarer in English than the *-er* ending to designate roles people play or jobs that people have. Tell students that most nouns that end in *-er* or *-or* are naming a person.

A

Ask small groups, "Which scenario goes with which word?" Put these in any order you want, and feel free to add your own examples.

- A man attends a soccer game where his favorite team is playing. (*spectator*)

- A woman interviews a famous football player and then shares her thoughts about the day's game. (*commentator*)

- A man starts doing the wave at a football game, and others follow his lead and do the wave too. (*instigator*)

- Your friend attends a rock concert. (*spectator*)

- A student goes to a political event and yells insults at the candidate and spectators. (*agitator*)

- Your neighbor starts a group that wants to end animal cruelty in your community. (*instigator*)

P

Place students in pairs. Assign each pair a word and have them collaborate and complete a modified Frayer model on that word. (See page 20 in chapter 2 for an explanation of modified Frayer models.)

Scaffolding

Tell students requiring scaffolding that a *spectator* sees, a *commentator* talks, an *instigator* starts trouble, and an *agitator* stirs the pot. These more colloquial definitions should help them understand these words better. Adjust as needed for English learners.

Acceleration

The word *aggressor* is similar to both *instigator* and *agitator*. Share this word if it seems appropriate.

▸ **Aggressor (n.):** A person who attacks first or starts a quarrel

Beyond the Lesson

Remind students not to be *agitators* or *instigators* when troublesome situations arise in your classroom, in the cafeteria, on the playground, and so on. Use these words in context when appropriate so that students have repeated exposure.

Lesson S18: *beggar, burglar, liar*

In this minilesson, teachers will teach the suffix *-ar* in people's roles, such as in the words *beggar, burglar,* and *liar*.

Difficulty level: 1

S

The following lists target words students should *see* and *say* for this minilesson.

▸ **Beggar (n.):** A person who asks others for money or resources because he or she has very little

▸ **Burglar (n.):** A person who steals things from other people

▸ **Liar (n.):** A person who doesn't tell the truth

A *beggar* is a person who may be homeless and forced to live on the street, or a *beggar* may be a person who has no job and therefore needs money. Some *beggars* are war veterans. Be sure to help students understand the difference between begging and stealing.

N

All these words are special because they end in *-ar*, which is a rare suffix in English. Because of the *-ar* suffix, students should be able to readily infer that all three words refer to people. The words also have verb forms: a *beggar* begs; a *burglar* burgles; a *liar* lies. These are words formed from the action named by the verbs. If you can identify the base word and you know it, then the *-ar* should tell you "a person who" about the verb.

A

Have small groups do some word association. Offer as many of these words as you like, and ask students to decide which of the three target words is most closely associated.

- Untrue (*liar*)
- Thief (*burglar*)
- Robbery (*burglar*)
- Intrude (*burglar*)
- False (*liar*)

- Deceive (*liar*)
- Plead (*beggar*)
- Mislead (*liar*)
- Criminal (*burglar*)
- Needy (*beggar*)

P

Ask each student to use one target word and one or more synonyms or associated words together in a sentence. Examples include the following.

- I stopped to give the *beggar* some spare change because I know he's *needy* and could use my help.

- I knew that character was a *liar* because she *deceived* others throughout the book.

- The *burglar* committed a *robbery* at a jewelry store.

Scaffolding

Use informal language as much as possible to help students understand these words' meanings. For example, you could use *break in* when talking about *burglar* and *street person* for *beggar* if these terms are more familiar. If students know the word *fib*, you can use that with *liar*. The caution here is to be as respectful as possible with these particular words, because they may be familiar to students from personal experience and carry a lot of (negative) weight. You wouldn't want any student to feel insulted or to insult another student or family when discussing these words.

Acceleration

There are not many words that end in *-ar* in English that name people's roles. There are far more words that are used as adjectives, like *similar, regular, polar,* and *nuclear*. Ask advanced students to come up with a list of ways to avoid mistaking an adjective ending in *-ar* for a "people word" ending in *-ar*.

Adjectives With *-ful* and *-ous*

Many adjectives in the English language end with the suffixes *-ful* and *-ous*, which mean "having" or "full of."

Lesson S19: *beautiful, wonderful, delightful, fabulous, gorgeous*

In this minilesson, teachers will teach adjectives with *-ful* and *-ous*, such as in the words *beautiful*, *wonderful*, *delightful*, *fabulous*, and *gorgeous*.

Difficulty level: 1

S

 The following lists target words students should *see* and *say* for this minilesson.

- **Beautiful (adj.):** Pleasing to the mind or the senses; pretty

- **Wonderful (adj.):** Extremely good

- **Delightful (adj.):** Enjoyable or charming

- **Fabulous (adj.):** Extremely good or extraordinary

- **Gorgeous (adj.):** Very attractive; extremely pretty

Almost all words that end in *-ful* or *-ous* are adjectives.

N

These words are all adjectives that mean something is very good or attractive. They can take the place of vague words such as *nice*, *good*, and *pretty* in students' writing.

A

Since *beautiful* and *gorgeous* have similar meanings, ask small groups of students to think about these two words and talk about when they might use one versus the other. For example, one might describe a sunset or a movie star as *beautiful* or *gorgeous*. But, since *gorgeous* is often used to mean a higher degree of beauty than *beautiful*, students might discuss the subtle differences. One student may think a certain pop star or athlete is gorgeous, while another student might think that same person is merely beautiful. As time allows, do the same thing with the other three target words, as their meanings are all about being better than just good.

P

 Ask each student to write a short paragraph using one *-ful* word and one *-ous* word from the list. If you like, you can read aloud the following example.

Last night, I had a wonderful *dinner with my friend Brooke. We had a yummy brick oven pizza. We sat outside at the restaurant and admired the* gorgeous *sunset. What a great evening!*

Scaffolding

Encourage students who require scaffolding to use the words *beautiful* and *wonderful* more often. Then, steer them to the other words in the list.

Acceleration

Students who have mastered these words might enjoy knowing the words *magnificent* and *phenomenal*.

- ▶ **Magnificent (adj.):** Breathtaking or striking; incredibly beautiful
- ▶ **Phenomenal (adj.):** Out of the ordinary; remarkable

Lesson 20: *shameful, disgraceful, dreadful, hideous*

In this minilesson, teachers will teach adjectives with *-ful* and *-ous*, such as in the words *shameful*, *disgraceful*, *dreadful*, and *hideous*.

Difficulty level: 2

S

The following lists target words students should *see* and *say* for this minilesson.

- ▶ **Shameful (adj.):** Causing disgrace or dishonor
- ▶ **Disgraceful (adj.):** Very unacceptable; shocking
- ▶ **Dreadful (adj.):** Extremely bad or very serious; causing fear or unhappiness
- ▶ **Hideous (adj.):** Very ugly or disgusting

N

These words are all adjectives that describe bad events or sights. One might describe a famous person who is caught in a lie as *shameful*. News broadcasts are often full of *disgraceful* events, especially when public servants don't do their duties or neglect their constituents. A natural disaster like an earthquake or tornado might be called *dreadful*. *Hideous* is often reserved for the exterior features of something, but a crime might also be called *hideous*.

A

In small groups, students can discuss examples that they feel could apply for each word. If you told a lie to your parents, that might be *shameful*. If you committed a crime, that might be *disgraceful* for you and your family. You could have a *dreadful* illness or know someone who does. Abusing or neglecting an animal might be described as a *hideous* act. Prompt students with examples as needed.

P

Have each student choose his or her two favorite words and write sentences using them.

Scaffolding

Shameful and *disgraceful* are very similar in meaning, so advise students to use them in similar situations. They will almost always be right.

Acceleration

Allow students to investigate some of the following synonyms for *shameful*: *deplorable, despicable, contemptible, dishonorable, reprehensible, scandalous, atrocious, appalling, vile,* and *unforgivable.*

Final Thoughts

Learning key suffixes in our language is important, as this knowledge, along with knowledge of roots, can unlock the meanings of hundreds of words students will encounter in school and beyond. The foundation laid in the lessons in this chapter can set your students on their way to being more powerful readers and communicators.

Testing Terms

S

tudents are bombarded with many forms of assessment these days—classroom assignments, including quizzes, tests, papers, and presentations; common assessments across a team, grade level, course, or entire school; systemwide benchmark assessments and writing prompts; and high-stakes assessments from the state or province level. At times, it seems that students are assessed more often than they are taught; as a matter of fact, I've heard many teachers express this sentiment. Obviously, instruction and assessment are two sides of the same coin—but various types of assessment, both formative and summative (both those the teacher generates and those generated from afar) are here to stay, and it behooves us to equip our students to deal with them. This chapter focuses on words that are most often used in assessing students on what they have learned.

We begin with some of the most common words from reading, writing, and language assessments. This seems a logical place to start since words are especially important to the discipline of English language arts. Also, from almost the first moment in the classroom, students are being read to. Teachers need to teach certain basic words about text immediately. This chapter also includes some of the most basic words used in mathematics, but many of them have application outside the discipline as well. And lastly, this chapter includes general words used in classroom discourse and formative and summative assessment. None of the words in this chapter are so specialized or rare that they are not worthy of discussing in any classroom. They constitute a foundational academic vocabulary for the earliest years of school.

Features of Print

Some of the earliest content-area learning our students need is about basic features of print. They need to know that books have covers, that text goes from left to right and down a page, and that photos, illustrations, and other visuals help us understand the information or the story better. The lessons in this section deal with very basic vocabulary about printed or digitally published text.

Lesson A1: *author, illustrator, title, subtitle*

In this minilesson, teachers will teach terms relating to features of print, such as the words *author*, *illustrator*, *title*, and *subtitle*.

Difficulty level: 1

S

The following lists target words students should *see* and *say* for this minilesson.

- **Author (n.):** The person who writes a book or other piece of writing, like a story or article
- **Illustrator (n.):** The person who draws or otherwise creates art for a book or other piece of writing
- **Title (n.):** The name of a book or other piece of writing
- **Subtitle (n.):** A secondary (lesser) title of a book or other piece of writing that gives more information than the title does; usually it appears below the title and in a smaller font size or a different font

These are basic words that students need to know for just about every book they will encounter, whether it's a physical book or an electronic one. Remind students that the suffix *-or* signifies that the word means "a person who." In this case, an *author* authors (as a verb) and an *illustrator* illustrates. If you feel it's appropriate, discuss these verb forms as part of this minilesson.

You may also need to define and describe the word *cover*. Ensure that you point out that the cover is made of different material and is sturdier than the inside pages.

N

Consider saying something like the following to your class.

These are words that educated people know. Educated people know the parts of a book and the proper names for them. The title *of a book is like a student's name—it's what we call it. The* subtitle *is a little like a nickname; it gives additional information about the book. And the two people involved with creating a picture book or other book with art are the* author, *who wrote it, and the* illustrator, *who created the art.*

A

Put students in small groups. Give each group a few books. Ensure that at least one book in each group has a *subtitle*. Have students point out the *authors, illustrators, titles,* and *subtitles* to each other. You could have the words prewritten on sticky notes and ask students to label the parts. Making the activity more hands-on by doing this may increase engagement.

P

Have each student find a book in the classroom (or, to save time, hand each student a book). Then, ask students to use the following sentence frame and fill in or circle the proper information. Students should write the entire paragraph, not just the words that go in the blank spaces.

▶ The *title* of this book is _____. The *author* of this book is _____. The book (*does* or *does not*) have a *subtitle.* The *illustrator* of this book is _____. I (*would* or *would not*) like to read this book.

Scaffolding

If necessary, precede step A with plenty of examples by holding up books, pointing to the pertinent parts, and having students repeat the target words again after you say them.

Acceleration

There are other common book features or components that students could learn. For advanced students, show them how hardcover books often have *jackets* (wrappers that can come off, but they help books stay clean). You may also want to show them what book *blurbs* are (the recommendations that are often printed on the back cover). Advanced students may want to locate books with *jackets* and *blurbs* instead of doing the writing in step P. As time allows, they can then share their findings with the class.

Lesson A2: *headline, byline, dateline, caption*

In this minilesson, teachers will teach terms relating to features of print, such as the words *headline, byline, dateline,* and *caption.*

Difficulty level: 2

S

The following lists target words students should *see* and *say* for this minilesson.

▶ **Headline (n.):** The title of a story in a newspaper, magazine, or other periodical

- **Byline (n.):** Usually under the headline; the line that tells who wrote the story and what his or her job or role is; sometimes includes an email address or social media contact information

- **Dateline (n.):** Usually under the headline; the line that gives the date the story was written; may also include the time and whether or not the story has been updated

- **Caption (n.):** Usually under a photograph; a short explanation or description; students often confuse this with a title or headline

If you can have a hard-copy newspaper available as you point these things out, that will make the words more concrete and memorable. You can also go to an online newspaper or news magazine site and scroll through, pointing out these parts. CNN (www .cnn.com) featured articles are excellent for showing headline, byline, and dateline, in that order. So are articles at the *New York Times* (www.nytimes.com) and *Washington Post* (www.washingtonpost.com). Check out *TIME for Kids* (www.timeforkids.com) and *News for Your Classroom* by Scholastic (http://magazines.scholastic.com) for student-friendly material. (Visit **go.SolutionTree.com/literacy** to access live links to the websites mentioned in this book.)

N

All these words are associated with journalistic writing (reporting the news). We usually don't apply this terminology to a wide variety of texts.

Point out that three of the words contain the word *line*. The word *line* should remind them that these words are all about text written in lines.

You may want to ask students if they've ever seen the TV show *Dateline*. This could help them remember that a *dateline* appears only in news reports and is information about when a story was written.

A

Have small groups work with a tablet or other device to practice finding examples of each term. You could use *TIME for Kids* (www.timeforkids.com) and have the site set to a different article for each group.

P

Have each student access one news article online, or hand him or her one page from a hard-copy newspaper or magazine. Have students write or annotate each part: *headline, byline, dateline,* and *caption.* Circulate and monitor to ensure no one struggles unproductively.

Scaffolding

Students often mistake *captions* for *headlines* or for actual parts of a news story. Be sure you explain that they describe only the photo or other visual that they are closest to. You can also use teacher gestures (see page 23) like pointing to the top of your head for *headline* and using your hand as if you are writing in the air for *byline* to help students remember those two particular words.

Acceleration

Allow advanced students to learn the terms *column* and *columnist* and, if possible, to find examples in an online or hard-copy newspaper that you provide for them—like, *Washington Post* columnists Dana Milbank and George Will and *New York Times* columnists Thomas Friedman and Maureen Dowd. You can find any number of examples like these online.

▸ **Column (n.):** A recurring piece in a newspaper or magazine, always written by the same person

▸ **Columnist (n.):** The person who writes a column in a newspaper or magazine; he or she shares his or her own views in the column, not just reports facts

Lesson A3: *table of contents, glossary, index*

In this minilesson, teachers will teach terms relating to features of print, such as the words *table of contents*, *glossary*, and *index*.

Difficulty level: 1

S

The following lists target words students should *see* and *say* for this minilesson.

▸ **Table of contents (n.):** A list of the parts of the book, in the order that the parts appear

▸ **Glossary (n.):** A brief dictionary at the back of a book; an alphabetical list of words found in that book

▸ **Index (n.):** An alphabetical list of names and topics that appear in a book; at the end of a book; contains where you locate each name or topic within the book

N

All these terms are alike in that they describe parts of a nonfiction book. Use a textbook or other familiar nonfiction book to hold up and point to these parts as you define them. Before teaching this minilesson, you may want to read Michelle

J. Kelley and Nicki Clausen-Grace's (n.d.) excellent online article "Guiding Students Through Expository Text With Text Feature Walks" (http://bit.ly/1K5e0xb).

A

Have small groups of students work together and find these parts in a book that is unfamiliar to them. Enlist the help of your media specialist beforehand to pull books for checkout that would look interesting to your students or that are popular. In that way, you will also be encouraging them to consider reading these books and not just use them for this activity.

P

Ask each student to write the following, filling in the appropriate term for each blank. Writing the entire sentence for each word helps students internalize correct sentence structure. Encourage them to do this instead of just writing the target term for each sentence.

> ▸ I would look up a word I don't know in the _____.
> (*glossary*)

> ▸ I would use the _____ to find the page number of a topic. (*index*)

> ▸ I would look at the _____ before reading the book so I could get an idea of what it was about. (*table of contents*)

Scaffolding

You can post these groups of related words to help students remember each term's components and functions. Also, Pinterest (www.pinterest.com) has examples of these terms shown in nonlinguistic ways on posters, anchor charts, PowerPoint slides, and so on. You may want to create a visual and post it in your room to support students during the minilesson and beyond.

> ▸ **Table of contents (n.):** Front of the book; titles; page numbers

> ▸ **Glossary (n.):** Back of the book; words; definitions

> ▸ **Index (n.):** Back of the book; names; topics; page numbers

Acceleration

Allow advanced students to view the slide show "The Parts of a Book" (Breitsprecher, 2007) on SlideShare (www.slideshare.net/bogeybear/parts-of-book).

Lesson A4: *heading, subheading, sidebar, diagram, bold type* or *boldface type*

In this minilesson, teachers will teach terms relating to features of print, such as the words *heading, subheading, sidebar, diagram,* and *bold type* or *boldface type.*

Difficulty level: 2

S

The following lists target words students should *see* and *say* for this minilesson.

- **Heading (n.):** A title of a section within a book
- **Subheading (n.):** A title of a smaller section of a book or other text
- **Sidebar (n.):** A narrow, vertical area beside the main text, which may contain additional information or suggestions of other resources
- **Diagram (n.):** A simple drawing or other figure that helps the reader better understand what's in the text
- **Bold (or boldface) type (n.):** Thicker, darker text than the rest of the text around it; used for emphasis; eye-catching

N

Consider saying something like the following to your class.

There are all sorts of ways that writers and publishers call our attention to information they're trying to share with us. Today's words are all about visual appeal in print. Just like a sound effect on TV or in a movie gets your attention, these text features are designed to get your attention. Headings and subheadings *are titles of sections of text. Their purpose is to show us where information is broken into smaller sections or chunks that we can more easily digest. Sidebars and* diagrams *appear outside of the sentences and paragraphs in the main chapter or article. They often have a box or lines around them, or they may have shading that shows they are different from the main text. They give information beyond the text that is supposed to help us understand more deeply, or they can even send us to look at other resources. Lastly,* boldface *print draws our eyes to the words that are in* bold. *These are usually important words. Also, headings and* subheadings *are in* boldface *so we can tell that they are section titles.*

A

Have small groups of students pull out various textbooks that may be available to them and point out to each other examples of all the terms. Circulate and monitor so you can ensure they are accurate.

P

Have each student pick two of the terms and write sentences showing he or she understands the meanings.

Scaffolding

Provide keywords to remember for each target word. Use the following keywords if you wish.

- **Heading (n.):** Title; part; big piece
- **Subheading (n.):** Subtitle; subpart; small piece
- **Sidebar (n.):** Extra; box
- **Diagram (n.):** Extra; drawing; visual
- **Boldface (n.):** Thick; heavy; dark; fat

Acceleration

Advanced students might like exploring other features, such as cross-sections. Visit Douglas County School District's (n.d.) page "Cross-section—Nonfiction" (http://bit.ly/2iA0dqP) for a good discussion of cross-sections.

- **Cross-section (n.):** Diagram that gives an inside look at an object to illustrate in detail how it works or how its parts fit together

Lesson A5: *margin, paragraph, indent, indentation*

In this minilesson, teachers will teach terms relating to features of print, such as the words *margin*, *paragraph*, *indent*, and *indentation*.

Difficulty level: 1

S

The following lists target words students should *see* and *say* for this minilesson.

- **Margin (n.):** Generally a border or edge around something; for printed materials or even for handwritten pages, the blank space around the paper's edges, usually one inch on the top, bottom, and sides
- **Paragraph (n.):** A group of sentences, all on one topic, indented or set off by a double-space in block-style writing; in handwriting, a new paragraph should be indented five letter spaces from the left margin
- **Indent (v.):** To start a line of handwritten or published text set in approximately five letter spaces from the left margin

▶ **Indentation (n.):** The act of setting a line in approximately five letter spaces from the left margin

N

Consider saying something like the following to your class.

These words are all related because they are all about how print looks on a page. Whether something is handwritten or typed, there must be margins and indentations (or block style for setting off paragraphs). The paragraph is the main unit of lengthy prose. All these words are words you need to know for reading and for writing.

A

Have small groups of students brainstorm a list of all the things they can think of that are made of *paragraphs*. This includes newspaper articles, magazine articles, stories, textbook chapters, and so on. It does *not* include poems, plays, and some other creative forms of writing.

P

Ask each student to sketch a quick diagram or other symbolic representation that shows the meanings of all the target words. For example, a student can sketch something that looks like an open book and then have arrows pointing to parts of one of the pages showing where paragraphs are, how they are indented, and where margins are.

Scaffolding

Show students who require scaffolding what a *blurb* is. A *blurb* is a short promotional piece accompanying a creative work, like a book. The author may write it him- or herself. Blurbs often contain praise from others.

Use a marker to draw over the margin lines on a piece of notebook paper and use this as a visual aid. Also, ask students to open any nearby book and to use their index fingers to touch all the paragraph indentations.

Acceleration

Other features of print include sidebars, diagrams, photographs, and so on. Ask advanced students to name as many features of print as they can.

Reading and Research

The lessons in this section all include basic terminology about the process of reading, the different genres and structures students will encounter in school, the most common literary devices, and reference materials.

Lesson A6: *text, composition, passage, excerpt*

In this minilesson, teachers will teach terms relating to reading and research, such as the words *text*, *composition*, *passage*, and *excerpt*.

Difficulty level: 1

S

 The following lists target words students should *see* and *say* for this minilesson.

▸ **Text (n.):** In English class, something that is written or printed, in hard copy or electronically, that we read

▸ **Composition (n.):** A work of literature (a piece of writing), or, more broadly, a work of art or music

▸ **Passage (n.):** A short piece of writing from a book or other longer original source—not the entire piece

▸ **Excerpt (n.):** Often a synonym for passage; a section or sample from a longer original source

N

 Consider saying something like the following to your class.

All of these words are about what we read in school for a class or for a high-stakes test. The word text *or* composition *means the whole thing, whatever it is—an article, a book, a poem, anything that we are reading and that we are possibly being asked about. The other two words mean only part of the whole composition or text. A passage or an excerpt is just one section of a larger whole. These words,* passage *and* excerpt, *are often used on important tests. A passage or an excerpt might appear on a test, and you would be asked to answer questions about it. Basically, this is a way to focus in on an important section or to save time. Obviously, I couldn't print an entire book out for you on a test! That would be way too much paper!*

A

 Have small groups of students discuss the following questions.

▸ Would you most likely read a whole *composition* or just an *excerpt* if you had only five minutes? Why? (probably an *excerpt*, although there are exceptions, like a very short article or a poem)

▸ Would a song be a *composition* or a *passage*? (*composition*)

▸ If you write a paper or a report for one of your classes, is that an *excerpt* or a *composition*? (*composition*)

P

 Ask students to pick the one word that they think will be hardest for them to remember, or the one that they feel they have the least experience with up to this point. Ask them to write a student-friendly definition for that word, using at least one complete sentence. These can be posted around the room for additional learning support.

Scaffolding

 Students can use sentence frames to build their sentences. Following is an example of a sentence frame you might provide.

▸ A _____ is a _____
that _____.

Student examples using this sentence frame might include the following.

▸ A *text* is a piece of writing that has everything included in it.

▸ A *passage* is a piece of text that leaves some things out.

Acceleration

Advanced students may enjoy learning synonyms for *excerpt*. Some you can share with them include *extract*, *portion*, *sample*, and *snippet*. As time allows, they can try to use one or more of these in a sentence. For example, I included a *snippet* from a Dr. Seuss book in my speech to my classmates.

Lesson A7: *visualize, symbolize, illustrate*

In this minilesson, teachers will teach terms relating to reading and research, such as the words *visualize*, *symbolize*, and *illustrate*.

Difficulty level: 1

S

 The following lists target words students should *see* and *say* for this minilesson.

▸ **Visualize (v.):** To see an image or picture in your mind

▸ **Symbolize (v.):** To stand for or represent something else

▸ **Illustrate (v.):** To provide pictures or artwork; to explain something

Teachers often use these words in class, but students may be surprisingly unfamiliar with what they mean. Give examples for *symbolize*, using images if possible. You could show a red rose to *symbolize* love and the American flag to *symbolize* patriotism. Be prepared to explain the second meaning of *illustrate*, which doesn't mean "to draw" or "to provide photos."

N

These words are all verbs that have to do with images, either real or imagined. When you *visualize*, you see images in your mind. A *symbol* creates associations in your mind when you see it. For example, a bald eagle often *symbolizes* the United States. To *illustrate* is to draw or paint something or to describe it in detail using words.

A

Ask small groups to talk about familiar *symbols* to them. If they start naming company logos, that's fine, too—but you may want to stop and teach the word *logo*.

P

Have each student answer the following on paper, or, if you wish, you could conduct this as a think-pair-share (see page 23) instead. It's fine if students debate the answers with each other.

▸ Does the illustrator of a book visualize in order to create his art? (*yes*)

▸ Does the author of a book visualize in order to write his story? (*yes*)

▸ What's something at our school that symbolizes something else? (*the school mascot, the country's flag*)

Scaffolding

Provide these simple definitions for students who struggle.

▸ **Visualize:** To see in your mind

▸ **Symbolize:** To stand for

▸ **Illustrate:** To draw

Acceleration

Advanced students can do a word talk with word questioning around the target words and related words such as *envision* (visualize) and *embellish* (illustrate). Teachers can ask students questions such as the following.

▸ "How are illustrating and visualizing related?"

▸ "Could a person embellish something while illustrating it?"

Lesson A8: *dictionary, thesaurus, encyclopedia*

In this minilesson, teachers will teach terms relating to reference sources, such as the words *dictionary*, *thesaurus*, and *encyclopedia*.

Difficulty level: 1

S

 The following lists target words students should *see* and *say* for this minilesson.

- **Dictionary (n.):** A book or electronic resource that lists the words of a language and gives their meaning, often also providing information about pronunciation, origin, and usage

- **Thesaurus (n.):** A book or electronic resource that gives synonyms (and often, antonyms) for words

- **Encyclopedia (n.):** A book or set of books giving information on many subjects

N

 These are all reference sources. Originally, they were in print form. Now they are also electronic. Show students a few examples by pointing them out in your room or showing websites like Dictionary.com (www.dictionary.com) and the Merriam-Webster dictionary (www.merriam-webster.com). (Visit **go.SolutionTree.com/literacy** to access live links to the websites mentioned in this book.)

Dictionaries and *thesauri* focus on words. An *encyclopedia* is full of information on hundreds of topics. An *encyclopedia* is the most comprehensive resource of those listed here.

A

 Ask students to discuss the following questions.

- Where would you look to find out more about penguins? (*encyclopedia*)

- Where would you look to find the perfect word to put in your story? (*thesaurus*)

- Which resource would you use to find out the meaning of the word *persnickety*? (*dictionary*)

P

Have each student choose two target words and write a sentence or two telling how the two items are different from each other.

Scaffolding

Students may need help with *thesaurus* and *encyclopedia*, as these are probably less familiar than a dictionary. Be prepared to show them hard-copy and online examples.

Acceleration

Advanced students could explore other reference sources, such as almanacs and atlases. You may want to have hard-copy or online examples ready for them to examine.

Lesson A9: *plot, theme, setting, characters, event*

In this minilesson, teachers will teach terms relating to what's happening in a story, such as the words *plot, theme, setting, characters,* and *event.*

Difficulty level: 1

S

The following lists target words students should *see* and *say* for this minilesson.

▸ **Plot (n.):** The main events that occur in a story, movie, and so on

▸ **Theme (n.):** A controlling idea that a work of literature presents; an insight that a reader comes to as a result of reading a work of literature; a lesson "taught" by a work of literature

▸ **Setting (n.):** The time and place in which a story takes place

▸ **Characters (n.):** The people, animals, or other beings in a work of fiction

▸ **Event (n.):** Something that happens, especially if it's important

N

These five components are the basics that any reader must know after having read a work of literature. The elements work in harmony to create a story.

A

Form small groups. Have students do word association by matching words and phrases to the correct literary element.

▸ The main character is in a terrible accident. (*plot* or *event*)

▸ The story is about a family in the 1800s in England. (*setting*)

▸ The ending of the story is surprising. (*plot* or *event*)

- A person in the story becomes friends with another person. (*characters*)

- After reading the story, you feel that you've changed your mind about an issue. (*theme*)

P

Ask each student to think about a story he or she recently read or a movie he or she recently saw. Ask students to identify the main event of the *plot* and to briefly comment on the *theme*.

You may want to provide an example from a book you read together or a movie most of the students have seen before you allow students to write. A classic like *The Wizard of Oz* may be familiar to students. The main event is the film's tornado, and the theme is the heroine's quote "there's no place like home." You may want to reference some Christmas movies, like *A Christmas Story* or *Rudolph the Red-Nosed Reindeer*, which are familiar to many students.

Scaffolding

The *plot* is what happens. The *characters* are the people or animals. The *theme* is what readers or viewers take away from the story. Think of simple ways to remind students what the terms mean.

Acceleration

The *conflict* and *climax* are considered the most important plot elements. The conflict is the main problem that must be solved. The climax is the moment with the highest point of tension, after which the resolution becomes clear—in other words, when the conflict can start to be settled. You may want to teach or review this with advanced students.

Lesson A10: *simile, metaphor, personification, analogy, hyperbole*

In this minilesson, teachers will teach terms relating to reading and research, such as the words *simile, metaphor, personification, analogy,* and *hyperbole*.

Difficulty level: 2

S

The following lists target words students should *see* and *say* for this minilesson.

- **Simile (n.):** A figure of speech involving the comparison of one thing with another thing that seems different

▸ **Metaphor (n.):** A figure of speech in which a word or phrase is applied to an object or action to which it is not literally applicable

▸ **Personification (n.):** The attribution of a personal nature or human characteristics to something nonhuman, or the representation of an abstract quality in human form

▸ **Analogy (n.):** A comparison between two things, typically on the basis of their structure and for the purpose of explanation or clarification

▸ **Hyperbole (n.):** Exaggerated statements or claims not meant to be taken literally

N

These words are all literary terms, but a few of them (*metaphor, analogy, hyperbole*) are also used in everyday speech.

All the words are based on comparing things to other things in some way. With *personification*, we compare nonhuman entities to humans, most commonly with animals, as in cartoons. *Similes, metaphors,* and *analogies* compare one thing to something that is unlike it, or in the case of *analogies*, a pair of things to another pair.

A

Have small groups of students brainstorm examples of *similes, metaphors,* and *personification.* Hungry as a bear, sly as a fox, busy as a bee, sick as a dog, eat like a bird, and swim like a fish are all common *similes.* A blanket of snow, the world's a stage, and I was a pig at dinner are *metaphors.* Nonhuman cartoon characters like SpongeBob SquarePants are examples of *personification.*

P

Ask each student to write one or more *hyperboles* and turn them in. This would be a good time to use a tool like Padlet (https://padlet.com) to display each hyperbole.

Scaffolding

Share the following examples of hyperbole to get students thinking.

▸ I'm so hungry, I could eat a horse.

▸ When I saw that, I almost died.

▸ I've asked you to do that a million times.

Acceleration

Hyperbolic is the adjective form of hyperbole. See if students who have mastered *hyperbole* are interested in this new word.

▸ **Hyperbolic (adj.):** Exaggerated or excessive

Beyond the Lesson

Remind students that they are being hyperbolic when they say things like "It's freezing in here!"

Lesson A11: *retell, paraphrase, summarize*

In this minilesson, teachers will teach terms relating to students telling what they've read, such as the words *retell*, *paraphrase*, and *summarize*.

Difficulty level: 1

S

The following lists target words students should *see* and *say* for this minilesson.

▸ **Retell (v.):** To tell a story again, making sure to cover all the events

▸ **Paraphrase (v.):** To tell a story again, or to tell something someone else said, but in your own words

▸ **Summarize (v.):** To give only the main points of something

These words may be familiar to your students. We ask students to do these things in class, but sometimes they may be confused about exactly what similar words mean.

N

These words are all about reading, listening, or watching something and then telling about it. To *retell* is to tell it as it was told by the author or creator. It's okay in a *retelling* to mimic or use the author or creator's actual wording. To *paraphrase* is to tell the original story but in your own words. And to *summarize* is to condense the original into only the key points. A *summary* is significantly shorter than the original, whereas *retellings* and *paraphrases* may not be.

A

Have students create comparisons to help them remember each word and how it differs slightly from the others. For example, a *summary* would be like a TV commercial, but a retelling would be like the whole show or a movie.

P

Ask each student which he or she would rather do after reading an exciting story—*retell*, *paraphrase*, or *summarize*. Also, ask each student to state why. This can be done in writing or aloud if you run short on time.

Scaffolding

Probably the most important of the three words is *summary*, as teachers and students will use it a great deal throughout the years in school. Help students understand the specifics of a *summary* (for example, that it does not include opinion).

Acceleration

The words *abstract* and *precis* are sometimes used in academia for special types of summaries. You may want to use these words if you have some students who are interested. (Make sure you pronounce *precis* correctly. It's tricky.)

- **Abstract (n.):** A summary of a book, article, or formal speech's content
- **Precis (n.):** A summary, usually of a speech or academic work

Writing

There are many assignments that call for writing as students proceed through school. They will be asked to write various types of papers for their classes and will also have to do many high-stakes writing pieces. The words in the following lessons are basic words that students must master in order to fully understand their writing assignments.

Lesson A12: *plan, prewrite, draft, revise, edit, publish*

In this minilesson, teachers will teach terms relating to the writing process, such as the words *plan*, *prewrite*, *draft*, *revise*, *edit*, and *publish*.

Difficulty level: 1

S

The following lists target words students should *see* and *say* for this minilesson.

- **Plan (v.):** To decide on, design, or arrange the writing in advance
- **Prewrite (v.):** To outline, diagram, storyboard, mind map, or otherwise plan what you will write before you actually write it
- **Draft (v.):** To prepare a piece of writing that is not yet the final version
- **Revise (v.):** To change a draft in order to improve it

▸ **Edit (v.):** To make sure a draft is correct and to get rid of errors

▸ **Publish (v.):** To get a draft ready to be read by its audience

If students have had writing process instruction throughout their years of school, they may know these words, but it's always good to review them.

N

Writers use these words to describe the process of writing and creating. The writing process mirrors other processes that we experience in life, such as the process of cooking a meal. When cooking a meal, you have to get all your ingredients ready; this is the *planning* or *prewriting* phase. The *draft* (writing) is when you cook and taste as you go along. The *drafting* is the act of creating. *Revising* is when you add salt, pepper, or other spices after tasting, and when you turn the temperature up or down. *Editing* is what you do last to get everything ready—perhaps even plate the dishes attractively. And *publishing* is when you serve the food.

A

Ask small groups of students to collaborate and draw a visual that captures these words all together. If you have a visual of the writing process displayed in your classroom, tell them they can't just copy it. If groups struggle, they could think of another process like the example of cooking a meal and depict that, explaining how each part is like writing.

P

Ask each student to pick just two of the target words and write a complete definition for each. As time allows, students could move around the room freely and visit with other students to view their definitions for the other terms.

Scaffolding

Students who require scaffolding may be confused about revising and editing. Revising is more than correcting errors. Emphasize this point.

Acceleration

Proofreading is a word that's often used to mean the final editing. Share this with students. Proofreading includes all checking for grammatical, syntactical, and usage errors, including correcting every punctuation mark if necessary.

Lesson A13: *narrative, expository, informational, opinion, persuasive*

In this minilesson, teachers will teach terms relating to writing genres and forms, such as the words *narrative, expository, informational, opinion,* and *persuasive.*

Difficulty level: 1

S

The following lists target words students should *see* and *say* for this minilesson.

- **Narrative writing (n.):** Writing that tells a story or is rooted in time as its basic structure

- **Expository writing (n.):** Writing that explains something in detail

- **Informational (or informative) writing (n.):** Writing that gives information about a topic, often even very technical writing, as in a brochure or poster

- **Opinion writing (n.):** Writing that tells how the writer feels about something or about his personal preferences

- **Persuasive writing (n.):** Writing that attempts to get the audience to agree with the writer's position and possibly to take action

N

These are the basic types of writing that students will be exposed to and expected to write in elementary school. Check your curriculum materials, and ensure that you also connect to terms and examples used there.

A

Put students in small groups. Assign each group one type of writing. Ask each to decide on three keywords that it can associate with that type of writing. For example, for *narrative*, the keywords might be *story, events,* and *time*. For *persuasive*, the key words might be *position, reasons,* and *action*.

P

Ask each student to choose his or her favorite type to either read or write and to write that down and say why. I might tell my students that my favorite type of writing to read is *informational* because I love to learn about new things. For example, I just read an article about all the ways teachers can use Twitter (https://twitter.com) with their students. Share your own example.

Scaffolding

If students can't think of what to write for step P or tell you they don't like to read or write any type of writing, ask them to write you a note about what they would like you to help them with in their writing. Tell them to give you one specific question or piece of advice.

Acceleration

You may want to have advanced students find Google images (https://images .google.com) or Bing images (www.bing.com/images) of the writing process and to decide on one or two they think you could display in the classroom.

Lesson A14: *evidence, introduction, body, conclusion, transition*

In this minilesson, teachers will teach terms relating to parts of an essay, such as the words *evidence, introduction, body, conclusion,* and *transition.*

Difficulty level: 2

S

The following lists target words students should *see* and *say* for this minilesson.

▸ **Evidence (n.):** Facts or information that could support someone's position

▸ **Introduction (n.):** The act of starting something, as an essay or report

▸ **Body (n.):** The part of an essay or report that develops the main idea

▸ **Conclusion (n.):** The portion that restates or amplifies the thesis or main point; it also closes the essay

▸ **Transition (n.):** Words and phrases that provide a connection between ideas, sentences, and paragraphs; they help to make a piece of writing flow better

If students don't know the word *essay,* you may have to insert it in this minilesson, too. Many students know the word *composition* but may not know *essay.*

▸ **Essay (n.):** A short piece of writing on one subject, usually presenting the author's own views; consists of multiple paragraphs

N

These words are actual components of an *essay.* Perhaps you could show a visual representation with these parts marked, or use a sample essay and mark

it up quickly to show students where these components appear. The parts of an essay are like the parts of a car. If something is not working right, the car won't run. If a part of an essay is left out or is not in good shape, then the essay will not be effective.

A

In pairs, ask students to discuss what part of the essay seems hardest (or easiest) to them.

P

Ask each student to write an original comparison for one of the parts of the essay. Following are some examples you can share or cue students with.

▸ The *introduction* of an essay is like a person's head. It's the first thing you see, and it helps you get to know what's coming next.

▸ A *transition* is like a link in a chain. It keeps all the ideas connected.

Scaffolding

Some students get *evidence* mixed up with *reasons*. Explain that *evidence* is material that supports your reasons. So, in order of importance or level of detail, the thesis or main point is most important. The reasons are the next level. The evidence then is the next level—and it must all support the reasons that then support the thesis. You can show this by quickly sketching an inverted pyramid.

Acceleration

Ask students who have mastered these words what other words they associate with writing essays. They may think of *thesis, thesis statement, claim, argument, title,* and so on.

Beyond the Lesson

Be cautious when using the word *essay*. Make sure that you and your colleagues understand that every essay must contain multiple paragraphs and state a position or central idea. Some teachers use the term "*essay* question" on a test when they want only a few sentences or a paragraph or two. These do not constitute *essays*.

Lesson A15: *describe, explain, persuade, argue, narrate*

In this minilesson, teachers will teach terms relating to an author's purpose, such as the words *describe, explain, persuade, argue,* and *narrate*.

Difficulty level: 1

S

The following lists target words students should *see* and *say* for this minilesson.

▸ **Describe (v.):** To give details about; to help a reader see something in his mind

▸ **Explain (v.):** To give information about

▸ **Persuade (v.):** To convince people to agree with you

▸ **Argue (v.):** To prove that you have a position or claim that is valid

▸ **Narrate (v.):** To tell a story, either real or imagined

N

These words are all verbs. They are all things that writers do. Writers write texts for many reasons. These words reflect some of the main reasons that writers decide to write. Sometimes a text combines reasons. For example, this book is partially to explain how to teach vocabulary minilessons, but it is also intended to be *persuasive*. You may want to give examples from recent materials read in class.

A

Which of the purposes most closely align with each of the following scenarios?

▸ A writer wants to capture the beauty of a sunset. (*describe*)

▸ A politician writes and gives a speech asking that you vote for him. (*persuade, argue*)

▸ A doctor creates a short video about how to prevent getting a cold. (*explain*)

▸ An elderly woman wants to write the story of her life. (*narrate*)

P

Ask each student to write only one or two sentences that show one of the purposes. For example, here is a sentence that is meant to *describe*: the party was full of people in colorful outfits and was filled with laughter and booming voices. You may want to provide examples of your own creation, too.

Scaffolding

Ask students to think about how *describe* and *explain* are different, or how *narrate* and *persuade* are different. Allow them to write about the key differences.

Acceleration

Ask students to think about songwriters and poets. Do they use these same purposes?

Lesson A16: *fact, topic, main idea* or *central idea, thesis* or *thesis statement*

In this minilesson, teachers will teach terms relating to writing, such as the words *fact*, *topic*, *main idea*, *central idea*, and *thesis* or *thesis statement*.

Difficulty level: 2

S

The following lists target words students should *see* and *say* for this minilesson.

▸ **Fact (n.):** Something that is true

▸ **Topic (n.):** What something is about; the subject

▸ **Main idea or central idea (n.):** The most important or central thought of a paragraph or larger section of text

▸ **Thesis or thesis statement (n.):** A short statement, usually a sentence, that summarizes the central idea or claim of an essay, research paper, and so on, and is developed in the text with examples and evidence

N

These words are all related because they are about the subject of a piece of writing. Most writing includes *facts*, unless the main purpose is simply to entertain or to narrate.

Main idea and *central idea* are synonymous. There can be several main or central ideas in any piece of writing. Each paragraph can also have a main or central idea. However, the term *central idea* is often reserved to refer to the entire text.

The *topic* is not the same as the main or central idea. A topic is simply a text's subject or the subject of a paragraph within that text. A topic can be stated in a single word or phrase, whereas a main or central idea must usually be a complete sentence or complete thought.

A *thesis* (also called a *thesis statement*) is the writer's main point. It guides the entire text's development.

A

Form small groups. Ask students if each of the following is a fact, a topic, or a thesis.

> ▸ Labrador retrievers (*topic*)
>
> ▸ A dog is a man's best friend. (*thesis*)
>
> ▸ Dogs have a keen sense of smell. (*fact*)
>
> ▸ Cats are nocturnal. (*fact*)
>
> ▸ Cats are the best house pet. (*thesis*)

P

Ask students to each write a fact and a thesis and turn these in. They should label which is which.

Scaffolding

Encourage students who require scaffolding to use either cats or dogs (or whatever animals you used for step A) to base their work on.

Acceleration

For extra challenge, ask students who have mastered these words to write two thesis statements for step P instead of a fact and a thesis. They can even write two statements that are in opposition to each other.

Speaking, Listening, and Presenting

The following lessons focus on terms that pertain to speaking, listening, and presenting and are often covered as part of language arts lessons starting in grades as low as 1 and 2.

Lesson A17: *speaker, audience, eye contact, volume, visual aids*

In this minilesson, teachers will teach terms relating to speaking, listening, and presenting, such as the words *speaker*, *audience*, *eye contact*, *volume*, and *visual aids*.

Difficulty level: 1

S

The following lists target words students should *see* and *say* for this minilesson.

> ▸ **Speaker (n.):** The person making a presentation

- **Audience (n.):** The people listening to a presentation
- **Eye contact (n.):** Looking at the audience as you speak
- **Volume (n.):** How loud you are as a speaker
- **Visual aids (n.):** Posters, slides, photographs, diagrams, charts, and other things you can use in a presentation to help the audience understand

N

These words are all about the basics of making a good presentation. These words may even appear on rubrics you use to give feedback to students. Review the terms as needed.

A

Pair students up. Have one of them role-play being a presenter and the other be the audience (you may want to pick the more extroverted student in each pair to be the presenter). Tell pairs to imagine they are doing a TV commercial for one of their favorite products—a cereal, toy, video game, and so on. Have the presenter in each pair use his or her best eye contact and volume. Let each student present for a minute or less. Then, ask the audience member to comment on how things went, sticking to eye contact and volume only.

P

Ask every student to write a brief statement about any images (visual aids) that would have helped the presenter during the role play.

Scaffolding

You could share the following template to support students in step P.

- A visual aid that would have helped _____ during the presentation is _____ because _____.

Acceleration

Students can watch Josh Brewer's (2013) video *Tips on Giving Oral Presentations* (http://bit.ly/1N1nPSi) to view a good two-minute tutorial about giving presentations. Brewer is a teacher and offers funny, helpful tips.

Lesson A18: *pronunciation, enunciation, emphasis, accuracy, credibility*

In this minilesson, teachers will teach terms relating to speaking, listening, and presenting, such as the words *pronunciation, enunciation, emphasis, accuracy,* and *credibility.*

Difficulty level: 2

S

 The following lists target words students should *see* and *say* for this minilesson.

- ▸ **Pronunciation (n.):** Saying a word correctly, with the right sounds and emphasis

- ▸ **Enunciation (n.):** Saying a word clearly so people can understand it

- ▸ **Emphasis (n.):** Stress laid on a word or words to get attention, or to indicate special meaning or importance

- ▸ **Accuracy (n.):** The state of being correct or precise

- ▸ **Credibility (n.):** The quality of being convincing or believable

N

Pronunciation, enunciation, and *emphasis* are all related because they are about the mechanics of saying words aloud. They are related to the word *volume,* which may have been studied earlier. A visual of an open mouth may help students remember these three words.

Accuracy and *credibility* are about the quality of the information and the speaker's believability. A visual of a bull's-eye with an arrow shot into it or of balanced scales might be good to represent these two attributes.

A

Have small groups of students discuss speakers they have seen on TV or online that exemplify these qualities. They may come up with ESPN commentators, YouTube celebrities, news anchors, or talk show hosts.

P

Ask each student to write you a brief note describing how he or she will try to enhance his or her *credibility* as a speaker. If this seems too difficult, ask students about *accuracy* instead.

Scaffolding

Speakers who mumble or say words incorrectly are hard to understand. You could demonstrate poor *pronunciation* and *enunciation* to help them see the qualities in action.

Acceleration

The Central Rappahannock Regional Library website provides the article "Speak Up: Giving a Good Oral Report" (Johnson, 2017; www.librarypoint .org/public_speaking) with a good discussion of presentations and links to other resources. You may want to send your students to this site.

Mathematics

Students in many nations are not showing that they have acquired the critical conceptual understanding that they need. Vocabulary is intricately connected with conceptual understanding in all subjects.

Much of mathematics vocabulary is highly specialized, or what Isabel L. Beck, Margaret G. McKeown, and Linda Kucan (2013) call *tier three vocabulary*. Because this book focuses mainly on general academic vocabulary, the lessons in this section include the most important, basic mathematics terms, many of which students should master before leaving the elementary grades. However, because schools are very diverse places, and students have a wide range of needs, teachers often find that students have a surprising lack of knowledge of even basic terms like *sum* or *estimate*. Additionally, many mathematics terms in this chapter are also cross-curricular words that reach beyond the discipline in various ways in reading, writing, speaking, and listening. For example, a poet or other creative writer can use the word *vertex*, figuratively to mean that two people or two forces collide. The word *capacity* is applicable in many settings, but people frequently use it to describe an amount of work that a person or organization can or cannot do, as in, "We simply don't have the *capacity* to fulfill the order right now." Some of the terms in the lessons in this section have precise mathematical meanings yet can also appear in everyday conversation (for example, *addition*, *total*, *accurate*, and *maximize*). Other words are not as common in nonacademic settings but are simply words that educated people know (such as *hypotenuse*, *perimeter*, and *theorem*).

Lesson A19: *addition, add, sum, total*

In this minilesson, teachers will teach terms relating to mathematics, such as the words *addition*, *add*, *sum*, and *total*.

Difficulty level: 1

S

The following lists target words students should *see* and *say* for this minilesson.

- **Addition (n.):** The act or process of joining something to something else

- **Add (v.):** To put together two or more things to increase the number, quantity, or size

- **Sum (n.):** The result of adding two or more numbers, amounts, or items

- **Total (n.):** The whole number or amount of something

You may want to use a teacher gesture when saying the words to help the students remember them. For example, you may have your hands apart, signifying the two parts of something, and then bring them together, making a new part.

For students that have a good understanding of the target words for this minilesson, you may want to teach the following terms.

- **Altogether (adv.):** In total; completely; wholly; totally

- **Combined (adj.):** Joined together; united

N

Consider saying something like the following to your class.

So, you can see that three of these words have to do with putting two or more items together ending with a bigger total. *The other two words refer to the effect of the items being put together. When we* add, *or have an* addition *problem, we are joining parts that end up being a larger part. The larger part that we end up with is the* total *or the* sum.

A

Small groups or pairs should discuss how the words are different and how they are the same (for just a couple of minutes). For example, they should notice that *addition* is the actual process of joining two or more items and that *addend* is the actual part that they are putting together to get a *sum*. Have groups share aloud one thing that they discovered through their discussion.

P

Have students use two or more of the target words in sentences that explain the process that each word represents. This can be done in writing or verbally or by conducting a Whip Around (see page 27) in which they must say aloud at least one of their answers.

Possible student answers include the following.

> ▸ I want chips in *addition* to the cookies.

> ▸ I had a pencil and a crayon to *add* to the supplies.

> ▸ I read for a *total* of thirty minutes yesterday.

Scaffolding

Offer students who struggle one or more of these sentences. They can place the correct word in each sentence instead of creating an original sentence. If you do the Whip Around, they will still have something to share aloud like the other students.

> ▸ What is the _____ number of students in class? (*total*)

> ▸ Could I _____ another book to my order? (*add*)

> ▸ The _____ of the problem was 5. (*sum*)

> ▸ There was a new _____ to the family. (*addition*)

Acceleration

Have students visit Math Is Fun's (n.d.b) "Definition of Addition" (www .mathsisfun.com/definitions/addition.html) to explore more about these words. Also, in the Whip Around in step P, you can challenge students to use two or more words in the same sentence, still ensuring that the sentence is grammatically correct.

Lesson A20: *accurate, accuracy, precise, precision*

In this minilesson, teachers will teach terms relating to mathematics, such as the words *accurate, accuracy, precise,* and *precision.*

Difficulty level: 2

S

The following lists target words students should *see* and *say* for this minilesson. Have the following words available for your students to see as you read and define each word. Reread the word list, and have students join you in saying the words. These words may be read with you or echoed.

> ▸ **Accurate (adj.):** Precise; exact; correct in details

> ▸ **Accuracy (n.):** The quality or state of being correct, true, or exact

> ▸ **Precise (adj.):** Exactly defined; marked by exactness of expression or detail

> ▸ **Precision (n.):** The state or condition of being exact or accurate

N

Consider saying something like the following to your class.

The commonality between these words is that they all mean to be exact. When you are exact there is no room for mistakes. These words mean that things are correct or are being done correctly. When we solve mathematics problems, we need accuracy *to be correct in our answers. If we are not* accurate *in work, we will have the wrong answers. We use* precision *when aligning numbers in a problem in order to have the equation be* precise.

A

Have small groups discuss the following questions.

▸ What are some things that must be *accurate* or *precise*? (Possible answers: An answer on a mathematics test, a measurement of your shoe size, an ingredient in a recipe for a cake, knowing the amount of money in your bank account)

▸ What are some things that don't have to be *accurate* or *precise*? (Possible answers: A prediction about the weather, an estimate of any type, an inference while reading)

P

Have two sticky notes (or use Padlet or TodaysMeet) for students to record their sentences explaining *accurate* or *accuracy* in one, and *precise* or *precision* in the second. The noun forms of the words may be more difficult for students, so be prepared to guide them.

Sample explanations include the following.

▸ Being *accurate* means that you are not careless in your actions to solve problems correctly.

▸ To have good *precision* means that you pay attention to details and are exact in what you do.

Scaffolding

Have students read Math Is Fun's (n.d.a) webpage "Accuracy and Precision" (www.mathsisfun.com/accuracy-precision.html) for additional help. (Visit **go .SolutionTree.com/literacy** to access live links to the websites mentioned in this book.)

Acceleration

Introduce students to the following two antonyms.

▸ **Imprecision (n.):** Something that is not accurate; vague; not
defined well

▸ **Inaccuracy (n.):** Something that is incorrect or untrue; a mistake

Although teachers don't use them often in mathematics instruction, these terms certainly have applications across disciplines. Challenge students to use each word in a sentence for step P.

Lesson A21: *approximate, approximately, estimate, estimation*

In this minilesson, teachers will teach terms relating to mathematics, such as the words *approximate, approximately, estimate,* and *estimation.*

Difficulty level: 2

S

 The following lists target words students should *see* and *say* for this minilesson. As you pronounce and define the following words, have a list of them available for students to see.

▸ **Approximate (adj.):** Close to a certain value or amount

▸ **Approximately (adv.):** Very close to, but not exact

▸ **Estimate (n.):** An approximate guess

▸ **Estimation (n.):** A rough calculation of a value, number, or quantity

N

These words are all words that are related to the concept of being inexact or imprecise but "in the ballpark," colloquially. Students may be familiar with the qualities of *estimation* from previous mathematics instruction. Ask them what they already know. Perhaps the best expression to use with the explanation of these terms is "an educated guess."

Add the noun *approximation* if it fits into the discussion at this point.

A

Have small groups discuss the following questions. Provide your own examples to get the groups started if you need to.

▸ How might a recipe be related to the word *approximate*? (*Some recipes tell you approximate amounts instead of exact amounts, like "a pinch of salt" or "a drizzle of oil."*)

▸ How could an *estimation* be related to money? (*People often estimate how much money they will need to pay their regular bills, how much will be taken out in taxes, and so on.*)

P

Have students choose two of the words to use authentically in sentences or a short paragraph.

Scaffolding

The word *estimate* can also be a verb and is pronounced differently than when it is a noun. Be prepared to clear up any confusion about this if the topic arises.

Acceleration

Students who have mastered these words might enjoy learning the informal word *guesstimate*. Ask them if they can create any other words that go along with the concept of estimation or approximation.

▸ **Guesstimate (n.):** An estimate based on a mixture of guesswork and rough calculation

Lesson A22: *area, perimeter, capacity, volume*

In this minilesson, teachers will teach terms relating to mathematics, such as the words *area*, *perimeter*, *capacity*, and *volume*.

Difficulty level: 2

S

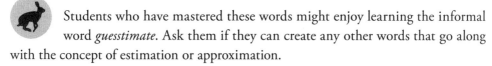
The following lists target words students should *see* and *say* for this minilesson.

▸ **Area (n.):** The amount of space inside a designated boundary

▸ **Perimeter (n.):** The distance around a boundary

▸ **Capacity (n.):** The largest amount that something can hold

▸ **Volume (n.):** The amount of space that something occupies

Clarify for students that this kind of volume is not about sound but instead is about the amount of space that an object fills.

N

These words are all about measuring space. People use the terms *area* and *perimeter* for measuring and marking space on the ground or in rooms (for fences, borders, sod, carpeting, tile, and so on). *Capacity* and *volume* are about how many or how much something can hold or the shape it takes.

A

Have small groups match the appropriate term with each of the following examples. Reorder the examples as you wish, and add your own.

- A grassy spot that's fenced in (*area*)

- Walking around the outside wall of the school (*perimeter*)

- All the marbles or pieces of candy that will fit into a large jar (*capacity*)

- Two liters of liquid in a bottle, like a soda bottle (*volume*)

- The maximum number of people that can safely be in our classroom (*capacity*)

- The mulch we would need in a flower bed (*area*)

P

Have each student choose two or more target words and draw a labeled diagram showing you an example of the use of the words.

Scaffolding

Step P can be done in pairs instead of individually. Ensure both partners are participating fully in the drawing and labeling process.

Acceleration

Students who have mastered these words may enjoy working more with volume, which is the most difficult type of measurement in this set of terms. See Learn Zillion's video about volume, titled *Understand Volume and How Volume Is Measured* (Nix, n.d.; http://bit.ly/2iKy0xD), for more information. You may want these students to view this and then write about it for their step P.

Lesson A23: *circle, circumference, diameter, radius*

In this minilesson, teachers will teach terms relating to mathematics, such as the words *circle*, *circumference*, *diameter*, and *radius*.

Difficulty level: 2

S

The following lists target words students should *see* and *say* for this minilesson.

- **Circle (n.):** A round plane figure whose boundary (the circumference) consists of points equally distant from a fixed point (the center)

- **Circumference (n.):** The outer boundary of a circle

- **Diameter (n.):** Any straight line segment that passes through the circle's center and whose endpoints lie on the circle

- **Radius (n.):** A straight line from the center of a circle to the outer boundary

N

These terms are all nouns and are all critical to understanding circles. Call students' attention to the first parts of *circle* and *circumference*—*circ* is a root from the Latin meaning "ring," and *circum-* is a prefix from the Latin meaning "around." Remembering these word parts can help them with words outside of mathematics content. *Diameter* and *radius*, however, must be remembered as they are because they can't be subdivided.

A

Allow students to work in pairs. Ask each pair to draw a circle and label it using all the terms.

P

Ask students to list all the common items they think of (in only a few minutes) that have a circumference (or, in other words, that are circular in shape). Some possible answers include a pencil, a can of soda or soup, a cup or glass, a bottle, or a flagpole.

Scaffolding

After step A is complete, post some of the diagrams to assist students visually as they do step P.

Acceleration

Students who have mastered these words may enjoy exploring other words that have similar word parts and that are used in academic text outside of mathematics, such as the following.

- **Circa (prep.):** Approximately or around; used when discussing dates

- **Circulate (v.):** To move in a circle or cycle, coming back to the starting point

- **Circumnavigate (v.):** To move around something, usually by sailing or flying

- **Circumscribe (v.):** To encircle or close within boundaries

Lesson A24: *compute, calculate, estimate*

In this minilesson, teachers will teach terms relating to mathematics, such as the words *compute*, *calculate*, and *estimate*.

Difficulty level: 1

S

The following lists target words students should *see* and *say* for this minilesson.

▶ **Compute (v.):** To determine; to have something make sense

▶ **Calculate (v.):** To find an answer by using mathematics

▶ **Estimate (v.):** To make a rough calculation or informed guess

These three words, in this order, can be said aloud and repeated with a memorable rhythm. This may enhance memory. The first two are basically synonyms for each other, but the third is different because it's not as precise.

N

All these words are verbs that involve mental action. They have specific mathematical meanings but are also used in general conversation and in other academic areas. Share some of your own examples such as *computing* how much your electric bill may be in the summer versus the winter or *calculating* how much you may need to save each month in order to afford a vacation next year.

A

Have pairs or small groups discuss the following questions.

▶ How are the words *compute* and *calculate* related?

▶ How is the word *estimate* similar to the word *predict*? How is it different?

P

Ask each student to write a sentence with each word. You can also challenge students to write a very short poem or rap if they prefer. Because *calculate* and *estimate* have the same syllable count and same last syllable, they can easily be part of a short, rhythmic text.

Scaffolding

Provide sentence stems like the following if you think they will support students who require scaffolding.

> ‣ *Compute* and *calculate* are similar because they
> both _____.

> ‣ *Estimate* is different because it _____.

Acceleration

Ask students who have mastered these words to explore the related words *appraise* and *enumerate*.

> ‣ **Appraise (v.):** To estimate the worth or value of

> ‣ **Enumerate (v.):** To list a number of things one by one

Lesson A25: *constant, variable*

In this minilesson, teachers will teach terms relating to mathematics, such as the words *constant* and *variable*.

Difficulty level: 2

S

The following lists target words students should *see* and *say* for this minilesson.

> ‣ **Constant (adj. and n.):** Staying the same, not changing; in algebra, a constant is a number on its own, or sometimes a letter to stand for a fixed number

> ‣ **Variable (adj. and n.):** Not always the same, able to change; in algebra, a quantity that may change within the context of a problem or experiment, usually represented by a single letter

N

The general meanings of the adjective forms of these words are also represented in the meaning of the mathematical terms, which are used as nouns. The two words in a general (nonmathematical) context are opposites, and this is also true for their specialized meanings. Emphasize that they are opposites, and provide as many examples of things that are constant and things that are variable as you can think of that will connect well with your students. For example, the outside temperature (and the temperature in one's own body) is *variable*, whereas the date an event occurred in the past is *constant*.

A

Have pairs discuss things from their own lives that are *constant* and *variable*. They may say that the love from a family member or pet is constant, for example, and that their ages are always variable.

P

Ask each student to write a short paragraph summarizing the conversation he or she had in step A. If time allows, students can compare their summaries with their partners and change anything they wish to change before turning in their paragraphs.

Scaffolding

Post some examples of *constants* and *variables* to assist students in steps A and P. Use the ones in table 7.1, or create your own.

Table 7.1: Examples of Constants and Variables

Constants	Variables
A grandmother's love	Body temperature
A pet dog's loyalty	The earth's temperature
The rotation of the earth on its axis	Your age
	The amount of food you eat
	The amount of sleep you get

Acceleration

Allow students to review or learn the term *coefficient* (because it's related to *variable*). Ask them to use both terms in a sentence.

▸ **Coefficient (n.):** A number used to multiply a variable

Lesson A26: *convert, reduce*

In this minilesson, teachers will teach terms relating to mathematics, such as the words *convert* and *reduce*.

Difficulty level: 2

S

The following lists target words students should *see* and *say* for this minilesson.

▸ **Convert (v.):** To change into another form; in mathematics, changing the form of a measurement to different units, without changing the size or total amount

▸ **Reduce (v.):** To make something smaller; in mathematics, rewriting any expression into a simpler form

N

These two words have a similar general meaning and a similar mathematical meaning. They are both about changing the form of something, but *reducing* is always about making something smaller and more efficient.

A

Ask small groups of students to discuss things outside mathematics that can be converted or reduced. For example, a person can *convert* glass bottles into mosaics by breaking the glass and using the pieces to make a new object. Also, a person can *reduce* his or her weight through diet and exercise.

P

Ask each student to write a short paragraph summarizing the conversation he or she had in step A. If time allows, students can compare their summaries with others and change anything they wish to change before turning them in.

Scaffolding

Students may know that a *convertible* is a type of car. Explain why they have this name; the car literally changes its features. This example may help students remember more about the general meaning of the word *convert*. Also, ask students if they know about food products that are *reduced* fat or *reduced* sugar. Obviously, this means that the items contain less of the particular substance.

Acceleration

Students can read Vocabulary.com's entry on the word *convert* (www.vocabulary .com/dictionary/convert) to access an interesting discussion of the word. Students may enjoy reading through this and discussing it with a partner or two.

Lesson A27: *maximize, maximum, minimize, minimum*

In this minilesson, teachers will teach terms relating to mathematics, such as the words *maximize*, *maximum*, *minimize*, and *minimum*.

Difficulty level: 2

S

 The following lists target words students should *see* and *say* for this minilesson.

- **Maximize (v.):** To increase something as much as possible
- **Maximum (adj.):** As high or as great as allowed
- **Minimize (v.):** To reduce something as much as possible
- **Minimum (adj.):** The smallest or lowest

N

Maximize and *minimize* are opposites, as are *maximum* and *minimum*. You may want to use teacher gestures as you discuss these words—perhaps place your arms out wide in a big circle for *maximize* and *maximum* and then clasp them together in a small ball for *minimize* and *minimum*.

You can tell students to remember *maximize* and *maximum* as "most" and *minimize* and *minimum* as "least." Point out that the word *mini* appears in *minimize* and *minimum* as a cue to help them remember that these words mean "just a tiny bit."

A

Have small groups of students discuss things they could *maximize* and *minimize*. For example, I might say that I'd like to *maximize* the amount of sleep I get every night and *minimize* the amount of unhealthy food I eat each day, but I'm not always successful at either of these. They might want to *minimize* their time studying or *maximize* their talent in a certain sport.

P

Each student should choose two of the words that are opposites and compose sentences with them.

Scaffolding

It's fine for students who require scaffolding to repeat something in writing that was said verbally in the group discussion. The key is for them to get practice using the words in writing.

Acceleration

Maximize is similar to *optimize*. Share this word with advanced students (or all students).

> **Optimize (v.):** To make the best or most effective use of a situation, opportunity, or resource

The Classroom Learning Environment

The following minilesson focuses on terms that pertain to the classroom learning environment. These are terms your students are likely to hear in instructions for activities or see in instructions for assignments or assessments.

Lesson A28: *cooperate, collaborate, create*

In this minilesson, teachers will teach terms relating to the classroom, such as the words *cooperate*, *collaborate*, and *create*.

Difficulty level: 1

S

The following lists target words students should *see* and *say* for this minilesson.

- **Cooperate (v.):** To work with others in an agreeable way
- **Collaborate (v.):** To accomplish something while working with others
- **Create (v.):** To make something original

N

Consider saying something like the following.

In our classroom, we will work together. We will work together when we learn and when we play. In order for that work to be done in a calm way we will use these words to help us: cooperate, collaborate, *and* create. *We will get along with others so that there is* cooperation. *When we work in groups to accomplish a task we* collaborate *on it. When I ask you to make something as a group, you* create *the work together so that I can see what you have done.*

A

Have students work in groups to brainstorm examples of how they collaborate, cooperate, and create in class. Have a few of the groups share out with the whole class until all three words have been described.

P

Students will create a vocabulary frame for each word. The frame will consist of the vocabulary term in the middle of a note card or sticky note, a definition of their own understanding (right corner), a sentence to remind them of the word's meaning (bottom left corner), and a quick sketch (lower right corner).

Scaffolding

Do a word match-up by listing the definitions and the words in separate columns and having students match each meaning with the correct term.

Acceleration

Ask students who have mastered these words to think about, talk about, and even write about how cooperation and collaboration differ.

Lesson A29: *sort, organize, arrange*

In this minilesson, teachers will teach terms about patterns, such as the words *sort*, *organize*, and *arrange*.

Difficulty level: 1

S

The following lists target words students should *see* and *say* for this minilesson.

▸ **Sort (v.):** To arrange in groups, often by similarities

▸ **Organize (v.):** To create a specific order for something

▸ **Arrange (v.):** To put into a specific order or pattern

N

Consider saying something like the following to your class.

> The three words that we are discussing today are synonyms. When we sort, organize, and arrange we are doing similar kinds of things to different objects or items. The difference in what we do is very subtle. When we sort *items, we decide on a way that we will separate them.* When we organize *those sorted items, we decide how we want them to be together.* To arrange *the items, we can create a display for others to see how we have* sorted *and* organized. We can do this with words, numbers, books, toys, and so on. Sometimes, the directions on an assignment or test will tell you how things need to be sorted, organized, or arranged. *Other times, you can come up with your own ways of figuring out the specific order.*

A

Have pairs of students brainstorm the different types of items in class or at home that they need to organize, sort, and arrange. For example, they see that the attendance list is organized in alphabetical order. The classroom library is arranged by book genres, and the books in those genres can be sorted in alphabetical order by author or title. Have pairs share out some of the categories that they discover around the classroom or that they remember from other contexts.

P

Have the students use each word in a sentence. They can use categories identified during their partner work from step A. Have students turn their work in.

Scaffolding

Arranging and organizing are basically the same action. However, to sort is to form groups for a certain reason. Help students understand this.

Acceleration

Have students sketch the words and write a sentence demonstrating their understanding of each word.

Lesson A30: *compare, classify, categorize*

In this minilesson, teachers will teach terms about similarities, such as the words *compare*, *classify*, and *categorize*.

Difficulty level: 1

S

The following lists target words students should *see* and *say* for this minilesson.

▸ **Compare (v.):** To look at two or more things to notice similarities and differences

▸ **Classify (v.):** To arrange items by how they are alike

▸ **Categorize (v.):** To put things in groups by how they are alike and different

N

Consider saying something like the following to your class.

> *When we want to notice characteristics about one or more things, we can com-pare them. We can find characteristics that are the same, and we can find differences. Once we have found common characteristics we can classify them or arrange them in a way by how they are alike. We can also have categories of items—groups of things that are the same or different. If we have two dogs, we can compare how they are the same and how they are different. We can then classify many dogs by characteristics that are the same, such as if they have long ears or curly tails. We can make categories of all types of animals and use a variety of characteristics for the categories. When we use the words compare, classify, and categorize, we are looking at specific things to create groupings.*

A

Have groups of students discuss as many examples as they can think of where things are classified or categorized. For example, in grocery stores, products are arranged by type. The cereal aisle might be one that students are familiar with. Ask them to think about how cereals are classified (by brand, type, and so on).

P

Ask students to create a poster for the three target words. Students should write the word, then write the definition in their own words and add at least three images representing the term. Collect their work.

Scaffolding

Have students compare two items, such as their shirts or shoes, and explain the comparison. Encourage the use of the word *compare*. Then have the students continue to demonstrate using *classify* and *categorize*, also including a verbal explanation. Insist that they use the vocabulary terms in their explanations.

Acceleration

Have students write a paragraph using the words *compare*, *classify*, and *categorize*. If you think it would be helpful, read the following example aloud to them first.

> *When I go grocery shopping, I compare prices. Many times, I buy the cheaper of two items. I like how items are categorized in the supermarket. For example, all the canned vegetables are in one area.*

Lesson A31: *connect, relate, associate*

In this minilesson, teachers will teach terms about relationships, such as the words *connect*, *relate*, and *associate*.

Difficulty level: 1

S

The following lists target words students should *see* and *say* for this minilesson.

▸ **Connect (v.):** To join two or more things together

▸ **Relate (v.):** To show or say how things go together or remind you of each other

▸ **Associate (v.):** To think how one thing goes with another

N

Consider saying something like the following.

> *The new words that we are learning today have the common meaning of how things go together. When we* connect *with something or someone it's because we might have common interests. We might need to show how two or more things* relate. *To do that, we would discuss or write about common characteristics or the things that we think link them together. When we use the word*

associate, it helps us to think of how one thing goes with another. For example, when I think of pancakes I automatically associate *pancakes with syrup. These two foods go together. They are* related. *They are* connected.

A

Have students work in pairs to discuss the terms and how they would use the words *connect* in mathematics, *relate* in social studies, and *associate* in reading. Have students share one example.

P

Students will use each word in a sentence demonstrating their understanding of the word. Collect the work from the students.

Scaffolding

For those students that need further assistance in understanding the terms, give them a word bank of things that go together so they can create their sentences. For example, peanut butter and jelly, movies and popcorn, rain and umbrella, wind and kite, and so on.

Acceleration

Have students who have mastered these words explore synonyms for the target words at WordHippo.

Lesson A32: *persevere, persist, perseverant, persistent*

In this minilesson, teachers will teach terms relating to work habits, such as the words *persevere, persist, perseverant,* and *persistent.*

Difficulty level: 1

S

The following lists target words students should *see* and *say* for this minilesson.

- ▸ **Persevere (v.):** To stick with doing something even though it may be difficult
- ▸ **Persist (v.):** To continue with a task despite the difficulties it presents
- ▸ **Perseverant (adj.):** Able to keep trying
- ▸ **Persistent (adj.):** Continuing to try to do something even though it is hard

N

Consider saying something like the following.

In this class, we work hard. We work hard to learn, to do our work, and to get along with each other. Sometimes it's hard to keep working hard, to get our work done—and sometimes it might even be hard to get along. When that happens, we use the meaning of the words persevere *and* persist. Persevere *and* persist *are synonyms. When we* persevere, *we stick with doing something even though it might be difficult and we want to quit. We* persist *in learning something new because most of the time, we're going to get new learning wrong before we get it right. And that is okay.* Persevere *and* persist *are verbs that are also synonyms; it's what we do and how we behave when tasks are difficult, but we don't give up. The words that describe those behaviors or students that exemplify that characteristic to sticking to it are* perseverant *and* persistent.

A

In small groups, have the students describe tasks or times in which they had to persist or persevere. Then have them brainstorm people that they know that are persistent or perseverant.

P

Have students create a vocabulary frame for each word. In the middle of the card or sticky note, they will write the vocabulary word. Then in the upper right corner, they should write the definition based on their own understanding, as well as the opposite in the upper left corner. Then they will write a sentence using the word in the lower left corner and draw a quick sketch in the lower right corner. Collect the students' work.

Scaffolding

Have students fill in the blanks of the following sentence frame using an appropriate target word.

▸ The boy kept walking through the rain until he reached the finish line showing his ability to _____ through difficult circumstances. (*persevere* or *persist*) He was very _____ in his actions. (*persistent* or *perseverant*)

Acceleration

Introduce the students to the word *tenacious*. Explain to them that being very determined to do something defines the word *tenacious*. Then, have the students use Wordle (www.wordle.net) to collect words and ideas for each of the terms.

They can use the new vocabulary word in a sentence demonstrating their understanding of the word. For example, "The boy was very persistent when learning to ride his bike."

Lesson A33: *respect, respectful, disrespect, disrespectful*

In this minilesson, teachers will teach terms relating to how we treat others, such as the words *respect, respectful, disrespect,* and *disrespectful.*

Difficulty level: 1

S

The following lists target words students should *see* and *say* for this minilesson.

- ▸ **Respect (v.):** To admire someone for his or her abilities

- ▸ **Respectful (adj.):** To show politeness to someone you admire

- ▸ **Disrespect (v.):** To have a lack of admiration for someone

- ▸ **Disrespectful (adj.):** To be impolite to someone

N

Consider saying something like the following to your class.

The words that we are learning about today are antonyms—they have opposite meanings. When we add the suffix -ful to the words, it changes the word from a verb to an adjective. The word goes from being something that you do to something that you can be described as. When we use the words respectful *or* disrespectful, *we describe someone that is admiring or not showing their fondness for a particular person or situation. In this classroom, we strive to have* respect *for others in the way we treat them and their belongings.*

A

In small groups have students discuss characters that they *respect* or *disrespect* from stories that you've shared with them or that they have read independently, and why they feel that way. Then have them discuss characters that they feel exhibit *respectful* or *disrespectful* behaviors toward others in the stories. Have a few students report out their examples of *respect* or *disrespect* and *respectful* or *disrespectful.*

P

Ask each student to choose either the word *respect* or *disrespect* and complete a concept circle (see chapter 2, page 16) for that word. You could pair students if you feel this would help the activity go more quickly.

Some possible explanations that you might see include the following.

▸ I respect my classmates by leaving their stuff alone.

▸ The players show respect by taking a knee when the injured player is on the ground.

Scaffolding

Emphasize that the *dis-* prefix in this case changes something from good to bad. See if they can think of other words in which the prefix has the same function.

Acceleration

Students may be interested in this related word.

▸ **Reverence (n.):** A feeling of awe and great admiration

Lesson A34: *responsibilities, procedures, consequences*

In this minilesson, teachers will teach terms about rules, such as the words *responsibilities, procedures,* and *consequences*.

Difficulty level: 1

S

The following lists target words students should *see* and *say* for this minilesson.

▸ **Responsibilities (n.):** Duties; things you are accountable for that are within your control

▸ **Procedures (n.):** The ways that things are done; rules

▸ **Consequences (n.):** The results of an action

N

Consider saying something like the following to your class.

When we set the guidelines for how we will behave in class and school, we talked about the responsibilities *that each of you has. This means that you have certain things that you need to do on your own that I am going to hold you accountable for or depend on you to do. For example, it is my* responsibility *to be prepared to teach you every day, and my principal is expecting me to do that. There are* consequences *for the times that* responsibilities *aren't met. A* consequence *can be a negative action for a* responsibility *not being done. At my house, it is my son's* responsibility *to empty the dishwasher, and when he does he can then play video games, but if he doesn't do it, then the* consequence *is that he cannot play video games. We have* procedures *in class that help us with our* responsibilities. *We have morning* procedures *which are the certain things that you need to do in order to be ready to learn for the day. Some procedures are putting your backpack away, turning in your homework, and having two pencils sharp and ready at your seat. Procedures really take away any questions about how certain things need to be done; they help create order.*

A

In small groups, have students brainstorm different responsibilities they have at school and at home, and what the consequences are if those responsibilities aren't met. Do they have any suggestions for additional responsibilities or consequences? Have them discuss how procedures help them at school, at home, and in life. Have students share their ideas.

P

Have students choose one of the words to do a Frayer model (see chapter 2, page 18) with. In the middle of their paper or notecard, have them write the word. In the upper left corner they will write the definition, in the upper right corner they will give characteristics of the word, in the bottom left corner they will give examples of the word, and finally in the bottom right corner they will give nonexamples. If you prefer, you can do a modified Frayer model instead.

Scaffolding

Help students who require scaffolding understand the words by carefully choosing real-life examples to use with them. Perhaps you can cite specific responsibilities they have in your class. You can also remind them of rules (*procedures*) in your classroom and the school and review consequences for breaking those rules.

Acceleration

Challenge advanced students to find as many synonyms as they can for these words. You may want to direct them to WordHippo or Thesaurus.com.

Final Thoughts

Students are subject to many tests as they progress through school. Certain words appear over and over again. The words in this chapter are a good basic set that can serve students well as they are exposed to numerous high-stakes tests.

Varied Voice

We teachers often bemoan the words that our students use—the slang that creeps in, the text message–like writing, the basic words that are used repetitively. In this chapter, the lessons will support you as you encourage your students to break out of the ordinary word rut and use more sophisticated, accurate words in both writing and speaking. First, we address perhaps the most tired word in all student writing, the ubiquitous *said*. Then we cover replacements for another tired and vague word, *nice*.

Words to Replace the Overused Verb *Said*

Students use common and unspecific words in much of their normal everyday conversation, and this lack of imagination and diversity often carries over to their writing. These first few lessons help students distinguish among various shades of meaning and choose better words for *said*.

Lesson W1: *announced, blurted, ordered, complained*

In this minilesson, teachers will teach words to use in place of *said*, such as the words *announced*, *blurted*, *ordered*, and *complained*.

Difficulty level: 1

The following lists target words students should *see* and *say* for this minilesson.

- **Announced (v.):** To have made something known in a loud and definite way
- **Blurted (v.):** To have told something without much thought, often interrupting something
- **Ordered (v.):** To have directed or instructed others
- **Complained (v.):** To have expressed unhappiness about something

N

Explain to students that this list of words can replace *said* in their writing. Students should understand that not all people simply say statements but say them in specific ways. This particular list of words replaces *said* by using words that have a stronger emotion behind them. For example, to demonstrate the use of the words you might do one of the following.

- Have students work quietly in groups, and then blurt something in their direction, interrupting the work.
- Give very stern orders to a group about a task it needs to accomplish.

Use of exaggeration in how you say the statements, exemplifying the use of the word, will help the students gain a better understanding of the word.

A

In small groups or pairs, have students choose two or more of the target words and collaborate on how they will demonstrate the words' use. They can act them out like the teacher modeling did. Allow time for all groups to share their examples.

P

From the following list, have students choose at least two words and write a sentence using each word. Collect student work. Possible student answers include the following.

- Tom *blurted* the answer out during the test.
- The coach *ordered* the team to run more laps.
- It started to rain before recess, causing the students to *complain*.

Scaffolding

Have students match each sentence with the correct vocabulary word that can replace *said*.

- _____ The principal said that students would no longer have recess after lunch. (*ordered*)

▸ _____ "I don't want to go to bed," said the little boy. (*announced*)

▸ _____ The student was so excited that she said, "Oh my goodness!" during silent reading time. (*complained*)

▸ _____ My big brother said I had to do his chores. (*blurted*)

Acceleration

Have students reread a notebook entry or other piece of writing and look for places in which they could replace *said* with one or more of the vocabulary words from the list.

Lesson W2: *demanded, exclaimed, informed, questioned*

In this minilesson, teachers will teach words to use in place of *said*, such as the words *demanded, exclaimed, informed,* and *questioned*.

Difficulty level: 1

S

The following lists target words students should *see* and *say* for this minilesson.

▸ **Demanded (v.):** To have said in a bossy way

▸ **Exclaimed (v.):** To have said something in a sudden, surprised, or angry way

▸ **Informed (v.):** To have said something that shows or shares knowledge with others

▸ **Questioned (v.):** To have asked for more information

N

Explain the value of using other words for *said* when writing and how it changes what the reader understands about the writing. Have the following sentences or something even more specific for your students available to see.

▸ I informed the class that we will be taking a test on Friday.

▸ My parents demanded that I pay for the window that I broke with my baseball.

▸ "Why do we need to take a test?" questioned the class.

▸ "Wow!" I exclaimed after I found one hundred dollars lying on the sidewalk.

A

Small groups can decide how the replacement words sound in a sentence. What are the emotions and tones that the variety of words represents? How do the words sound? What kinds of things would characters be doing or feeling to make them use these words? Have each group give a demonstration using their replacement word for *said*.

P

Have students choose two of the replacement words for *said* and use them in a paragraph. Collect student work.

Scaffolding

Have students fill in the missing word for *said*, using context about the situation to determine how the character might be speaking.

▶ "We will be going on a field trip next week," _____ the teacher. (*informed*)

▶ The teacher _____ the students be on their best behavior as they would be visiting a museum. (*demanded*)

▶ "Not a museum!" _____ the student. (*exclaimed*)

▶ "Yay! A museum," another student _____. (*exclaimed*)

▶ "Is there a gift shop?" _____ a boy. (*questioned*)

Acceleration

The expressions "spill the beans" and "let the cat out of the bag" are related to the words *exclaim* and *inform*. Help students understand these expressions.

Lesson W3: *pleaded, snapped, gasped, whispered*

In this minilesson, teachers will teach words to use in place of *said*, such as the words *pleaded, snapped, gasped,* and *whispered*.

Difficulty level: 1

S

The following lists target words students should *see* and *say* for this minilesson.

▶ **Pleaded (v.):** To have asked for something in an emotional way; to have begged

▶ **Snapped (v.):** To have replied quickly or in an irritated way

- **Gasped (v.):** To have said something while out of breath, often because of feeling strong emotion or experiencing pain

- **Whispered (v.):** To have spoken very softly or to have said something in secret

You may choose to cover this list multiple times, making sure you actually exemplify the type of speaking as you share the definitions.

N

Explain to the students that this list of words can replace *said* in their writing. Students should understand that not all people simply say statements, but say them in specific ways. This particular list replaces *said* by using words that have a specific tone or amount of breath being used when the words are spoken. For example, demonstrate the word *plead* to your students by using it to convince them to use words other than *said* in their writing assignments to make them more interesting for you to grade. Have students group the replacement words for *said* from softest to loudest as they would be heard from the reader's perspective.

A

In those same groups, have students role-play as a character acting out their replacement word for *said*. They may use the words in a sentence, or they may simply act out the word.

P

Have students reread a recent piece of their writing and revise the sentence using two or three of the replacement words for *said*. Collect the revisions.

Scaffolding

In the following sentences, have students fill in the missing word for *said*, using context about the situation to know how the character might be speaking.

- "May we get a puppy?" _____ the kids. (*pleaded*)

- "No," _____ the mother. (*snapped*)

- The children _____, "We always get our way with dad." (*whispered*)

Acceleration

Have students create their own comic strip, applying their new vocabulary words.

Lesson W4: *acknowledged, boasted, chimed in, interjected*

In this minilesson, teachers will teach words to use in place of *said*, such as the words *acknowledged*, *boasted*, *chimed in*, and *interjected*.

Difficulty level: 2

S

The following lists target words students should *see* and *say* for this minilesson.

- **Acknowledged (v.):** To have shown acceptance or to have admitted that something is true or correct

- **Boasted (v.):** To have spoken with pride about oneself; to have bragged

- **Chimed in (v.):** To have joined in or broken into a conversation

- **Interjected (v.):** To have abruptly said something that interrupted a conversation

N

These words are replacements for *said*. These words are connected by the way they would be used. Two of the target words, *chimed in* and *interjected*, are ways to interrupt a conversation in order to join. *Acknowledged* and *boasted* are words that replace *said* that convey a certain attitude about the speaker when they are used. Demonstrate the use of the words by saying something like the following: "When Jim won the award, he *acknowledged* it graciously. He was then later able to *boast* about his achievement to his friends."

A

Small groups discuss how the words *acknowledged* and *boasted* can be used to share information about oneself. How are the words similar, and how are they different? How are *chimed in* and *interjected* the same or different? (*Acknowledging* something has a more positive connotation than *boasting* about something does. Likewise, *chimed in* has a more positive connotation than *interjected*.)

P

Have each student write a short bit of dialogue using one or more of the target words. They can even use characters from familiar works of literature or television shows. You can show them an example like the following: "Sheldon asked Leonard, 'When are we going to the comic book store? You promised we'd go soon!' Leonard finally *acknowledged* him and answered with, 'Maybe tomorrow night.'"

Scaffolding

Have students fill in the blank in the following sentence frames, using the appropriate replacement word for *said*.

▸ I was discussing the practice schedule with the coach when an assistant _____ to remind the coach about a meeting that was about to take place. (*interjected*)

▸ While I was explaining my reasons about why I was late, my brother _____ at my defense. (*chimed in*)

▸ "I believe that I know the answers," _____ the student. (*acknowledged*)

▸ "Yes!" _____ the student. "I had the answers correct and received the highest score in class." (*boasted*)

Acceleration

Have students brainstorm additional words that are synonyms for the listed words.

Lesson W5: *divulge, disclose, betray, expose*

In this minilesson, teachers will teach words related to secrets to use in place of *said*, such as the words *divulge, disclose, betray,* and *expose.*

Difficulty level: 2

S

The following lists target words students should *see* and *say* for this minilesson.

▸ **Divulge (v.):** To make something that was private publicly known

▸ **Disclose (v.):** To make secret information known by revealing it

▸ **Betray (v.):** To share information to hurt someone else; to reveal a secret

▸ **Expose (v.):** To harm someone by sharing secret or hidden information about him or her

N

Consider saying something like the following to your class.

To divulge, disclose, betray, *and* expose *information about someone or something is to share information that was not intended for public knowledge. When you share private information, you are putting yourself at risk for being an untrustworthy friend or colleague. These words are examples of words that have shades of meaning—words that have the same basic meaning but degrees of difference.*

A

Small groups collaborate to discuss if there are varying degrees of distrust when sharing secret information. For example, if you *betray* someone by sharing information, is that worse than *disclosing* information about someone?

P

These words lend themselves to shades of meaning. Have students rank the words from strongest verb to weakest verb and explain their reasoning for the ranking.

Scaffolding

Have students use Studyladder (2017; http://bit.ly/2jGkqgp) to practice with other words that have different shades of meaning. Students will need to set up a free account.

Acceleration

Have students give real-life examples of individuals that have divulged, disclosed, betrayed, or exposed someone or something, and what the effects were because those individuals shared that information.

Words to Replace the Adjective *Nice*

Students often describe their personal friends, fictional characters, and even historic figures as *nice* in their writing. There are so many more specific and engaging words to use! This lesson contains three basic replacements.

Lesson W6: *pleasant, agreeable, charming*

In this minilesson, teachers will teach words to use in place of *nice*, such as the words *pleasant*, *agreeable*, and *charming*.

S

The following lists target words students should *see* and *say* for this minilesson.

- ▸ **Pleasant (adj.):** Friendly and likable

- ▸ **Agreeable (adj.):** Likable; easy to get along with; agrees with others

- ▸ **Charming (adj.):** Polite; friendly; can talk other people into things

N

These words all describe a person and are similar to the word *nice* in that they mean "friendly." A *pleasant* person is easy to spend time with and makes others happy. An *agreeable* person does not argue with others. A *charming* person is friendly and fun to be around but can also use his or her personality to convince other people to do things.

A

Place students in pairs. Ask them to discuss characters from stories read in class, TV shows, and movies and name characters who are pleasant, agreeable, and charming.

P

Have each student write three sentences, one for each target word.

Scaffolding

Support struggling students by providing sentence stems like the following.

- A pleasant person _____ (does what?).

- An agreeable person _____ (is like what?).

- A charming person _____ (does what?).

Acceleration

Use word talk with word questioning for advanced students. You may want to ask the following questions.

- How is a pleasant person like or unlike an agreeable person?

- Do charming people have things in common with pleasant people?

Final Thoughts

Hopefully your students will remember and apply some of the words in this chapter to add strength and variety to their writing. Avoiding the repetitive overuse of undescriptive or vague words like *said* and *nice* will encourage your students to seek more sophisticated, specific, and accurate alternatives.

Appendix: Index of All Vocabulary Words Appearing in the Book

S

T

References and Resources

AISLyle. (2015). *How to use Padlet in the classroom* [Video file]. Accessed at www.youtube .com/watch?v=KHWRi54nCn8 on April 18, 2017.

Allen, J. (2007). *Inside words: Tools for teaching academic vocabulary, grades 4–12.* Portland, ME: Stenhouse.

Allen, J. (2014). *Tools for teaching academic vocabulary.* Portland, ME: Stenhouse.

Aronson, E., & Patnoe, S. (1997). *The jigsaw classroom: Building cooperation in the classroom* (2nd ed.). New York: Longman.

Beck, I. L., McKeown, M. G., & Kucan, L. (2013). *Bringing words to life: Robust vocabulary instruction* (2nd ed.). New York: Guilford Press.

Belyeu, F. O. (Producer). (2016). *The big bang theory* [Television series]. Burbank, CA: Warner Brothers Television Distribution.

Biemiller, A., & Slonim, N. (2001). Estimating root word vocabulary growth in normative and advantaged populations: Evidence for a common sequence of vocabulary acquisition. *Journal of Educational Psychology, 93*(3), 498–520.

Breitsprecher, W. (2007). *The parts of a book.* Accessed at www.slideshare.net/bogeybear /parts-of-book on February 21, 2017.

Brewer, J. (2013). *Tips on giving oral presentations* [Video file]. Accessed at www.youtube .com/watch?v=QKOO99UjsSE on February 21, 2017.

Cal High News. (2015). *CLR: Whip around* [Video file]. Accessed at www.youtube.com /watch?v=9LJ50g-u4dI on April 18, 2017.

Christa. (2013, March 20). *Audi and Volvo: The Latin origin of the car company names.* Accessed at http://highnames.com/audi-volvo-car-company-names-origin on October 31, 2016.

Colker, L. J. (n.d.). The word gap: The early years make the difference. *Teaching Young Children, 7*(3). Accessed at www.naeyc.org/tyc/article/the-word-gap on March 23, 2017.

Coxhead, A. (2000). A new academic word list. *TESOL Quarterly, 34*(2), 213–238.

Cunningham, A. E., & Stanovich, K. E. (1997). Early reading acquisition and its relation to reading experience and ability 10 years later. *Developmental Psychology, 33*(6), 934–945.

Data. (2016). In *Dictionary.com*. Accessed at www.dictionary.com/browse/data?s=t on January 3, 2017.

Davis, V. (n.d.). *How to use Padlet: A fantastic tool for teaching*. Accessed at www .coolcatteacher.com/how-to-use-padlet-fantastic-tool-teaching on April 18, 2017.

Dictionary.com. (2015, October 7). *What percentage of English words are derived from Latin?* [Blog post]. Accessed at http://blog.dictionary.com/word-origins on April 13, 2017.

Douglas County School District. (n.d.). *Cross-section—Nonfiction*. Accessed at https://sites .google.com/a/dcsdk12.org/nonfiction/text-features/cross-section on February 2, 2017.

Dr. Seuss. (1957). *How the Grinch stole Christmas!* New York: Random House.

English for Students. (n.d.). *Demo & dem*. Accessed at www.english-for-students.com /demo.html on February 21, 2017.

EnglishClub. (n.d.). *Animal vocabulary*. Accessed at www.englishclub.com/vocabulary /animal-terms.htm on February 2, 2017.

esu6pd. (2011). *Choral Response.mov* [Video file]. Accessed at www.youtube.com /watch?v=eKkR0EpvrcM on May 30, 2017.

Fact Monster. (2017). *Animal group terminology*. Accessed at www.factmonster.com/ipka /A0004725.html on February 16, 2017.

Fox, M. (1984). *Wilfrid Gordon McDonald Partridge*. Brooklyn, NY: Kane Miller Books.

Frayer, D. A., Frederick, W. C., & Klausmeier, H. J. (1969). *A schema for testing the level of concept mastery: Report from the Project on Situational Variables and Efficiency of Concept Learning*. Madison: Wisconsin Research and Development Center for Cognitive Learning.

Fry, E. B., & Kress, J. E. (2006). *The reading teacher's book of lists* (5th ed.). San Francisco: Jossey-Bass.

Gordon, S. (2014). *"Aud" words*. Accessed at https://prezi.com/ggdthqwezkdk/aud-words on February 21, 2017.

Grammarist. (2014). *Negative prefixes*. Accessed at http://grammarist.com/usage/negative -prefixes on February 21, 2017.

Graves, M. F. (2006). *The vocabulary book: Learning and instruction*. New York: Teachers College Press.

Graves, M. F., & Hammond, H. K. (1980). A validated procedure for teaching prefixes and its effect on students' ability to assign meaning to novel words. In M. L. Kamil & A. J. Moe (Eds.), *Perspectives on reading research and instruction* (pp. 184–188). Washington, DC: National Reading Conference.

Hart, B., & Risley, T. R. (2003). The early catastrophe: The 30 million word gap. *American Educator, 27*(1), 4–9.

Humphrey, A. V. (2006). *How to pluralize Latin & Greek nouns*. Accessed at www .telusplanet.net/~alfvaen/latin.html on January 3, 2017.

Hyerle, D. (2009). *Visual tools for transforming information into knowledge* (2nd ed.). Thousand Oaks, CA: Corwin Press.

imb1999. (2017). *Photo- words*. Accessed at https://quizlet.com/15319226/photo-words -flash-cards/ on February 16, 2017.

Johnson, V. (2017). *Speak up: Giving a good oral report*. Accessed at www.librarypoint.org /public_speaking on February 21, 2017.

Jones, C. (Director), & Washam, B. (Director). (1966). *How the Grinch stole Christmas!* [Motion picture]. United States: CBS.

Kelley, M. J., & Clausen-Grace, N. (n.d.). *Guiding students through expository text with text feature walks*. Accessed at www.readingrockets.org/article/guiding-students-through -expository-text-text-feature-walks on January 3, 2017.

Kenning, C. A. (2012, October 3). *Latin root word luc means light, bright*. Accessed at http://tellingvoice.com/blog/latin-root-word-luc-means-light on February 2, 2017.

Kinney, B. (2013, April 13). *Word endings foldable {freebie}* [Blog post]. Accessed at http://ilove2teach.blogspot.com/2013/04/word-endings-foldable-freebie.html on January 3, 2017.

Learner's Dictionary Ask the Editor. (2015). *Doubling the final consonant before adding -ed and -ing*. Accessed at www.learnersdictionary.com/qa/Doubling-the-final-consonant -before-adding-ed-or-ing on February 2, 2017.

Marzano, R. J. (2004). *Building background knowledge for academic achievement: Research on what works in schools*. Alexandria, VA: Association for Supervision and Curriculum Development.

Marzano, R. J. (2007). *The art and science of teaching: A comprehensive framework for effective instruction*. Alexandria, VA: Association for Supervision and Curriculum Development.

Marzano, R. J., Pickering, D. J., & Pollock, J. E. (2001). *Classroom instruction that works: Research-based strategies for increasing student achievement*. Alexandria, VA: Association for Supervision and Curriculum Development.

Marzano, R. J., & Simms, J. A. (2013). *Vocabulary for the Common Core*. Bloomington, IN: Marzano Research.

Math Is Fun. (n.d.a). *Accuracy and precision*. Accessed at www.mathsisfun.com/accuracy -precision.html on February 16, 2017.

Math Is Fun. (n.d.b). *Definition of addition*. Accessed at www.mathsisfun.com/definitions /addition.html on February 2, 2017.

McCarthy, C. (2010). *Words starting with 'Un'*. Accessed at www.ecenglish.com /learnenglish/lessons/prefix-words-starting-with-un on February 2, 2017.

Membean. (2017a). *Root word of the day: Clud*. Accessed at http://membean.com/wrotds /clud-shut on February 21, 2017.

Membean. (2017b). *Root word of the day: Port*. Accessed at http://membean.com/wrotds /port-carry on February 21, 2017.

Membean. (2017c). *Root word of the day: Scrib*. Accessed at http://membean.com/wrotds /scrib-write on February 21, 2017.

Morgan, P. L., Farkas, G., Hillemeier, M. M., Hammer, C. S., & Maczuga, S. (2015). 24-month-old children with larger oral vocabularies display greater academic and behavioral functioning at kindergarten entry. *Child Development, 86*(5), 1351–1370.

Most things that end in -ly are adverbish. These aren't. (n.d.). Accessed at http://srufaculty .sru.edu/david.dailey/words/lys.html on February 9, 2017.

Nagy, W., Berninger, V. W., & Abbott, R. D. (2006). Contributions of morphology beyond phonology to literacy outcomes of upper elementary and middle-school students. *Journal of Educational Psychology, 98*(1), 134–147.

Neuman, S. B., & Wright, T. S. (2013). *All about words: Increasing vocabulary in the Common Core classroom, preK–2.* New York: Teachers College Press.

Nix, K. (n.d.). *Understand volume and how volume is measured: Direct instruction* [Video file]. Accessed at https://learnzillion.com/lesson_plans/7163-understand-volume-and -how-volume-is-measured on February 2, 2017.

Orphal, D. (2014). *Stealing business ideas for my classroom.* Accessed at www .teachingquality.org/content/blogs/dave-orphal/stealing-business-ideas-my-classroom on February 2, 2017.

Oxford University Press. (n.d.). *Plurals of English nouns taken from Latin or Greek.* Accessed at https://en.oxforddictionaries.com/grammar/plurals-of-english-nouns -taken-from-latin-or-greek on February 2, 2017.

Peery, A. B. (in press). *Vocabulary in a SNAP: 100+ lessons for secondary instruction.* Bloomington, IN: Solution Tree Press.

Quizlet. (2017). *Quizlet: Company and mission.* Accessed at https://quizlet.com/mission on April 18, 2017.

Rasinski, T. V., Padak, N., Newton, J., & Newton, E. (2011). The Latin-Greek connection: Building vocabulary through morphological study. *Reading Teacher, 65*(2), 133–141.

Rippel, M. (n.d.). *How we teach prefixes.* Accessed at http://blog.allaboutlearningpress .com/prefixes on February 21, 2017.

Rodgers, R. (2011). *Adjectives ending in -ly.* Accessed at www.englishcorner.vacau.com /vocabulary/lyadjs.html on February 9, 2017.

Roth, F. P., Speece, D. L., & Cooper, D. H. (2002). A longitudinal analysis of the connection between oral language and early reading. *Journal of Educational Research, 95*(5), 259–272.

rtalkows. (2017). *Vid, vis, view—root word.* Accessed at https://quizlet.com/140594/vid -vis-view-root-word-flash-cards on February 2, 2017.

Speakspeak. (2017). *Spelling: When to double a consonant before adding -ed or -ing to a verb.* Accessed at http://speakspeak.com/resources/english-grammar-rules/english-spelling -rules/double-consonant-ed-ing on February 2, 2017.

studntz. (n.d.). *Root word → AUTO.* Accessed at www.slideshare.net/studntz/root-word -auto on February 21, 2017.

Studyladder. (2017). *Shades of meaning.* Accessed at www.studyladder.com/games /activity/shades-of-meaning-22775 on February 3, 2017.

Tech in 2. (2014). *How to use Kahoot! in the classroom* [Video file]. Accessed at www .youtube.com/watch?v=BJ3Er1-tCMc on April 20, 2017.

Tyson, K. A. (2012, December 6). *Concept circles {12 days: Tool 2}.* Accessed at www .learningunlimitedllc.com/2012/12/concept-circles-vocabulary on December 12, 2015.

Tyson, K. A., & Peery, A. B. (2017). *Blended vocabulary for K–12 classrooms: Harnessing the power of digital tools and direct instruction.* Bloomington, IN: Solution Tree Press.

Vacca, R. T., & Vacca, J. L. (1986). *Content area reading* (2nd ed.). Boston: Little, Brown.

Vocabulary.com. (n.d.). *Convert.* Accessed at www.vocabulary.com/dictionary/convert on February 21, 2017.

Vocabulary.com. (2015). *Elements of the universe: Sol.* Accessed at www.vocabulary.com /lists/724755#view=notes on February 21, 2017.

Wasko, B. (2014, March 14). *Non-adverbs that end in -LY* [Blog post]. Accessed at http:// blog.writeathome.com/index.php/2014/03/non-adverbs-that-end-in-ly on June 22, 2017.

White, T. G., Sowell, J., & Yanagihara, A. (1989). Teaching elementary students to use word-part clues. *Reading Teacher, 42*(4), 302–308.

Wiktionary. (2013). *Category: English words prefixed with tele-.* Accessed at https://en .wiktionary.org/wiki/Category:English_words_prefixed_with_tele- on February 2, 2017.

Willis, J. (2006). *Research-based strategies to ignite student learning: Insights from a neurologist and classroom teacher.* Alexandria, VA: Association for Supervision and Curriculum Development.

WordHippo. (2017a). *What is another word for revise?* Accessed at www.wordhippo.com /what-is/another-word-for/revise.html on February 2, 2017.

WordHippo. (2017b). *Words starting with AUTO.* Accessed at www.wordhippo.com /what-is/words-starting-with/auto.html on February 16, 2017.

WordHippo. (2017c). *Words starting with MANU.* Accessed at www.wordhippo.com /what-is/words-starting-with/manu.html on February 16, 2017.

WordHippo. (2017d). *Words starting with SUB.* Accessed at www.wordhippo.com/what-is /words-starting-with/sub.html on February 2, 2017.

WordsinaSentence.com. (2016a). *Recede in a sentence.* Accessed at https:// wordsinasentence.com/recede-in-a-sentence on February 21, 2017.

WordsinaSentence.com. (2016b). *Secede in a sentence.* Accessed at https://wordsinasentence .com/secede-in-a-sentence on February 21, 2017.

Zwiers, J. A. (2014, November). *Meeting new standards with oral language activities to build academic thinking and language* [Audio recording]. Presented at Using Brain Science to Engage Attention in a Distracted World: Fall Conference of Learning and the Brain, Boston, MA.

Index

Blended Vocabulary for K–12 Classrooms
Kimberly A. Tyson and Angela B. Peery

Discover a research-based model you can implement to help all students master tiered vocabulary. With greater understanding of how to teach vocabulary effectively and incorporate digital tools, you can develop a blended approach to word learning that makes a significant impact on achievement.

BKF630

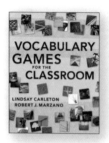

Vocabulary Games for the Classroom
Lindsay Carleton and Robert J. Marzano

Make direct vocabulary instruction fun and successful with this simple, straightforward, and easy-to-use book. Hundreds of vocabulary terms handpicked by Dr. Marzano cover four content areas and all grade levels.

BKL007

Vocabulary for the New Science Standards
Robert J. Marzano, Katie Rogers, and Julia A. Simms

Impact science education with direct vocabulary instruction. With this three-part resource, you'll discover a six-step process for successfully incorporating vocabulary from the science standards into student learning. Identify the crucial aspects of vocabulary education, and learn targeted strategies to actively engage students.

BKL026

Vocabulary for the Common Core
Robert J. Marzano and Julia A. Simms

The Common Core State Standards present unique demands on students' ability to learn vocabulary and teachers' ability to teach it. The authors address these challenges in this resource, helping you create a successful vocabulary program.

BKL014

Wait! **Your professional development journey doesn't have to end with the last pages of this book.**

We realize improving student learning doesn't happen overnight. And your school or district shouldn't be left to puzzle out all the details of this process alone.

No matter where you are on the journey, we're committed to helping you get to the next stage.

Take advantage of everything from **custom workshops** to **keynote presentations** and **interactive web and video conferencing**. We can even help you develop an action plan tailored to fit your specific needs.

Let's get the conversation started.

Call 888.763.9045 today.

SolutionTree.com